CULTURE SHOCK!

Ukraine

Meredith Dalton

Graphic Arts Center Publishing Company
Portland, Oregon

In the same series

Argentina	*France*	*Malaysia*	*Sweden*
Australia	*Germany*	*Mauritius*	*Switzerland*
Bolivia	*Greece*	*Mexico*	*Syria*
Borneo	*Hong Kong*	*Morocco*	*Taiwan*
Britain	*Hungary*	*Myanmar*	*Thailand*
Burma	*India*	*Nepal*	*Turkey*
California	*Indonesia*	*Netherlands*	*UAE*
Canada	*Iran*	*Norway*	*Ukraine*
Chile	*Ireland*	*Pakistan*	*USA*
China	*Israel*	*Philippines*	*USA—The South*
Cuba	*Italy*	*Singapore*	*Venezuela*
Czech Republic	*Japan*	*South Africa*	*Vietnam*
Denmark	*Korea*	*Spain*	
Egypt	*Laos*	*Sri Lanka*	

Barcelona At Your Door	*Paris At Your Door*	*Living and Working*
Chicago At Your Door	*Rome At Your Door*	*Abroad*
Havana At Your Door		*Working Holidays*
Jakarta At Your Door	*A Globe-Trotter's Guide*	*Abroad*
Kuala Lumpur, Malaysia	*A Parent's Guide*	
At Your Door	*A Student's Guide*	
London At Your Door	*A Traveller's Medical Guide*	
New York At Your Door	*A Wife's Guide*	

Illustrations by TRIGG

© 1999 Times Editions Pte Ltd
© 2000 Times Media Private Limited
Reprinted 2000

This book is published by special
arrangement with Times Media Private Limited
Times Centre, 1 New Industrial Road, Singapore 536196
International Standard Book Number 1-55868-420-4
Library of Congress Catalog Number 99-60172
Graphic Arts Center Publishing Company
P.O. Box 10306 • Portland, Oregon 97296-0306 • (503) 226-2402

Printed in Singapore

To the good people of Ukraine
and to those expatriates genuinely dedicated
to a better Ukraine
a better life for Ukrainians
a better world
peace.

CONTENTS

ACKNOWLEDGMENTS

Although my heritage includes no Slavic blood, something about Slavic culture seized me many years ago in John Bowlt's art history classes in Austin. In 1996 while living in Kyiv, a Ukrainian interpreter and dear friend told me that I was now half-American, half-Ukrainian. At the time I wished it were so. My little brother once described himself as three-eighths Irish (true, although I always preferred the one-third joke), half Southern, and a quarter Okie, plus I think he threw in some Nordic percentage (of which, like Slavic, we Daltons possess none). John, a veritable math scholar, couldn't get his proportions to add up. I too am intrigued by questions of national identity, ethnicity, and multi-culturalism—the world's as well as my own. At the same time, all of us are aware of the tragic consequences of insisting on a particular lineage.

Today I view myself as a sort of collector of places; the topographical features range from the mundane to the elegiac. But in the end it is the people whom I have met that have individually and collectively colored my perceptions. Like those American crazy-quilts that I have loved since my youth, my impressions of Ukraine have been molded through interactions with fellow American, Canadian, Ecuadorian, English, Irish, Belgian, French, German, Swiss, and other expatriates who shared their own observations and experiences with me. Ukrainian friends and colleagues likewise and indelibly shaped my experiences.

Special thanks to the following Ukrainians and expatriates; I apologize for any significant omissions: Jim Asher; Mark Baillie; Jennifer Baker; Cynthia Bakle; Igor Bandarenko; Amanda Barley; Betsy Bassan; Marco Berchtold; Joe Bidnez; Lesia Bihun; Carrie

Braxton; Len Brockman; Zakhar Bruk; Andrey Cheban; Evgeny Chernyak and Irina, Natasha and Oleg; Bohdan Chomiak; Jim Davis; Lena Davis; Roger Dean; Geoff Elkind; Bob Evans; Gary Fickemeyer; Igor Fotiev; Randy Fortenbery; H^3; John Helmuth; Dwight Hewitt; Laura Hoover; Ty Jagerson; Myron Jarosewich; Kathy whose kids attend New Hope School; Patricia Koch and Brian Foster; Marta Kolomayets; Andrey Kolomiets; Peter Koshukov; Nikki Lemley; Tom Lemley; Allison Lynch; Carlyse Marshall; Shannon Matthews; Joe MacFarlane; Tim McQuillin; Nigel Mukherjee; Igor Musiyuk; Boris Najman; Andrew Pearson; Hugh Patton; Meagan Plagge; Ron Prescott; Randy Regan; Linda Rogers and Jeff Berstein; Jeff Rosenberg; Hermanito Willie Salinas Zambrano; Skip Sayer; Kevin Scallan; Dick Shriver; David Snelbecker; Doug Stephenson; Kathryn Stevens; Nick Stevens; Aleksei Strelnik; Annelise Tarnstrom; Kristi Tarnstrom; Tanya of Coopers & Lybrand; Glenn Tasky; Pavel Ustimenko and Valentin, Lena and Olga; Harry Walters; Greg Welling; and Sasha Zinchenko.

Additional thanks go to my dear friend Jacqueline Curzon Price, who shared her photographs after so many of mine were stolen last year, and to my little sister Catherine, whose photographs proved invaluable (and superior to mine). I love you, Twin. Special thanks to Clifton Warren, who is consistently available to me and whose heart is huge; to Lori and Andrew for opening their home and hearts to me in the thirteenth hour, and to Keith Bowden of the University of Central Oklahoma who helped me with Photoshop in my time of need. Especial thanks to Olena Czebiniak for converting my Russian into Ukrainian. Thanks also to the editors at Times Editions, who encouraged me without overwhelming me. It's a harder task than most people realize.

As always, thanks to my loving and supportive family; to Tia and Cuz, and to all my friends who genuinely encouraged me. This includes Alyssa, Andrew, Karen, Eve and many others—not only do I know who you are, I also know where you live (that's more than you can say for me!)

Thank you, one and all.

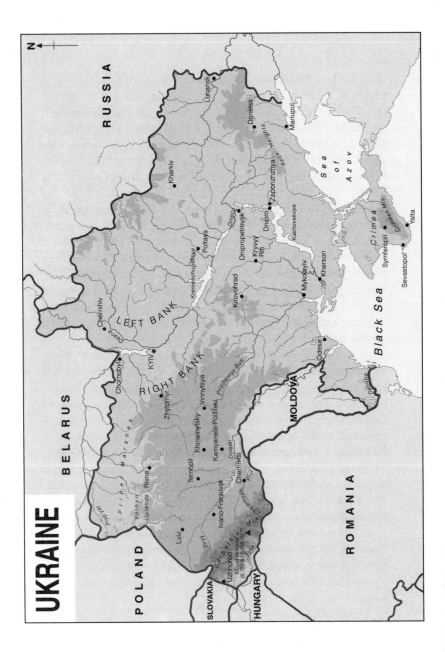

Chapter One

INTRODUCTION TO UKRAINE

Ukraine is today well-known as the breadbasket of the former Soviet Union (FSU); as the site of the world's most horrific nuclear accident in 1986; for its post-independence disputes with Russia over Crimea and the Black Sea Fleet; for its delicious borshch, Ukraine's national soup that was subsequently adopted by other Soviet republics; for its unique peppered vodka, *horilka z pertsem*; and for fine, native handicrafts, including beautifully decorated Easter eggs that predate the Christian era. But Ukraine is much more than this—and far more complex.

A COUNTRY IN TRANSITION

Ukraine's strategic geographical position made it an ancient cross-roads between the Black Sea, the Sea of Azov (Oziv in Ukrainian), and the Baltic Sea. This same location between modern-day Germany and Russia proved particularly inauspicious during the Great Patriotic War (World War II), as a disproportionate number of battles was fought on Ukrainian soil.

Today Ukraine is an independent nation somewhat divided by language, history, and religion. The Dnipro River reflects a physical and cultural demarcation between eastern and western Ukraine. Left-Bank (or eastern and southern) Ukraine is predominantly Russian-speaking and often favors Russia, whereas Right-Bank Ukraine speaks Ukrainian and is at times staunchly nationalistic.

These distinctions are somewhat changing as Ukrainian, once described as a language for peasants and the intelligentsia, is now the official language used by the government and in the schools. In practice, Russian is the dominant—and most practical—language for business today, as historically more Ukrainians spoke Russian than Ukrainian (since Russian was the official language of all Soviet republics). Also, Russia is Ukraine's primary trading partner.

The main difference today is that Ukrainians don't discriminate against Russian-language speakers, whereas the Soviets vehemently discouraged any displays of Ukrainian solidarity or culture—especially language, as it was considered the most important component of nationality. However, the roots of Russification in Ukraine were not a distinctive Soviet feature but may be traced to the Russian Empire during the mid-18th century.

For centuries, Poland and Russia fought over Ukrainian soil, and their influences and territorial divisions have continuing ramifications today. The Ukrainian Uniate Church in western Ukraine is essentially a hybrid of Ukrainian Orthodoxy with Catholic Poland's influences. The Ukrainian Orthodox Church has the larger following in Ukraine and is similar to the Russian Orthodox Church. A second contender to Orthodoxy reemerged in 1990, the Ukrainian Autocephalous Orthodox Church which had been banned since the 1930s. The fate of Ukraine's Jews is another bloody chapter in Ukraine's turbulent history, and discrimination against Jews remains one of the Soviet Union's legacies. There are reports especially in Russia that anti-Semitism is on the upswing since the Soviet Union imploded, but, like Russification, its roots predate the communist era.

The paucity of information available on Ukraine is striking, and most often Ukraine is relegated to the back sections of books on Russia. Many outsiders erroneously believe that Ukraine is today a part of Russia. The histories of the two nations are inextricably connected, and in fact Ukraine, Russia, and Belarus all trace their roots to the great state of Kyivan Rus that emerged in the 9th century. But let us mince no words here: Ukraine is not Russia.

Among Ukraine's most infamous chapters in recent history was the forced collectivization of farms and Stalin's deliberate starvation of some six to ten million Ukrainians in the early 1930s in an effort to break the Ukrainian spirit. Stalin failed, but his actions must be considered among the foremost factors that have informed modern-day Ukrainian identity.

Like its megalithic neighbor, Ukraine is in a period of painful transition, and it is difficult at times to unravel where Russian and Ukrainian cultures overlap or diverge. Chauvinism and its associated handicaps are prevalent, and isolated reports by outsiders have suggested that Ukraine is on the verge of ethnic combustion. This is unreasonable. Far more likely, albeit unacceptable, is financial collapse, despite the fact that the country weathered the financial and consequential social crisis in the latter half of 1998 better than Russia did. This is partly because Ukraine never attracted the attention—and investments—anywhere near the scale of Russia. One legitimate concern in 1999 is that without additional help from foreign financial institutions Ukraine's financial straits may force the country back into Russia's expanding sphere of economic and political influence.

The name "Ukraine" originates from a Slavic word meaning "borderland." "Little Russia" and "South Russia" were two former names for the region that have since been rejected for their derogatory implications. Today, Ukrainians prefer the English name "Ukraine" to "the Ukraine" for reasons given below. Like their Slavic brothers, Ukrainians are proud people and generous hosts. Their national anthem, *Ukraine is Not Yet Dead*, underscores a bittersweet history and unique national character.

GEOGRAPHY AND ETHNICITY

With an area slightly larger than France's or just under the size of Texas, Ukraine is today the largest country completely in Europe. The Ukrainian Soviet Socialist Republic was the third largest of the fifteen Soviet republics after Russia, today the world's largest country, and Kazakhstan, which is also significantly larger than Ukraine.

To Ukraine's north lies Belarus, the former Soviet republic called Byelorussia or White Russia. To the east (and northeast) is Russia. West of Ukraine are Poland, Slovakia, Hungary, Romania, and Moldova, formerly the Soviet republic called Moldavia. Ukraine's southern border lies along the Black Sea and Sea of Azov and includes the Crimean peninsula.

The Cyrillic letters resembling CCCP in English are actually SSSR; they stood for the Union of Soviet Socialist Republics (USSR). In Russian, USSR referred to the Ukrainian Soviet Socialist Republic. (If all this is confusing, study the Cyrillic alphabet in Chapter Three.)

The Ukrainian SSR was the second most populous republic after Russia. Today, Ukraine's population is around 51 million (and slightly declining each year), in contrast to Russia's 143 million, also declining. (Belarus, the third Eastern Slavic state, has a population of roughly 10 million.)

Ethnic Ukrainians represent 72% of Ukraine's population; ethnic Russians comprise 22%. More Ukrainians today speak Russian than Ukrainian, although the majority of the population is bilingual. These numbers will continue to increase in independent Ukraine, since the official language is now Ukrainian.

Jews are considered a distinct nationality in Ukraine. As of late 1998, Ukraine's Jews comprise just over one-half of 1% of the population, or roughly 300,000. What is particularly disturbing is that ten years ago there were roughly 500,000 Jews, and every year one in ten emigrates to Israel, Europe, or North America. At this rate alone, in ten years there will be no Jewish population. Moreover, it is the young who are emigrating so quickly, and half of the current Jewish population is over 50 years old. It is estimated that for every Jewish child born today, there are nine deaths. Unlike Poland, there are Jews today in the smaller towns, but the bulk lives in urban areas. Jews are distressed to watch as their numbers are being thinned out.

Other minorities in Ukraine today include Belarusians, Poles, Hungarians, Romanians, Moldovans, Slovaks, Bulgarians, and gypsies. Where applicable, these ethnic minorities tend to live near the borders of their ancestral homelands; consequently, with the notable exception of the Belarusians, most minorities live in western Ukraine. Similarly, the bulk of ethnic Russians is today in Ukraine's more populous eastern and southern parts.

Five Ukrainian cities today boast populations of over one million citizens: Kyiv, Kharkiv, Dnipropetrovsk, Odesa, and Donetsk. Each of these is predominantly Russian-speaking, and all but Odesa are located in what is known as Left-Bank Ukraine. (Odesa is about 75 miles west of the Dnipro.) This is why one often hears references to "Left-Bank Ukraine plus Odesa."

The Dnipro River (Dnepr in Russian) roughly halves the country in a sort of yin-yang fashion. Right-Bank Ukraine is comprised of western and central Ukraine, whereas Left-Bank Ukraine includes the eastern and southern regions. The Dnipro's physical division also evinces a psychological demarcation.

Right-Bank Ukraine is predominantly Ukrainian-speaking and home to some of Ukraine's most ardent nationalists. The unofficial capital of western Ukraine is Lviv, a city with a unique history and a particularly Central European feel. Activists here spearheaded the independence movement. Because of this, and also because Lviv is the largest city in western Ukraine (with fewer than one million people), there is a tendency to mistake the people of Lviv as a prototype for western Ukraine. However, Lviv and its immediate surroundings were not ruled by Moscow prior to 1939. As a result, its wayward populace never fully succumbed to the Soviet stronghold in Moscow. Also, between 1941 and 1944, Lviv was occupied by the Germans. When the Red Army seized control of the city in 1944, things did not necessarily improve for Lviv's residents, many of whom were accused of collaborating with the Germans.

The emergence of Ukrainian nationalism is often associated with the art and writings of Ukraine's national hero, Taras Shevchenko, born into serfdom in 1814. Shevchenko was responding in part to the suppression of Ukrainian culture (and later language), traceable to the mid-18th century. Ryszard Kapuściński, a contemporary Polish journalist, has observed that nationalism cannot exist in a conflict-free environment; there will always be grudges and claims. Consequently, whenever nationalism does surface, there will be an immediate reaction on the part of the group's enemies. Not surprisingly, Ukrainian nationalism was criminalized under the Soviets.

By contrast, Left-Bank Ukraine (plus Odesa) speaks Russian and at times favors Russia, although a 1998 motion to join the proposed Russian-Belarusian union was dismissed without consideration by all of Ukraine. Of Ukraine's ten million ethnic Russians, some 80% live in the eastern and southern regions. President Leonid Kuchma, elected in 1994 largely by Ukraine's Russian-speaking populace, has learned Ukrainian in office and now delivers all speeches in the country's official language. (Native Ukrainian speakers nonetheless scoff at his grammar. Compare this, however, with a Party meeting in 1939 where the Georgian-born Stalin made a Russian grammatical error; every speaker who followed him repeated his error out of fear.)

Today when you hear a Ukrainian speak disparagingly about Ukrainian nationalists, odds are good that the speaker is from Left-Bank Ukraine and his targets, from the right.

Ukraine's sequential domination by other peoples, further complicated by its history of changing borders, helps explain Ukraine's personality complex. It is important to recognize the coexistence of pro-Ukrainian and pro-Russian factions; equally important is recognizing current ethnic tensions without exaggerating them.

The rise of so-called hate journalism is a legitimate concern today for former Eastern European and Soviet countries. The communist tradition of using the media to denounce enemies of the state is being reworked to new, propagandistic ends: manipulative journalists are capable of arousing ethnic strife among rural and less educated people; they are also encouraging voters to turn against the intelligentsia. Kosovo's ongoing strife as of early 1999 is among Eastern Europe's most recent chapters; likewise, Aleksandr Lukashenko, Belarus's authoritarian leader, has proved repeatedly that he will seize any excuse to crack down on alleged subversive activities.

Ukraine too perpetuates many of its chauvinistic traditions. Ethnic minorities in Transcarpathia today complain of discrimination. Prior to 1945, this region was part of Hungary, and many here still set their watches back one hour to Hungarian time. (Some also insist that Subcarpathia is a more accurate name than Transcarpathia.)

Crimea, with its ethnic Russian majority, is marked by external and internal divisiveness. Ukraine and Russia have clashed over the fate of the Black Sea Fleet. Further, while Crimeans would prefer autonomy above all else, the fallback position for many would be Russian citizenship, not Ukrainian. (They tried for dual citizenship but lost this battle in 1995.) Ethnic issues are further muddied as many Crimean Tatars who were banished by Stalin to Central Asia are returning to their ancestral homeland, without fanfare or assistance. Many of them do not possess Ukrainian citizenship or passports, and the bureaucratic process for obtaining these is daunting.

15

Ethnic tensions in neighboring Moldova in the Transdnistr region continue to affect Ukraine, although these have diminished since war erupted here in 1992. This small strip of land borders on Ukraine and is populated by ethnic Ukrainians and Russians, whereas Moldova's population of 4.4 million is mostly ethnic Romanian. Residents of Transdnistr feared that Moldova would soon join Romania. Although a peace agreement was brokered here in 1994 by Aleksandr Lebed, Russian troops are still stationed in Transdnistr to ensure peace. Not everyone wants this presence.

In light of these ethnic tensions—and further scuffles within Ukraine's ethnic mix are conceivable—there are those who would have you believe that independent Ukraine is a pressure-cooker, another Yugoslavia waiting to happen. It is not.

Climate and Topography

Most of Ukraine is gently sloping steppes, and its moniker "the breadbasket of the Soviet Union" stems from the fertility of its celebrated black soil—as rich as the best soil of the American Midwest. Ukraine's northern steppes, bordering on Belarus, are forested, providing sources for food, fuel, and building materials as well as excellent hiding places from invaders and difficult rulers. On its western border, Ukraine is flanked by the Carpathian Mountains, where opportunities exist for downhill skiing and hiking expeditions.

Crimea in the south has a Mediterranean climate and is known for its vineyards, spas, and health resorts, along with a spectacular coastline. The Russian or Ukrainian Riviera refers to this peninsula.

The capital Kyiv is slightly above the latitudes of Frankfurt and Prague. It is generally known for its warm summers and mild winters, although like elsewhere the past decade has left its mark on recent records. The winter of 1995–96 was reportedly the worst winter in over fifty years. When the thaw at last arrived in mid-spring, outdoor life rebounded quickly as Kyiv's café culture unfolded in its streets.

UKRAINE IS NOT RUSSIA

It is not possible to speak of Ukraine without addressing Russia at length, as their Slavic histories are inextricably linked. But these are today two distinct countries, and it is incorrect to lump Ukraine as a part of Russia. The third Eastern Slavic nation is Belarus, whose independence from Russia is much more tentative than Ukraine's.

On August 24, 1991, Ukraine's Supreme Rada (equivalent to Russia's Duma or Parliament) adopted a declaration of independence; this was contingent upon a national referendum. December 1, 1991, saw an unprecedented voter turnout of 84% with some 90% voting for independence.

Ukraine, Russia, and Belarus all trace their origins to Kyiv, the "mother of Russian cities" that was once the capital of the great state of Kyivan Rus. All three countries have separate, but related, languages, although Belarus recently scrapped Belarusian for Russian as its official language.

In Ukraine today, there are three primary churches, in addition to Protestant, Muslim, and Jewish minorities. The Ukrainian Orthodox Church is essentially the Russian Orthodox Church in Ukraine with allegiance to Moscow's patriarchate (and semi-autonomous authority in Kyiv). The Ukrainian Autocephalous Orthodox Church maintains allegiance to the Ukrainian patriarchate in Kyiv, and the Uniate (or Ukrainian Catholic) Church is essentially a hybrid of Orthodoxy and Catholicism, recognizing papal authority in Rome. (Like the Chechens, Crimea's Tatars practice Islam.)

Despite shared elements of history and Slavic culture, many differences between Ukrainians and Russians are more subtle than church authority and language issues—and sometimes far more inflammatory. An understanding of Ukraine's history of colonization by Russians and Poles (and earlier Lithuanians) helps to explain the unique character of Ukrainians. For centuries, Ukrainians have viewed their country as the underdog, and this was naturally reinforced through the years of suppressing Ukrainian culture; in 1876 the

Ukrainian language was banned in schools and in all publications. In more recent history, Stalin clearly targeted Ukrainians, but he didn't necessarily spare other Soviet peoples.

WHAT'S IN A NAME?

An overview of the origins of the name "Ukraine" summarizes aspects of Ukraine's changing borders and its self-perception as inferior to Russia, the world's largest country.

The name "Ukraine" or *Ukraina* (say *ooCRYeena*) originates from the Slavic word meaning "borderland." From the 12th to 15th centuries, "Ukraine" meant "borderland," "bordering country," or "country." Continuing into the 16th century, documents made references to various Ukraines (Galician Ukraine and Kyiv Ukraine, among others), but over time "Ukraine" came to mean the Cossack territory stretching along both sides of the Dnipro River, then part of the Polish Commonwealth. In the 17th century the concept of Ukraine was extended farther east to include not only eastern Ukraine but also territory of the Muscovite state of Slovidska Ukraine, which attracted Cossack settlers. After Hetman Bohdan Khmelnytsky's successful uprising against the Poles in the mid-17th century, "Ukraine" referred to the rise of a Cossack state in central Ukraine. This was not its official name, but the Hetman territory was usually known as Ukraine in both Ukrainian and Polish sources at this time.

The 1667 and 1668 partitions between Muscovy and Poland interrupted the evolution of Ukraine as a unifying concept. Indeed, this period sowed the seeds for much of the east vs. west conflict we encounter today in Left-Bank and Right-Bank Ukraine. The former, then a Muscovy protectorate, was transformed into a province of the Russian Empire; it became officially known in Russian as Malorossiya or Little Russia. It was also sometimes called Southern Russia.

The larger part of the Ukrainian territories was unified with the Russian Empire during the Partitions of Poland between 1772 and 1795. This paved the way for the concept of Ukraine as Ukrainian national territory as well as the emergence of Ukrainian nationalism in the 1840s. Only Ukraine's far western territory, the region around Lviv, was excluded; this went instead to the Hapsburg Empire.

Taras Shevchenko associated "Ukraine" with a proud Cossack past whereas "Malorossiya" reinforced national humiliation and colonial status. From the mid-19th century, "Ukraine" at last displaced all other names for this territory.

The years immediately following the Russian Revolution and World War I were chaotic and unstable, and civil war broke out and lasted until 1921 or 1922. This was really a prolongation of revolution. In 1918, for example, there were at least thirty governments in what had been the Russian Empire. After 1920, parts of western Ukraine were divided between Poland, Romania, and Czechoslovakia. In 1921, the Bolsheviks gave formal recognition to Ukraine's independence; then in 1922, Ukraine was seized and incorporated into the newly formed USSR as the Ukrainian Soviet Socialist Republic. The Communist Party had established its one-party rule.

Finally, in its 1991 declaration of independence, the new state adopted "Ukraine" as its official name. The name in English is not "the Ukraine" as it was formerly called in English. In fact, the articles "the" and "a" do not exist in the Ukrainian, Russian, or Belarusian languages. The larger issue, however, is that "the Ukraine" suggests to Ukrainians a geographical region, when in fact Ukraine is today an independent country.

Language and Identity: Kyiv, Kyyiv, or Kiev?

Years of practice have meant that "Kiev" still appears more frequently in print than "Kyiv," just as "the Ukraine" is more commonly used than "Ukraine." Nevertheless, the statement "Kiev is the capital of the Ukraine" no longer sounds or looks correct to me.

The traditional English spelling of Ukraine's capital city was a direct transliteration from the Russian. "Kyyiv" was proposed as a more accurate Ukrainian transliteration, but this never really took hold. Independent Ukraine has now adopted "Kyiv" as the official English spelling for its capital. The stress in all cases is on the first syllable. In practice, it falls somewhere between *KEYyiv* and *KAYyiv*.

In the post-Soviet era, Russian remains the language of business and more people speak Russian than Ukrainian in the capital. But most street signs, storefronts, and billboard advertising are in Ukrainian. For example, you'll see the abbreviation *vul.* in Ukrainian for *vulytsia* (meaning street) whereas you'll more likely hear *ulitsa* (Russian) spoken. This gets confusing at times, but such is life in contemporary Ukraine; many speak a mixture of both languages.

The situation is further complicated because so many of the Soviet names have been replaced, sometimes reclaiming the pre-revolutionary name. Not all cities have adopted new names for communist ones. For example, Kharkiv's Karl Marx and Lenin Streets remain unchanged, whereas Kyiv's have been renamed. Skeptics claim that changing the communist names is merely window-dressing.

In Ukrainian and Russian, the names of many Ukrainian cities and towns are slightly different. For example, the Ukrainian transliteration for Odessa (on the Black Sea) is Odesa; because the dominant language here is Russian, you will encounter the Russian transliteration far more often. Slightly more confusing is nearby Mykolayiv (the Ukrainian name), called Nikolaev in Russian. Kharkov in the east and only 25 miles from the Russian border is a "Russian" city; it seems more appropriate to use its Russian transliteration, thereby respecting the wishes of the majority of Ukrainian citizens living here. Officially, however, the city is now Kharkiv. (My friend Zhenia joked that that's like telling someone that I was raised in Oo-klahoma.)

Go to Lviv (Lvov in Russian, Lwow in Polish, and Lemberg under the Germans and the Hapsburgs), and you will find that the people speak Ukrainian, or perhaps Polish, but not Russian. (The rest of western Ukraine speaks Ukrainian.) Kyiv's international airport, Borispol, is "Borispil" in Ukrainian. A few places have the same name (and English transliteration) in both languages, e.g. Donetsk.

Below is a list of places whose Ukrainian and Russian differ:

Ukrainian name	*Russian name*
Borispil	Borispol (Kyiv's international airport)
Chernivtsi	Chernovtsy
Chernihiv	Chernigov
Chornobyl	Chernobyl
Dnipropetrovsk	Dnepropetrovsk
Dnipro (River)	Dnepr
Ivano-Frankivsk	Ivano-Frankovsk
Kamyanets-Podilski	Kamenets-Podilsky
Kharkiv	Kharkov
Khmelnytsky	Khmelnitsky
Kirovohrad	Korovograd
Krivy Rih	Krivoy Rog
Kyiv	Kiev
Lviv	Lvov
Luhansk	Lugansk (the Soviet name was Voroshilovgrad)
Mariupol	(the Soviet name was Zhdanov)
Mykolayiv	Nikolaev
Odesa	Odessa
Pochaiv	Pochaev
Rivne	Rovno
Ternopil	Ternopol
Uzhhorod	Uzhgorod
Vinnytsya	Vinnitsa
Zaporizhzhya	Zaporozhie
Zhytomyr	Zhitomir

See Chapter Three for a more detailed discussion on language.

UKRAINE'S REPUTATION ABROAD

Ukraine is today one of the largest recipients of international aid, yet its financial balance sits precariously on the brink of collapse. In 1996, the last of Ukraine's nuclear warheads was transferred to Russian hands, as encouraged by the international community and in exchange for much-needed fuel.

Ukraine is probably most known in the West for its strong agricultural production and the 1986 Chornobyl disaster. (The Ukrainian transliteration, Chornobyl, more accurately reflects its pronunciation than the Russian Chernobyl.) The widespread adoption of Orthodox Christianity in Kyivan Rus, the history of Jews in the so-called Pale of Settlement, and Ukraine's tragic consequences as crossroads between Germany and Russia during World War II are further subjects more or less known in the West today. Fewer outsiders are familiar with Stalin's deliberate starvation of more than six million Ukrainians during 1931–32. While this chapter needs to be told, it is hardly uplifting. (See Collectivization below for more.)

Post-independence disputes with Russia concerning Crimea and the Black Sea Fleet have made recent headlines, and this debate today reinforces aspects of Ukraine's overlapping and separate history from Russia's. Crimea was made a gift to Ukraine by Nikita Khrushchev (who was of Ukrainian peasant stock) in 1954 in recognition of 300 years of Russian-Ukrainian unification. Although the peninsula is predominantly Russian today, it rightfully belongs to Ukraine now.

Ukraine has been hailed as the breadbasket of the Soviet Union, Eastern Europe, or simply Europe. Its rich, black soil called *chornozem* (meaning "black earth") produced one-quarter of the wheat and much of the sugar beet for the USSR. Livestock, rye, sunflowers, and flax were also important. Today, agricultural production is roughly one-half of its highest Soviet levels due to the high cost of energy and agricultural inputs, languishing equipment, and general mismanagement. Moreover, the state is unable to relinquish its long-standing tradition of market interference. Grain bans occur on a regular basis,

Kyiv's controversial arch, colloquially called by some "The Yoke." This monument is dedicated to the 1654 unification of Russia and Ukraine. Many Ukrainians equate this to the beginning of the Russian yoke over their country. (Photo courtesy of Catherine Isabel Dalton.)

sometimes couched in new rhetoric but with the same results: grain that is contracted for sale but not yet delivered is effectively seized by regional and *oblast* (state) administrations in an effort to supply local needs. The old days of state control are, sadly, not old enough.

In agriculture and in all areas of industry, stultifying bureaucratic obstacles abound, and corruption is rife. These are not distinctive features of post-Soviet life: Nikolai Gogol (who was born in Ukraine) satirized bureaucratic inefficiencies over 150 years ago, and corruption (and crime) was a growing problem under the Soviets, particularly in the later Brezhnev years. Only during Stalin's reign was corruption kept to a minimum.

Soviet salaries were always maintained at very low levels, but housing and energy costs were practically free, and education and pensions were guaranteed. It was not a cashless society, but access and influence were generally more powerful and more valuable than money. Today's officials continue to receive such low wages that bribes are often perceived as necessary income supplementation (by the payee) or as a cost of doing business (by the payer). Indeed, people with ordinary amounts of cash can buy off officials at reasonable rates, although your company or employer might have other ideas about bribery.

The Soviet system also laid the foundations for today's enormous and expanding barter economy. One of its salient features is the absence of tax revenues. While the Ukrainian government is working hard to improve its collections, the prohibitively high tax rates mean that even those who want to work within the law are often forced to maneuver around it. For other Ukrainians, avoiding taxes is considered a matter of national pride, and tax collectors are universally regarded as among the most corrupt and despicable government officials. In general, people also vehemently mistrust the police (called *militsia*), and many rely on the protection afforded them by their "security firm." After all, they are paying for it, aren't they?

Both the crime and corruption of the later Brezhnev era have escalated since independence, and Ukraine, like Russia, is stigmatized for its problems with the mafia. The international press is filled with tales of mafia infiltration into practically every business venture, and violent crime, while far more common in Russia, is negatively impacting Ukraine's incipient democratic struggle. Western businessmen are by no means immune to the mafia's deleterious actions, but at the end of the day most of them can pack their bags for home if they so desire. There are isolated stories of foreigners who have lost their lives in mafia turf wars. By all accounts the situation is serious and goes well beyond the repeated tales of ineffective police (many of whom are reputed to be in cahoots with the mafia), the labyrinthine bureaucracy, and inbred governmental corruption. Stephen Handelman's *Comrade Criminal: Russia's New Mafiya*

(Yale University Press, 1995) is the best source of information for understanding the complexity and spectacular tentacles of this unwieldy beast.

From a foreign perspective, constantly changing tax laws, including retroactive ones, may prove unmanageable. Visibility here extracts a much higher cost than elsewhere, for with it often come numerous inspectorates looking for baksheesh. One critical lesson for surviving Ukraine, according to some foreigners, is to consciously separate the actions of the government from its citizenry. Elaboration on these subjects will be given below. Suffice it to say that the more you get to know Ukrainians, the more you will marvel at their ability to carry on.

Chornobyl

The explosion at Chornobyl and its tragic aftermath underscores the pernicious nature of government actions and—in this case—inaction on the part of the former Soviet government. For many, it came to symbolize all that was wrong with the Soviet Union.

Historically, Ukraine was considered the second most important Soviet republic after Russia. Some might disagree with this assessment, but the role played by the Chornobyl disaster in undermining the Soviet Union warrants further consideration.

April 26, 1986 marked a black day in world history. Chornobyl, Ukraine was the site of the world's worst nuclear disaster, and the Soviet government deliberately downplayed the gravity of the situation. In the face of upcoming Labor Day celebrations on May 1, the government didn't want widespread panic to disrupt the annual event. After all, May Day and October Revolution Day (November 7, according to the Julian calendar) were important vehicles for commemorating the triumph of the Soviet system.

The foreign press reported the incident before the Soviets did. Swedish scientists recorded high radioactivity levels, which Americans then traced via satellite to the radioactive plume above Chornobyl.

The deliberate, delayed response on the part of the Soviets effectively lost time in containing the contamination, contributing to greater radiation exposure and the loss of more lives. This complicity on the part of the government irrevocably altered the history of the Soviet Union; some say that ultimately it cost the Soviet Union its existence.

Chornobyl is located 60 miles north of Kyiv and very close to the Belarusian border. Belarus suffered more significantly than Ukraine due to prevailing wind patterns; estimates hold that nearly one-quarter to one-third of Belarusian soil was seriously damaged. Parts of western Russia were also severely contaminated. Ukrainians and Belarusians contend that had this tragedy occurred on Russian soil, or closer to Moscow politics, the reactions would have been swifter.

Many Ukrainians express fear of having children in the wake of Chornobyl. One friend in Kyiv remarked that his sister-in-law had miscarried in Ukraine and subsequently given birth to a healthy child in New York. This was de facto proof to him that the Chornobyl tragedy was a contributing factor in the loss of the first child. Moreover, environmental hazards are rife in the most industrialized of the Soviet republics. The Leninist credo "Production is always necessary" (with its corollary "Production at all costs") bestowed upon Ukraine a daunting environmental legacy.

A sizeable increase in vodka and red wine consumption followed the Chornobyl catastrophe, based on the belief that these drinks help to flush radiation from the body. Ostensibly the liquidators (Chornobyl's clean-up crew) were given vodka rations for this reason; however, it is more likely that vodka was needed to mollify fears of contamination.

Access to iodine in the days immediately following Chornobyl was grossly inadequate. When it was available many people drank it without proper instruction, burning their throats and stomachs. Fearing a panic, the government even curtailed its availability at one point. Used properly, iodine attaches itself to the thyroid; otherwise, radio-active iodine will. If there is no space available for the radioactive isotope, it will be flushed from the system as an unneeded nutrient. Reports of thyroid damage, especially among children, are staggering. Similarly, bones latch onto calcium—and radioactive strontium. After Chornobyl, inadequate supplies of "clean" milk put children at greater risk of strontium poisoning. In any case, radioactive cesium can find many hosts in the human body and is not easily flushed.

An Incomplete Summary of Facts about Chornobyl
Chornobyl's explosion was the result of a failed experiment. Engineers had advised Moscow that they would perform a test on the morning of April 26, 1986, but Moscow didn't respond. The Ukrainians opted to proceed with the experiment. They wanted to know what would happen if some of the systems failed, so they intentionally shut down part of the reactor.

The problem lay in the reactor's design. (This type of reactor is known as the RBMK, and calls to eliminate all RBMK nuclear reactors were widespread.) Specifically, in slowing down these systems, other functions were actually sped up temporarily. The plant itself had been hastily constructed to substandard specifications. Defective metal was used so that construction could stay on schedule. Also, a lot of cement had been stolen during construction; sand was then added as filler, resulting in adulterated cement.

In cesium levels alone, Chornobyl has been described as equivalent to 300 Hiroshimas. A problem arises, however, in comparing the victims of Chornobyl, Hiroshima, and Nagasaki. Chornobyl victims had been exposed to small doses of radiation over a long period (including regularized releases of radioactive steam in order to prevent a sizeable build-up of noxious contaminants) prior to the 1986 explosion. Scientists and medical specialists have confirmed that the Soviet and Japanese problems don't correlate well.

The Soviet government repressed its scientists, physicians, and journalists after Chornobyl. Doctors were forbidden from ascribing illnesses and deaths to radiation exposure. The government intervened in the press to pinpoint the Chornobyl engineers as scapegoats rather than the fallible reactor design itself. Also, when acceptable levels of radiation rocketed off the scale, the scale was changed to accommodate amounts twenty times the originally acceptable levels.

For some communities, maps of irradiated areas were not drawn for years after the explosion. Some evacuations were planned for as late as five years after Chornobyl. Four radiation zones were mapped, Zone One being most contaminated and unfit for human habitation, although some elderly people later moved back there. Some say all of Kyiv is Zone Four with Zone Three hot spots. But Zone Four residents are exempt from taxation, and Kyiv could not survive without its already limited tax revenues if it were classified as Zone Four.

The evacuations were puzzling. Some began within a few days, quietly out of fear of widespread hysteria. While high-ranking government officials were sequestering relatives, most adults and children were unaware of the burgeoning cover-up. Many recall an unseasonably warm May Day parade during which children marched in the Kyiv streets with bare legs, unknowingly kicking up radioactive dust. Later, the government had these same schoolchildren rake all the leaves and bury them. All mutant animals were destroyed, as were evacuees' pets. In other cases where people weren't evacuated, their farm animals were seized but not necessarily destroyed.

People who wanted to leave contaminated areas were prevented from moving by law. In the Soviet era and today, citizens cannot relocate simply because they want to live elsewhere. (See Chapter Two on internal passports and the *propiska* registration stamp.) Others later returned to their contaminated homes. Thieves raided contaminated homes and sold the furniture to unsuspecting buyers.

In some contaminated areas millions of rubles were spent to dig ditches to bury radioactive soil (which soon regained its high levels of radioactivity); so-called clean homes were built in areas where the residents should have been relocated altogether. In other cases, people were relocated to contaminated areas.

Subsidies (colloquially referred to as "coffin money") were offered to members of certain villages, while neighboring villagers received nothing. The system was arbitrary at best, and even though some people were offered clean milk and tinned meat, supplies of clean provisions were always inadequate. Consequently, many were forced to consume their own irradiated milk, cattle, fruit, and vegetables; irradiated wood was burned for heat. Because of the system of subsidies, people wanted to be reclassified for additional benefits.

The government disbursed much of the contaminated products throughout the Soviet Union, declaring that some should be diluted with uncontaminated products. In this way, it was hoped that no single community would be overloaded; rather, contaminated products were offered to Soviet citizens at large.

In Bryansk (one of Russia's western regions hardest hit by Chornobyl) locals insist that Moscow ordered planes from the Bryansk and Oryol military bases to fire cloud-seeding missiles, causing rain to fall; this ostensibly diverted radioactive clouds from Moscow. In 1994 Russian scientists performed similar cloud-seeding in St. Petersburg to prevent rain from washing out the Goodwill Games.

Chornobyl was not the first major nuclear catastrophe in the Soviet Union, but it was its last. *Glasnost* (openness) and *perestroika* (restructuring) may have been the new Soviet buzzwords, but to many Soviet citizens Chornobyl's tragic unfolding showed how little these were put into practice. Gorbachev's appearance on national television more than two weeks after the explosion marked the first time in history that a Soviet premier had admitted an error, and this a grave one. The growing cynicism of the later Brezhnev era was strengthened by the government's egregious behavior and cover-up. Chornobyl's aftermath also sparked an environmental movement that addressed issues beyond nuclear problems.

The subsequent break-up of the Soviet Union means that the corpus of information on Chornobyl, clandestine and public, is no longer part of the Soviet Union. Whose information is it? Alla

Yaroshinskaya, a Ukrainian journalist who has studied the subject extensively, is convinced that without the failed coup of August 1991 we would have far less information. Still, no records were kept on the liquidators, many of whom had helped to build Kyiv's metro but were then relocated throughout the Soviet Union.

The cover-up was extensive and by all rights criminal, but this fact is really moot now. The bigger issue is the ongoing waste in the name of humanitarian aid. Millions of dollars have helped to line the pockets of bureaucrats, while Chornobyl's victims have rarely seen the 12% tax collected on all paychecks. There is currently a proposal to scrap this tax, which has been regarded almost universally as a sham since its inception.

Travel Advice vis-à-vis Chornobyl

Western experts generally agree that today's visitors to Ukraine need not worry about Chornobyl's residual effects. However, do observe some basic precautions. For example, although locals do it, think before swimming in the Dnipro River in the vicinity of Kyiv; some of the silt was contaminated by radioactivity and then carried downstream. This also means drinking local water is not advised. If you must, make sure you boil it first. (More on this in Chapter Four.) Also, while Ukrainians love their wild berries and mushrooms, avoid them if their origin is uncertain. Other foods are not generally specified.

Environment, Energy, and Mineral Wealth

In addition to Chornobyl's vast consequences, there is extensive air, land, and water pollution in Ukraine. Under the Soviet system, the republics were marked by different specialities. Uzbekistan, for example, was celebrated for its cotton production; Minsk, (then) Byelorussia concentrated on domestic appliances; and Ukraine with its rich soil and large population base emphasized agriculture as well as chemical and heavy industry, including metallurgy, machine-building, energy-intensive manufacturing, and nuclear missile production. Consequently, Ukraine attained dubious distinction as the most industrialized of the Soviet republics: in Soviet terms, this also means that today it is among the most contaminated; widespread environmental pollution accompanied all Soviet industrialization. Improper disposal of toxic wastes and a general lack of ecological controls in mines and industrial plants wreaked havoc on Ukraine.

The Donetsk region is exceptionally rich in coal deposits; this coal, along with Ukraine's rich iron ore deposits, is used in the steel-making process and is highly polluting. Coal also served as an energy source for much of Ukraine's strong manufacturing base; this was necessary to perpetuate the large working class that was the basis of Soviet legitimacy and power. Coal has thus contributed adversely to Ukraine's already daunting environmental legacy.

Since independence, the government has enacted environmental protection laws in an effort to halt additional pollution. Still, Ukraine lacks the financial resources to repair the widespread damage sustained during the communist period.

Further, under the Soviet paradigm, end users paid virtually nothing for energy, and waste was rife, as it is today. Moreover, increasing demand ostensibly signaled a more powerful country. Today, Ukraine's tradition of wastefulness combined with gross inefficiency translates into a heavy reliance on imported fuel from Russia. One solution widely practiced is exchanging Ukrainian wheat for Russian oil and gas. In these barter transactions no money exchanges hands, nor are the transactions taxed. Nevertheless, by late 1998, Ukraine was in debt to the tune of $1 billion to the Russian natural gas monopoly Gazprom; this was after significantly reducing the size of the Ukrainian debt throughout that year. An agreement was worked out by year's end whereby the Ukrainian government provided grain and industrial equipment valued at $1.1 billion in exchange for writing off the debt. (Russia in 1998 had not only seen its ruble plummet; its crop yields were disastrous and insufficient for feeding its population.)

Nuclear Energy and Missile Technology

Obviously, an alternative energy solution has been the production of nuclear energy. Ukraine currently depends on its five nuclear power plants for roughly half of its energy needs. These reactors will reach the end of their safe life span around 2010. One significant drawback is that Ukrainian nuclear power plants exclusively use Russian-made (and low quality) nuclear fuel.

In 1998, only Chornobyl's third reactor (of four) was in operation. In 1995, Ukraine signed a memorandum with the Group of Seven (G7) to close down Chornobyl by 2000; in exchange Ukraine received aid to construct two new nuclear reactors to replace Chornobyl's lost capacity. There is continuing debate about these new reactors at Rivne and Khmelnytsky, which by late 1998 were 70% complete.

Among its other specialities, Ukraine was the center for producing nuclear missiles. The United States paid Ukraine's nuclear fuel bill through 1998 in exchange for Ukraine relinquishing its Soviet-era warheads—the world's third largest arsenal—to Russia in 1996. The United States also contributed money to completely destroy the missiles and silos that once housed the warheads. This process is well under way, although Ukraine stills lacks an effective method for reprocessing the highly toxic solid fuel that was used in the missiles.

THE CRIMEAN QUESTION

Today Crimea is predominantly Russian (63% vs. 25% Ukrainian and 9% Muslim Tatar), although it was officially gifted to Ukraine in 1954 in recognition of Ukraine's 300 years of unification with Russia. Crimea is Ukraine's only region where Moscow time is observed. Moscow time (GMT+3) is one hour ahead of Kyiv (GMT+2). An experiment in 1997 to unite all of Ukraine under one time zone failed quickly, and Moscow time was resumed in Crimea.

Tatars ruled Crimea before the 18th century when Russians occupied the peninsula. Following World War II, the Soviet dictator Iosif Stalin accused the Crimean Tatars of collaborating with the

Germans during the latter's three-year occupation. Stalin banished some 250,000 Tatars to Central Asia with the largest numbers deported to Uzbekistan. Many died en route. Khrushchev later said that Stalin would have deported far more Ukrainians, but their numbers were too large. As it was, he had attacked Ukraine's peasantry in the early 1930s and its intelligentsia later in the decade.

In recent years, some 250,000 Tatars have returned to their ancestral homeland; their presence is altering the peninsula's ethnic makeup. In early 1998, violent protests erupted when repatriated Tatars were not allowed to vote.

Many of Crimea's Tatars do not possess a passport, having relinquished citizenship rights when they left former Soviet states. For those holding Uzbek passports, efforts are under way to simplify the process for obtaining Ukrainian citizenship. Tatar leaders are calling for similar measures to ease naturalization for repatriated Tatars banished to other countries in the Soviet Union.

This is not Crimea's only issue. In 1995, Ukraine declared Crimea's separatist constitution and presidency under Yuri Meshkov invalid. (Crimea had declared self-rule in 1992 which Ukraine did not recognize.) For a time war between Ukraine and Russia seemed a possibility, although by 1995, Russia's war with Chechnya was under way; the Kremlin told Meshkov that this was an internal affair. Ukraine was clearly wise in having never sent troops to Crimea; for its part, Crimea recognized that tourism, unlike wheat and iron ore production, does not continue during wartime. Because tourism was its foremost priority, Crimea withdrew its claims for independence, and further conflict was averted.

TRANSDNISTR

In 1994 Moscow signed a peace agreement with Moldova in which Russia agreed to close its 14th Army base in Moldova's separatist Dnistr region. In late 1998, the Ukrainian and Moldovan presidents were still urging Moscow to withdraw its troops as agreed.

In 1990 pro-Moscow forces in Transdnistr had proclaimed independence from Moldova. Moldova has not yet recognized independence in this sliver of land between the Dnistr River and Ukraine's western border. The Dnistr region is populated mainly by ethnic Russians and Ukrainians, who feared that Moldova, dominated by ethnic Romanians, would seek to reunite with neighboring Romania.

In 1992 a brief war was fought between the separatists and Moldova. The separatists were armed with weapons from the former Soviet 14th Army. A ceasefire was brokered by Aleksandr Lebed, then the base's commanding general. Although tensions between the Dnistr separatists and the Moldovan government have since abated, neither side has budged on its stance. In 1998 Ukraine began insisting on its right to send peacekeepers to Transdnistr, and Russia remains uneasy about Ukrainian presence there.

Moldova is a small country with a population of 4.4 million. It is dependent on Russian gas and is not needed by Russia for shipping gas to Europe. Its official language is Romanian, a Romance language, written in Cyrillic script during Soviet times.

Collectively, Romania, Ukraine, and Moldova have expressed interest in establishing a Lower Danube Free Economic Zone for the shipment of Caspian oil across their countries. Part of Ukraine's interest in Transdnistr stems from weak border controls. Ukraine is also concerned about potential border and visa issues with Poland and Hungary, both of which received EU membership in May 1999.

SIMILARITIES WITH RUSSIA AND POLAND

Ukraine is distinct from Russia in that there are two dominant languages and three primary churches today, and for centuries the nation was dominated by outsiders, namely Poles and Russians (and Lithuanians and Poles before the Russians). Culturally, Ukraine shares more traditions with its Eastern Slavic brothers, the Belarusians and Russians, than with its neighboring Poles, although much of its cuisine falls somewhere in between.

The so-called Russian soul is really the Slavic soul, and Ukrainians and Russians alike have strong predispositions toward mysticism and superstition. The role of vodka traditions among the Eastern Slavs is historical and significant (both Russians and Poles claim to have invented the intoxicating elixir). Drunkenness and alcoholism are unfortunate corollaries attached more to Ukrainians and Russians than to Poles. The Eastern Slavs also share a tendency toward fatalism that is often linked to their excessive drinking.

Graft and corruption are also legitimate concerns for those traveling to the former Soviet Union or establishing business relations there. Seventy-plus years of communism, including some twenty-five years under Stalinist absolutism, have molded Soviet citizenry and individual character in ways different from communist rule in Eastern Europe.

Ukraine's financial woes are acute, but the country possesses vast mineral wealth, including iron, coal, manganese, zinc, sulfur, mercury, petroleum, and natural gas (even if the last two are insufficient for the country's needs). Ukraine's ultimate wealth, however, is its people, and outsiders who fail to recognize this should look to other countries for their international exploits.

EARLY HISTORY IN A NUTSHELL

Ukraine's early history essentially concerns several important and competing clans. Most significant were the Scythians and Varangians, but others are worth noting.

The mother of Russian cities, Kyiv was founded in the late 5th century. In 1982 the city observed its 1500th anniversary, whereas Moscow celebrated its 850th birthday in 1997, and St. Petersburg was founded by Peter the Great some three hundred years ago. The ancient chronicles refer to the kingdom of Kyivan Rus, the huge Eastern Slavic state that was precursor to modern-day Russia, Ukraine, and Belarus and whose capital was Kyiv. At its height it stretched from the Danube to the Volga and from the Baltic to the Black Sea. Its prosperity grew in large measure to its trade route along the Dnipro River.

The Scythians were Central Asians who settled the steppes north of the Black Sea around the 7th century B.C. The Scythians distinguished themselves as horsemen and gold craftsmen. Warriors were encouraged to drink the blood of the first enemy killed and to make chalices out of enemies' skulls. Ruthless toward their enemies, they valued friendship and loyalty above all else. Their civilization was based on commerce, and they established contacts with Greeks from Asia Minor who had settled along the Black Sea coast around the same time. By the 4th century B.C., the Greek coastal cities were booming and continued to do so until the 2nd century B.C. The Greeks and Scythians intermarried, and both groups crafted many of the famous Scythian ornaments and decorations characterized by animal motifs. (The finest examples of Scythian art in Ukraine can be seen in Kyiv's Monastery of the Caves.)

With the exception of Crimea (until the 3rd century A.D.), the Scythians were defeated by the Macedonians in 339 B.C.; a century later, they were overwhelmed and assimilated by the Sarmatians, an eastern nomadic group. The Sarmatians dominated this area for the next 400 years, until the 2nd century A.D. (Sarmatian women were not permitted to marry until after they had killed in battle.)

In the 2nd century A.D., Germanic Goths arrived from what is today northern Poland; they set up a state covering most of modern Ukraine. Around A.D. 370, the Huns, a nomadic tribe originating in Mongolia, drove out the Goths; the empire established by the Huns potentially threatened the Roman Empire.

The migrations of the Slavs (the direct ancestors of Ukraine's current population) began early in the Christian era, no later than the 2nd century A.D.; but the big wave did not come until the 6th and 7th centuries. The Slavs were able to spread throughout the region while the Huns focused on other territories. Linguistic and cultural differences mark the Western Slavs (forerunners of today's Poles, Czechs, and Slovaks) and the Southern Slavs (forerunners to the Bulgarians, Macedonians, Serbians, and Croatians) from the Eastern Slavs, ancestors of the Ukrainians, Russians, and Belarusians. By the 7th century, the Eastern Slavs were based on the right bank of the Dnipro.

Trade among the Eastern Slavs was poorly developed. In the 8th century, the Khazars (nomadic Turkic and Iranian tribes from the Caucasus) penetrated much of Ukraine. The Khazars, who adopted Judaism in the 9th century, built an empire based on their military and equestrian strengths as well as their Iranian and Jewish trading skills: they were both conquerors and traders. Their capital was then near the mouth of the Volga, but Kyiv proved to be an important trading base, helping to bridge the Arab and Byzantine peoples. The Slavs were valued by the Khazars for their honey, wax, furs, and slaves. But many conflicts with the Arabs and encroachments by the Turkic Pechenegs weakened Khazaria; meanwhile, the Varangians began appearing with increasing frequency and force. The Varangians were Swedes known as the Vikings who beginning at the end of the 5th century had set up a southern outpost in Kyiv. In the 6th century, they set up trading posts east of the Baltic.

A matter of historical debate has been the etymology of "Rus," with some contending that the Slavs called the Varangians "Rus." In any case, there is consensus that the Scandinavian impact on Eastern Slavic language and culture was minimal. In reality, the rise of Kyivan Rus was the result of a complex interrelationship of ethnic peoples.

The Varangians obtained furs, honey, and slaves from the natives; seeking further profits, they continued to move southward and in 860, they raided Constantinople, prior to fighting the Khazars.

In 882 Oleh of Novgorod proclaimed himself ruler of Kyiv which was by then some 400 years old. (Twenty years before, when he first established himself in Kyiv, he declared it would become "the mother of all Rus cities.") Kyiv and Novgorod were now successfully united as the main depots on the "Greek" trade route. The highlight of Oleh's rule was when he attacked and pillaged Constantinople in 911.

After Oleh, the reign of Ihor was much less successful. Ihor's wife, Olha, ruled from 945 to 962 after Ihor was ambushed and killed for repeatedly forcing his subjects to pay tribute. Olha was depicted in the chronicles as beautiful, crafty, and wise. She recognized that the arbitrary collection of tribute had to be changed and instituted the first reforms in Kyivan Rus, which specified certain tributes at certain intervals. Her foreign relations were marked by diplomacy, not war, and she went to Constantinople to negotiate with the Byzantine emperor.

Finally, Kyivan Rus expanded in the later 10th century under Svyatoslav. After crushing the Khazars, the greatest competitors for hegemony in Eurasia, he conquered the northern Caucasus. All of the Eastern Slavs came under Kyivan rule. The problem was that the Khazars had kept eastern nomadic tribes, such as the Turkic Pechenegs, from advancing along the Ukrainian steppes.

The founders of Kyiv, according to legend: brothers Kiy, Shchcek, and Horiv, and sister Lybid. (Photo courtesy of Meredith Dalton.)

In 968, Svyatoslav agreed to help the Byzantines against the powerful Bulgarian kingdom. With a huge army, the rich cities along the Danube were captured. Svyatoslav's empire now stretched from the Volga to the Danube, and he preferred the Balkans to Kyiv. Byzantium worried about its aggressive neighbor and turned against him in a brutal campaign. Forced to return to Kyiv in 972, his army was ambushed by Pechenegs, and Svyatoslav was killed.

Ukraine's Christian Origins

In 988 Volodymyr (Vladimir in Russian) accepted Christianity from Constantinople, thereby strengthening the role of Byzantine culture—including art, education, literature, and imperial authority—within Kyivan Rus. Christianity had arrived at least in the previous century (Olha had converted circa 955), but Volodymyr is recognized for introducing Christianity to his realm on a significant scale. According to legend, Volodymyr forced a large part of Kyiv's population to be baptized in the Dnipro River despite freezing temperatures. His reign was marked by another significant point, the annexation of what is now western Ukraine, which set the scene for the centuries-long struggle against the Poles. As a result of his conquests, his realm became the largest in Europe.

After Volodymyr's death, his eldest son killed three of his younger brothers; two of them, Borys and Hlib, were later canonized by the Orthodox Church. The second son, Yaroslav the Wise, defeated the eldest brother, then split the realm with yet another brother to avoid bloodshed. Yaroslav received the land west of the Dnipro, and Mstyslav won the east. Kyiv was too valuable to divide.

Yaroslav's reign is usually considered the high point of Kyivan Rus. He continued to expand his empire and won back lands that had been lost to the Poles. He also successfully destroyed the Pechenegs. In gratitude for winning this battle, Yaroslav built *Sofiyivskiy Sobor* or St. Sofia's Cathedral between 1017 and 1031; it was dedicated in 1037. St. Sofia's is named and modeled after the Hagia Sofia (Holy

Wisdom) in Constantinople, now Istanbul. In addition to its religious role, St. Sofia's was the seat of the metropolitan and a center of learning, culture, and politics in Kyivan Rus. It housed the first school and library of Kyivan Rus.

Yaroslav the Wise is considered the "Peter the Great" of Kyivan Rus, although he looked south, not west. The construction of churches was very important to him; during his rule, Kyiv boasted over 400 churches. Yaroslav is also noted for his codification of the legal code. Finally, in an effort to prevent the internecine fighting that had arisen among his brothers, he divided his territories among his sons before his death and established rules of seniority and rotation. Problems arose, however, when one of the sons died; often sons of the deceased ignored the rules of rotation and instead fought against their uncles who had seniority for that territory.

Political fragmentation contributed to the decline of Kyiv as more and more principalities split off and Kyiv lost its wealth, population, and territory. It became a principality like all the others. At the same time, Kyiv's assets had always been its liabilities. Whereas Khazars and Slavs had successfully exploited Kyiv's favorable location, making it the strongest and richest town on the Dnipro trade route, this also meant that Kyiv attracted marauders. At the same time, other trade routes opened up, making this one less important. The pillage of Constantinople in 1204 by the Crusaders was a blow to Kyivan commerce. The final blow came in 1240 when the Mongols, called Tatars by the Eastern Europeans, sacked Kyiv and its inhabitants fled.

St. Sofia's was badly damaged by the Mongols in 1240 and suffered further damage by the Poles and Lithuanians. By the late 17th century, it lay in ruins until its reconstruction early in the 18th century on orders of Peter the Great. Yaroslav the Wise is buried in St. Sofia's.

The Orthodox Churches Today

The Ukrainian Orthodox Church was formerly called the Russian Orthodox Church in Ukraine. This name was officially changed in

1990, in part because the church was concerned that it was losing ground to the resurgent Catholics who were linked with the reviving of national consciousness in Ukraine's western region. Allegiance is to the Moscow patriarchate, although a fragmented group under Metropolitan Filaret claimed Kyiv authority in 1992.

The year 1990 also marked the second re-emergence of the Ukrainian Autocephalous Orthodox Church or UAOC. "Autocephalous" means self-governing. In 1686, the Ukrainian Orthodox Church was forced to recognize authority from the Russian Orthodox Church. In 1921 the UAOC emerged for the first time during a brief flowering of national identity following the Russian Revolution. By 1930, however, this autocephalous church was forced underground again. Today all services are in Ukrainian, and allegiance is to the Ukrainian patriarchate in Kyiv.

The third primary church in Ukraine is the Uniate (also called Ukrainian Catholic or Greek Catholic) Church, which follows Orthodox rituals but recognizes the Pope as its leader. (Uniate priests are the only Catholic priests allowed to marry.) This church principally exists in Ukraine's western, Polish-influenced half. In 1946, Stalin abolished the church and seized all of its property, handing over parts of it to the Russian Orthodox Church. Like the UAOC, the Uniate Church was thus forced underground and did not resurface until the late 1980s. This was when the independence movement was garnering support in Right-Bank Ukraine.

Yaroslav's Golden Gate

Zolaty Vorota (say *ZOlatee vaROta*) was the main entrance to Kyiv, which in Yaroslav's day was surrounded by a high defensive wall. Like St. Sofia's, this gate, built in 1037, was inspired by Constantinople's Golden Gate and was famous throughout Europe. It was covered with gold and precious metals and topped with a tiny church. Destroyed in the 1240 Mongol-Tatar raid, it was presumably covered in earth around 1750. In 1982 this stone and wood structure was rebuilt in honor of the city's 1500th anniversary. Minor renovations were completed in recent years.

Genghis Khan never traveled as far as Kyiv. But, according to legend, his grandson, Batu Khan, entered the city here at the time of the Mongol capture.

Kyiv's Pecherska Lavra

St. Sofia's Cathedral and Kyiv's *Pecherska Lavra* (say *peCHERska LAvra*) or Monastery of the Caves are World Heritage sites. They are also Ukraine's most important religious sites. The Lavra's origins date to the 11th century and it was a monastery of the highest order.

You might want to check out the guided tour (in English) on the Lavra's website at www.lavra.kiev.ua. Here you'll find a layout of the 50 acres including buildings no longer standing; there are also photos of some buildings seen on the grounds today. For example, you can see the courtyard where the Assumption Cathedral (*Uspenskiy Sobor*) once stood. This masterpiece dated to the end of the 11th century and was influenced by Byzantine architecture. Damaged by the Mongols in 1240, religious life was not revived until the 15th century when the cathedral was restored. Plundered by the Tatars in 1482, the cathedral was again restored in the 16th century but burned in a fire in 1718. It was rebuilt for the last time in the 1720s.

During the time of Russian Tsar Peter the Great (1672–1725), the Lavra was an important pilgrimage site. In the mid-18th century, the monastery owned some 80,000 serfs, and there were three glassworks on the grounds. The cathedral was the centerpiece of the Lavra architectural ensemble. The most revered relics were cherished here, and Kyiv princes (and later prominent religious people and high-ranking military) were buried here. In 1941, during the German occupation, the Assumption Cathedral was blown up. Some sources still charge the Nazis with this act, although it was later said to be the work of the Red Army attempting to trap the German forces. (Like-wise, it was the Red Army that destroyed Kyiv's main street, the

Kyiv's Pecherska Lavra (Monastery of the Caves). This fascinating site dates back to the days of Kyivan Rus. (Photo courtesy of Catherine Isabel Dalton.)

Kreshchatyk, immediately following the arrival of the Germans. Babi Yar [see below] was among the Germans' retaliatory responses.)

The bell tower was completed in 1745. This was built to replace the one that had burned in 1718 along with the cathedral. At 315 feet, it was the highest bell tower in the country and the tallest structure in the Russian Empire before St. Isaac's Cathedral in St. Petersburg surpassed it. The tower was so high that the monks were afraid it would collapse and therefore refused to pay the architect for his work. The architect, J.G. Schedel, had to sue the monastery for his fee.

Finally, we turn to the story of the caves. *Perchery* in Ukrainian means "caves." A monk settled in these caves in the mid-11th century to pray and was soon followed by a second monk. More monks chose to go underground, and eventually they turned their attention to the construction of the Assumption Cathedral.

The tradition of burying monks in the catacombs began with the arrival of the second monk and continued until the 17th century. In the

43

14th century monks presumably discovered that dead bodies in the catacombs do not decompose, so the corpses were put into coffins and displayed for visitors as the relics of saints. In 1643 Metropolitan Petro Mohyla (for whom the university is named) canonized 69 monks buried in the catacombs.

At present the near caves, where the bodies are better preserved, contain 73 coffins, and the far caves have 45. You can tour the caves for the price of a candle, which will help you to see your way through this short but claustrophobic maze. (Visitors should dress conservatively out of respect for the monks; I've also heard not to look at monks unless their palms are up.)

In 1927 the monastery was closed and converted into a museum; the caves were given to the Museum of Historical Treasures of Ukraine. This is one of several museums housed on the monastery grounds and well worth a visit. Jewelry exhibits date from the 6th century B.C. to the 19th century A.D. Golden ornaments made by the Scythians and masters of Kyivan Rus are displayed.

Other museums of note on the grounds include the Museum of Microminiatures and the Ukrainian Museum of Folk and Decorative Art. During the Soviet era, there was even a Museum of Atheism on the grounds. It was housed in the refectory, and among its displays was a mummified rat. The curators explained that climactic conditions had preserved the rat, which, like the mummified saints, had no religious value!

In 1987 the state returned the caves to the church, and in 1988 it recognized the 1000th anniversary of Kyiv's mass baptism.

The Cossacks and Bohdan Khmelnytsky

Princedoms developed over time, splintering the great Kyivan Rus state, and in 1240 Kyiv was sacked by the Mongols. This effectively ended the empire, whereupon the power base was moved north and west. In the mid-14th century, parts of western Ukraine were absorbed into Polish and Lithuanian kingdoms, with eastern Ukraine held by Russia. Sovereignty changed hands repeatedly. The Crimean Tatars devastated, sometimes completely and sometimes in parts, much of present-day Ukraine.

The Cossacks (*Kozak* in Russian and Ukrainian) were originally refugees who fled serfdom, beginning in the 15th century, to hide out in what was then the borderland, now Ukraine. The name *Kozak* is derived from a Turkish word meaning "free man." Later its meaning was broadened to include Ukrainians who went into the steppes to fish and hunt and practice other trades, such as beekeeping. The Cossacks are today lauded for winning independence from Poland and for establishing the state that made up the central part of modern Ukraine. The western part remained with Poland.

The Cossacks were the most militant of the Ukrainian population. They set up democratic military communities whose elected leaders were called hetmans. The most famous of these was Bohdan Khmelnytsky (1595-1657), who gained fame for leading the Ukrainian people in the war of liberation against the Poles. One way that he succeeded in doing this was to strike an alliance with the traditional enemies of the Cossacks, the Crimean Tatars. Khmelnytsky is also recognized for his ability to mold unruly peasants and Cossacks into powerful and organized armies; today one hears that the Soviet army was well stocked with Ukrainian officers because of the Cossacks' strong military traditions. Further, Khmelnytsky instilled pride and self-confidence in a group that had previously lacked a sense of identity, and he repeatedly stressed that defending Orthodoxy was a major goal of his revolt. According to some historians, he succeeded in building the platform for Ukrainian statehood; however, the poet Shevchenko and others have criticized him for bringing Ukraine into Russia's sphere.

Sovereignty didn't last, and central Ukraine was quickly annexed to Russia. As a result of Khmelnytsky's efforts toward unification with Russia, Ukraine was essentially divided during the late 17th century, with Poland controlling the western half and Muscovy controlling the eastern part. This strengthened the foundation for the east vs. west division that persists today.

Western Ukraine remained with Poland for another century—until the Partitions of Poland between 1772 and 1795 transferred much of Polish Ukraine to Russian hands. By now roughly 85% of Ukraine had fallen under Russian control. Only the far western region of modern Ukraine, around Lviv, remained with Poland; this fell under the reign of the Austro-Hungarian Empire after 1867. With the decline of the Polish kingdom, the Cossack period also ended. This new period marked the beginnings of Russification and suppression of Ukrainian culture.

That Khmelnytsky is regarded as a hero by many is a source of great tension in Ukraine. As many as 200,000 Jews were slaughtered during his reign; thus Jews and Poles universally hate him. Furthermore, according to Soviet history, Khmelnytsky's greatness lay in his understanding that the salvation of Ukrainians lay only in unity with the Russian people. Some predict that he, like many communist-era heroes, may later be relegated to oblivion, in part because he signed the treaty of unification with Russia. At the same time, his achievements have been compared to the impact of Oliver Cromwell on England. His impact on Ukrainian history is significant and irrefutable. It will be interesting to observe whether propaganda and fashion continue to revise history.

A monument to Khmelnytsky on a rearing horse—frozen mid-gallop and with mace drawn—was erected in 1888, on the site where Kyiv residents had welcomed their triumphant hero more than two centuries earlier. (After independence, this square, formerly called Khmelnytsky Square, was renamed Sofiyivska Square. At the same time, neighboring Lenin Street was renamed Bohdan Khmelnytsky Street.) The mace is a Ukrainian symbol of authority, with Cossack, anti-Russian implications and should you have any interest in owning a mace like the one on the monument, you can find wooden versions for sale in all the souvenir shops.

Jewish History Prior to World War II

Kyiv historically boasted one of the world's most important Jewish communities. The center of Kyivan Rus was a commercial crossroads between Central Asia and Western Europe and attracted itinerant Jews and later settled communities. The Jewish population tried to convert Prince Volodymyr to Judaism. (Volodymyr's first choice was presumably Islam until he learned of its stance of alcohol abstinence.)

Jews in Ukraine were intermittently persecuted and expelled, only to return again. At times, Jews could reside in the city; at others, merchants could only enter the city for business but had to be out by day's end; still at other times, they could not enter at all. Bohdan Khmelnytsky massacred Jews in his efforts to free Ukraine from Poland's yoke and to defend Orthodoxy; with eastern Ukraine's subsequent annexation to Russia, the ban on Jewish settlement was renewed. Eastern Ukraine did not have a Jewish community again for another century, when the Polish Partitions of the late 18th century brought in half a million Jews. These Jews were confined to the occupied lands: present-day Ukraine, Belarus, Lithuania, and eastern Poland comprised the "Pale of Settlement."

The notion of a "Jewish problem" grew in the 19th century. In 1835, Jews were expelled once again from Kyiv, but they continued to enter the city as tradesmen. In the 1860s, the city sections of Podil (Podol in Russian) and Lyebed were assigned for Jews with residency permits. With the exception of the German occupation years, Podil has been the center of Kyiv's Jewish life ever since. Prior to World War II, one-fifth of Kyiv's population (or 175,000) was Jewish, whereas Lviv was one-third Jewish. Odesa boasted the highest Jewish percentage of all: one hundred years ago half of its population was Jewish, and it was one of the largest Jewish centers in the world.

In Ukraine, generalizations can be made about urban dwellers and villagers. The cities were typically populated by non-Ukrainians, notably Jews and Russians, who were closely associated with urban growth and industrial expansion. To a Jew, the Ukrainian represented the backward, ignorant villager; to a Ukrainian, the Jew represented that foreign, exploitative city element that bought his produce cheaply and sold all goods at high markup.

Pogroms occurred in 1881 and 1905, but Jewish life and culture flourished in Kyiv. The University of Kyiv attracted more Jews at the turn of the century than any university in the Russian Empire. Both Isaac Babel and Golda Meir recalled the pogrom of 1905. Meir, Israel's first ambassador to the Soviet Union, also recalled seeing the writer Sholem Aleichem who then lived at Chervonoarmyiska 5 (No. 5, Red Army Street). Aleichem is one of the great Yiddish writers best known for capturing the Ukrainian Jewish experience; *Fiddler on the Roof* was derived from his Tevye stories. (Anatevka Village in the stories is based on Boyarka, a village about 15 miles from Kyiv.)

The possibility of large-scale pogroms arose after a Jew assassinated Russian Prime Minister Pyotr Stolypin in 1911. In Kyiv that year, Mendel Beilis was charged with the murder and mutilation of a 12-year-old Christian boy. Beilis, a Jew, had supposedly killed the boy for his blood, which was to be used for ritual purposes. Police actually traced the crime to a gang of thieves, but Beilis was nonetheless imprisoned for two years before his trial; he was acquitted.

Several fictionalized accounts of this case have been written, including *The Bloody Hoax* by Sholem Aleichem and *The Fixer* by Bernard Malamud. The latter won the Pulitzer Prize and was adapted to the screen in 1968, starring Alan Bates. For a detailed, nonfictionalized account, look at Maurice Samuel's *Blood Accusation: The Strange History of the Beilis Case* (Knopf).

In the earliest years of communism, Kyiv was a major center of Jewish culture with its Yiddish schools, newspapers, literature, and theaters. Many Jews fought in the Russian Revolution with its promises of religious tolerance. Trotsky (né Lev Bronstein) was a Ukrainian Jew, although he later denied it. Beginning in the 1930s Jewish culture was systematically destroyed throughout the Soviet Union.

Babi Yar and Its Monument

In August 1941 the Germans captured or killed over half a million Soviet troops in Kyiv. On September 21, the Germans captured Kyiv. They were to occupy the city for nearly 800 days, until the Red Army retook the capital on November 6, 1943.

On September 24, 1941, the Soviet Army set off fires in downtown Kyiv in reaction to the Nazi occupiers, and on September 26, retaliation was planned. On September 29, Jews were ordered to report to the designated site with their documents and warm clothes; those who did not show faced execution. Germans spread rumors that the Jews would be relocated to ghettos or labor camps. The posters appearing in Russian, Ukrainian, and Yiddish gave unclear instructions about the meeting place; however, the general proximity to a rail station appeared to bode well for relocation.

Instead, more than 33,700 Jews were killed in a two-day period after being stripped of all their belongings. Their bodies were then dumped into a ravine, Babi Yar, which means Granny's Ravine. Over the next two years, the total killed at this site reached 100,000; some estimates suggest the total was closer to 150,000. Those executed were primarily Jews, but they included Ukrainian partisans and nationalists, prisoners of war, and gypsies. Evidence shows that Ukrainian guards were willing participants in the massacre.

Babi Yar will live on in infamy as a powerful symbol of Jewish suffering. For years Soviet authorities refused to acknowledge that most of the victims killed in this Kyiv ravine were Jews. To erase this horrific memory, the government even tried to build a housing project at Babi Yar in the 1960s; the project was canceled when Jews and non-Jews protested.

In 1959, a monument had been erected on the site of a wartime German prison camp. It was several hundred yards from the ravine. The monument referred only to "fascist occupiers" and "citizens of Kyiv." The only hint that the vast majority of victims was Jewish was that one plaque to the "citizens of Kyiv" was in Hebrew.

Also in 1959, a plaque was erected at the home of Sholem Aleichem on Red Army Street. Aleichem's Jewish origins were acknowledged on the plaque, thereby betraying cracks in the official anti-Semitism. However, this plaque was replaced a year later by another that did not mention his Jewish roots. In 1992 the three-story building built in the 1880s was gutted to make way for a museum.

In 1961 Yevgeny Yevtushenko, the internationally renowned poet, wrote his most celebrated poem, *Babi Yar*, lamenting the absence of a monument and acknowledging the murdered Jews. Dmitri Shostakovich set this to music in his 13th Symphony in 1963.

On September 28, 1991, the 50th anniversary of Babi Yar, an explicitly Jewish monument was dedicated closer to the site of the killings. Representatives from the Soviet and Ukrainian governments, Israel, and the United States attended the ceremony. The Soviet Union officially ended in mid-December, so the sanctioning of this memorial was one of its last official acts.

There are further plans today to create a museum and archive dedicated to all Ukrainian Jews killed during World War II. A list of those killed at Babi Yar is under way.

Historically Ukrainian Jews spoke Russian (and Yiddish), not Ukrainian. (Babi Yar is "Babyn Yar" in Ukrainian, but the Russian is the more familiar name.) Since independence, a number of Hebrew schools have opened, but they are preparing the younger Jewish population for emigration to Israel and elsewhere. Despite attempts to revive Yiddish, the historic Ukrainian-Jewish tongue is dying.

Jews Today

Many Jews returned to Kyiv after the war despite continued suppression of Jewish life. One infamous case concocted by Stalin (the "Doctors' Plot") accused nine doctors, including six Jews, of planning to murder communist leaders. Their public executions were planned in Moscow to be accompanied by a massive anti-Semitic campaign and deportations of Jews. Stalin's death in 1953 spared their lives.

Monument to Babi Yar, Kyiv. (Photo courtesy of Catherine Isabel Dalton.)

51

During the 1970s and 1980s, the Soviets allowed emigration from time to time. Since independence, emigration has continued steadily, and Ukraine's Jewish population is down to nearly half of what it was just ten years ago. Anti-Semitism survives, although the Ukrainian Nationalist group RUKH has staunchly supported a Jewish role in independent Ukraine. Many Jews still express a desire to emigrate.

The blue and white Puppet Theater at Shota Rustaveli and Rognedinska Street was once Kyiv's Great Synagogue, built in 1902. Church property seized by the communist regime has been returned to the Orthodox Church; thus, Jews also eagerly await the return of the Great Synagogue. There are plans to create a Jewish community complex around Shota Rustaveli which was once home to Kyiv's wealthiest Jews, whereas the Podil area was and remains the center of Jewish cultural life. Podil in the late 1990s is undergoing a revival of sorts; people especially like that it retains much of the flavor of the early 20th century. (By contrast, 90% of Warsaw was destroyed during the war.) Kyiv's synagogue on Shovkovychna Street was opened in 1894. It has been in continuous use except when the Nazi occupiers used it as a stable.

Reading Sources for Ukrainian and Russian History

For practical and space considerations, it is not possible to include a detailed history of Ukraine. Yet certain historical facts are necessary background information for a better understanding of Ukrainian profiles today. In the chapters that follow subjective impressions and observations—mine and those of many people interviewed—are described, with occasional detours into historical facts intended to help the reader better understand modern Ukrainians. (See also Select Bibliography.)

There are several good social histories, primarily about Russia during the late Soviet era, which I highly recommend. I direct the reader's attention to Hedrick Smith's *The Russians* and *The New Russians*, both revised in paperback editions, and to David Remnick's

Pulitzer Prizewinning *Lenin's Tomb: The Last Days of the Soviet Empire*. Remnick's *Resurrection: The Struggle of a New Russia* was issued in paperback with a new afterword in 1998 (but before the August financial collapse). These books by Smith and Remnick collectively examine changes in daily life beginning in the mid- to late Brezhnev era, the late 1980s and final years of the Soviet Union under Gorbachev, and the early to mid-1990s in Russia under Yeltsin.

An assessment of recent events in Ukraine is much harder to come by than information on Russia. Two of the better current sources are on the Internet—www.russiatoday.com gives information on Russia, Ukraine, and the FSU; the free, English-language newspaper available twice a week in Kyiv and Odesa posts the bulk of its articles online at www.kiev.thepost.ua. This newspaper tends slightly toward the melodramatic, which fairly reflects its expatriate hard-copy readers in those two cities. Other good sources for current information on Ukraine and Russia include *The New York Times*, *The Economist,* and *The Financial Times*.

Orest Subtelny's *Ukraine: A History* provides an alternative to the mostly Russian history books available. It is necessary to outline some of the reasons why Ukrainians view themselves the way they do; one reason was the disastrous response and failure to resolve the Chornobyl disaster of 1986. Another was Stalin's deliberate starvation of Ukrainians in the early 1930s. Both reasons contributed adversely to the Ukrainians vs. Russians mentality.

Indeed, in order to better understand the Soviet people at large, it is necessary to examine the reign of Iosif Vissarionovich Dzhugashvili, best known to the world as Iosif Stalin. (The word *stal* in Russian means "steel.") Robert Conquest's *Stalin: Breaker of Nations* is a brief, readable overview of Stalin's life and cruel legacy. (The cult of Stalin that exists today is another topic unto itself.)

Collectivization and the Faked Famine

In the late 1930s, Stalin targeted his purges against the intelligentsia

53

and Communist Party itself. *The Great Terror*, another book by Robert Conquest, is the name frequently ascribed to this period in Soviet history. Earlier in the decade, Stalin had focused his energies on destroying the Ukrainian peasantry who had militantly resisted the push toward collectivization. A third book by Robert Conquest is *Harvest of Sorrow: Collectivization and the Terror-Famine*. Myron Dolot also wrote a book on this period entitled *Execution by Hunger*.

In 1932, Stalin's response to the peasants opposing collectivization was to demand grain deliveries that were impossible to achieve. His scheme was ruthlessly enforced; people starved to a slow, hideous death (there were even tales of cannibalism), while Stalin's henchmen were dispatched throughout the countryside to unearth hoarders of grain. People who were not visibly starving were suspected of stealing. The sentences for all manner of crime were rarely confiscation of property or ten-year prison minimums; execution was far more common.

While grain producers in regions bordering Ukraine were included in this hysterical sweep, the Ukrainian peasants were the actual target precisely because they were more fiercely resistant than the Russians. Ostensibly, it was the kulak class that was the most hated. *Kulak* comes from the word for "fist," and it was a derogatory reference to the so-called rich peasants who very often had no more than one or two cows to their name. This "famine" was a mad attempt to break the independent spirit of the Ukrainian peasant and to destroy the kulak class.

Estimates range from six to ten million deaths as a direct result of this famine, sometimes called a drought in Soviet history books in which the dates were also changed. Actual truths about the famine were unspeakable for many years; ten-year prison sentences and even executions were the price for such talk, long after the terror famine was over. Only in 1988–90 was the hideous truth fully revealed, although people had been quietly making reference to it for years. Prior to the *glasnost* period, there was no official mention that the famine was premeditated. Of all the Soviet falsifications, this was perhaps the most massive lie.

Some Ukrainians have told me that whatever horrific deeds were committed in the name of war, the far greater insult to the Ukrainian people was this deliberate famine engineered by the megalomaniac Stalin. To the Soviet peoples at large, Stalin was responsible for thinning the intellectual ranks, and he targeted nationalities and minorities without compunction or conscience. These same friends tell me that Stalin was worse than Hitler ever was, as he directed his purges against his own people. He destroyed the best of the best. While I don't want to split hairs over who was the greater evil, this ugly piece of Ukrainian history helps to explain why Ukrainians view their agricultural and peasant traditions as separate from the Russian experience.

De-Stalinization

The aftershocks from Khrushchev's 25,000-word "secret speech" in 1956 denouncing Stalin were sensational, and thus the period of de-Stalinization was launched. The cult of Stalin was partially resurrected under Brezhnev (1964–84) with plans for a full rehabilitation of his name in 1969 and 1979; this was only narrowly averted thanks to foreign communist leaders and prominent Soviet intellectuals.

It is interesting that Khrushchev's speech focused on repression against high Party officials and crimes committed following the celebrated murder of Leningrad Party leader Sergei Kirov in 1934. The exclusion of Stalin's crimes of collectivization distressed Gorbachev, whose own family came from Russian "middle peasant" stock (as opposed to the vilified kulak class). The middle peasantry was often swept away in the anti-kulak hysteria, as were many kulaks who were not particularly wealthy. Gorbachev was not in attendance for Khrushchev's historic speech, but Khrushchev's focus on violence against the upper Party echelons, to the exclusion of mass terror, struck some Party members who were present. Khrushchev's public denunciation was nevertheless a remarkable feat.

UKRAINE'S NATIONAL HEROES

Taras Shevchenko is the beloved national hero of Ukraine. While the fate of so many Lenin statues throughout Ukraine is uncertain, Shevchenko's monuments are secure. The man who distinguished himself equally as a great artist and poet was born into serfdom in 1814. The prominent artist Karl Bruillov, whom Shevchenko met and impressed in St. Petersburg, helped Shevchenko purchase his freedom. Shevchenko then became a leader in the fight against serfdom. After his arrest in 1847, he spent ten years in internal exile. He was released in 1857 but never returned to Kyiv. He was frail in his last years and died in 1861 at 47. His home in Kyiv is now a museum filled with drawings, paintings, and manuscripts.

Both Shevchenko and Bohdan Khmelnytsky are recognized as Ukrainian national heroes, although the latter is far more controversial. Shevchenko criticized the hetman for bringing Ukraine into Russia's sphere, while others have credited him with uniting a disparate and unruly group. They argue that Khmelnytsky instilled both the pride and identity necessary for the further development of the concept of Ukrainian statehood. Some people claim that the proximity of Sholem Aleichem's home in central Kyiv to Bohdan

Khmelnytsky's imposing equestrian monument just a few blocks away betrays a fragile balance in contemporary Ukraine. This juxtaposition of Jewish and Cossack experience is a reminder of trenchant ethnic conflicts of the past amidst today's rapidly dwindling Jewish population.

More Cultural Heroes

Lesya Ukrainka and Ivan Franko are names you'll frequently hear in Ukraine. Ukrainka was a famous poet; Ivan Franko was the writer for whom Lviv's university is named. Franko is considered second in stature to Shevchenko. Sholem Aleichem was mentioned above; Isaac Babel and Isaac Bashevis Singer were born in Ukraine as was Nikolai Gogol (1809–1952). While Gogol distinguished himself in St. Petersburg, he greatly admired and recorded Ukrainian folktales and carols. *An Evening at Dikanka* (first published under the pseudonym Rudy Panko, Beekeeper) reflects his strong Ukrainian roots.

Aleksandr Pushkin lived in Odesa for a while, and Anton Chekhov enjoyed Crimea, the leisure destination of heads of state and wealthy people. Josef Conrad was born in present-day Berdichev. In the early 20th century, the so-called Russian avant-garde included Ukrainian artists Aleksandra Exter, Iosif Chaikov, and the Burliuk brothers.

Mikhail Bulgakov (1891–1940) was Ukrainian; you can visit his house on the winding Andriyivskiy Uzviz, which served as inspiration for the *White Guard*. His most celebrated work is *Master and the Margarita*. The 1995 English translation by Diana Burgin and Katherine O'Connor is excellent.

MOTHER RUSSIA AND OTHER MONUMENTS

In Kyiv you cannot escape Mother Russia. This gaudy, oversized (236 feet) stainless steel monument dedicated to the Defense of the Motherland is often criticized for its imposing, static design. Note that the sword is disproportionately small; it looks as if it were cut off in space. In fact, the monument's design had to be altered so that it

Monument in Lviv to the Ukrainian writer Ivan Franko, for whom Lviv's university is named. (Photo courtesy of Meredith Dalton.)

wasn't higher than the bell tower at the Monastery of the Caves. To many locals, this monument exemplifies the wasteful spending of the Brezhnev era.

Two museums are located at the site. One of them is dedicated to the Afghan War, the Soviet Union's tragic nine-year war that has been compared to America's Vietnam. The other is the Ukrainian Museum of the Great Patriotic War (World War II), which focuses on children and their suffering.

The Arch of Unification, or "the Yoke" as some locals call it, is a monument to Ukrainian and Russian unity. Whatever you call it, this monument, like Mother Russia, is remarkable, if only for sheer size.

The Soviet Union was renowned for its monumental and public sculptures, and Kyiv and other Ukrainian locales are no exception. Check your guidebooks for more information. Lenin still stands in Kyiv facing Bessarabskiy Rynok, although there was a hot debate about his survival a few years ago. Several notable post-independence monuments have been erected, including the Olga Triad and Archangel Michael. My personal favorite public sculpture is from the Soviet era. It's what Kharkiv citizens call their *Five Men Carrying a Refrigerator* monument; once you've seen this Socialist Realist ensemble, it's hard to think of another name. (Its official title is "Monument in Honor of Proclaiming Soviet Power in Ukraine.")

The Trident

Whereas the troika (with its three horses abreast) has long been associated with Mother Russia, the trident or *tryzub* is the official coat of arms of Ukraine. It is seen on state buildings and on currency notes. During the Soviet era, it was outlawed as a nationalist symbol—and immediately reintroduced after independence.

The *tryzub* has its roots in Kyivan Rus, and there are various theories about its origins. One theory is that the trident is a symbol of Poseidon, the Greek god of the sea. The oldest examples found on Ukrainian soil date to the first century A.D.; it was later stamped on the coins issued by Volodymyr, who may have inherited this symbol from his ancestors. Later rulers chose a bident as their coat of arms, and in the 12th century, the state emblem was the Archangel Michael, but the trident continued in usage as a dynastic coat of arms until the 15th century. It was also used as a religious symbol.

Nearly 200 variations on the medieval trident have been uncovered. Prince Volodymyr's was adopted by the short-lived Ukrainian National Republic. In February 1992, the Verkhovna Rada selected the trident as the chief element in the state's coat of arms.

Various versions of the trident are used today, for example, by the Ukrainian Catholic Church and other nationalist organizations.

The Flag

The Ukrainian flag is divided into two equal horizontal bands. The top is azure and the bottom is golden yellow. Most believe that the top band represents a blue sky, and the yellow represents Ukrainian wheat or sunflowers. In the past, however, these colors have been reversed.

Flags became popular with the inception of heraldry in medieval Europe. The standard flag in Kyivan Rus was predominantly red with a golden trident or bident, but there were others. One flag of the Galician-Volhynian period in western Ukraine was azure with a golden lion. (The symbol of Lviv is the lion, from which its name is also derived.)

There were many banners and variants on flags within the Ukrainian territories. Archangel Michael appeared on Kyiv flags of the Lithuanian-Polish period; a two-headed eagle is another symbol of this period. In the Cossack period, there were two hetman standards: one was the Archangel Michael; the other had the coat of arms of the individual hetman. Red was the predominant color for both.

With the annexation of central and western Ukraine by Russia and Austria, the various flags disappeared. The Russian Empire had no territorial flags, whereas western Ukraine had three: a golden lion on azure, horizontally striped yellow-azure, or azure-yellow. The order of colors was then not fixed. (There was also a Soviet Ukrainian flag with a hammer and sickle, a five-pointed star, and Cyrillic initials.)

The National Anthem

Before delving into some of the Ukrainian stereotypes, it is noteworthy that Ukraine's national anthem is entitled *Ukraine is Not Yet Dead*. The above overview of select points in Ukrainian history helps to put this title in perspective. The anthem evokes a mixture of hope and desperation; it is poignant and befitting for this nation that has collectively suffered and labored hard for independence. Not only is Ukraine not yet dead, it proclaims, but neither is its glory nor its freedom. "Luck will still smile on us brother-Ukrainians."

Not unlike the trident above, this anthem was adopted by the short-lived Ukrainian National Republic. This was naturally replaced during the Soviet era and again adopted after Ukraine's independence in 1991.

— Chapter Two —

UKRAINIANS AND THE FOREIGNERS WHO MAKE IT HERE

IMPRESSIONS AND STEREOTYPES

Ukrainians, Russians, and Belarusians share Slavic roots and Soviet inculcation. However, to simply lump them together as Slavic peoples (or Russians, as is more often the case) and to ignore historical differences is naive at best. So how are we to fairly characterize Ukrainians? In ethnic and linguistic terms, Ukrainians most closely resemble their Eastern Slavic cousins, the Russians and Belarusians. For historical reasons mentioned in Chapter One, Right-Bank Ukrainians share traits with the Western Slavs, particularly the Poles, but don't mistake the people of Lviv as a prototype for the rest of western

Ukraine. Further, the transition to a market economy has been far easier for Poles and other Eastern Europeans than for the Ukrainians who struggled for 70-plus years under the Soviet yoke.

In temperament, Ukrainian tendencies toward spirituality and fatalism elicit comparisons to the Russian, or more aptly, Slavic soul. The Mongols or Tatars, who sacked Kyiv in 1240 (thereby ending Kyivan Rus as the whole of Kyiv dispersed), are credited with staving off the expanding states of Poland and Lithuania (and their Catholic intentions) from Russia. However, along with protecting both the region and the Orthodox Church, the Mongols cut off Western cultures and contributed to the region's backwardness.

Specifically, neither the Renaissance nor the Protestant Revolution ever reached Russia or Left-Bank Ukraine, meaning that neither did the spirit of individualism and the spirit of free inquiry. The collective spirit that survives today in Russia (slightly diluted in Ukraine) derives in part from Mongol autocracy and the institution of state service (wherein every member of the group has a paramount obligation to that group). In Ukraine, however, the situation is complicated since Right-Bank and Left-Bank Ukraine were divided during this critical period in Europe's history. The Renaissance and Reformation did infiltrate Poland's sphere, which in turn influenced Right-Bank Ukraine. The net result may have contributed to the recalcitrance of the Ukrainian peasantry that Stalin strove to destroy.

Ukrainians are especially superstitious and yet well educated. Ukraine boasts a strong tradition of higher education, and the Soviet educational system maintained high standards for educating (and indoctrinating) its youth. In theory, a schoolboy studying at a particular location within the USSR should have been able to pick up his studies on the following day—in any other Soviet location—at the precise point where he had left off. One negative aspect of Soviet education was limited exposure to certain problem-solving skills. Because the system patently discouraged its citizens from thinking critically or questioning their superiors, today's new-found freedoms offering unprecedented choices can be overwhelming. The educational system that stressed rote memorization above all else did not encourage active decision-making. Older people especially complain that it is difficult to adapt to society's accelerated (and often unwanted) changes.

Time and again, Ukrainians distinguish themselves as gracious hosts and generous folk. Ukrainian women are very attractive and make great efforts to maintain stylish dress. They are generally submissive in this patriarchal society, which is both sexist and racist. Men show their age more quickly, often ravaged by excesses of alcohol and cigarettes. Attitudes toward work and money are obfuscated by seven decades of communism, just as issues of privacy were informed both through Soviet legacy and years of communal living. Society (and consequently business relations) is clearly based on relationships rather than contracts, and petty to excessive bribery and corruption are aspects of the culture.

Alongside limited democratic reforms of the past decade, the scourge of homelessness, prostitution, and pornography has blighted Ukrainian society. The increasing stranglehold of the mafia is also a post-independence phenomenon. One response in this age of lawlessness, poverty, inflation, and worthless pensions has been the strengthening of pro-communist sympathies. Advocates of communism argue that turning back the clock will help to repair society's ills, and individual freedoms should be sacrificed for the collective good.

New stereotypical profiles have emerged in independent Ukraine. Today's strata of society, including pensioners, bureaucrats, the New Rich (or New Russians), the mafia, young entrepreneurs, and an incipient middle class, are distinctive from their Soviet forebears. A reasonable question might be, what happened to the Soviet stereotypes of the late Brezhnev era: specifically, the *nomenklatura*, the military, the intelligentsia, and dissidents?

One overriding observation distinguishes for me Ukrainian national character, if there is such a thing: Ukraine is not for the meek.

This is true for the expatriate community in very different, and deliberate, ways, but more importantly for the Ukrainian people. Their history is a troubled one, and personality traits have emerged from their collective experiences. In contrast to Americans who take very seriously their right to "the pursuit of happiness," Ukrainians aggressively pursue their right to survival.

KYIV VS. THE REST OF UKRAINE

Chapter One's outline of historical events, which points to the coexistence of pro-Russian and Ukrainian nationalist factions, helps to describe various Ukrainian profiles today. While extreme nationalist factions do exist, the vast majority of Ukrainians lies somewhere between the two poles, and indeed much of what is said about Ukrainians at large is also applicable to East Slavs. Nevertheless, a 1998 proposal to unite Ukraine, Belarus, and Russia as one Slavic state was promptly rejected by Parliament. Ukraine had fought too hard for independence to relinquish it so easily (whereas Belarus's leadership favors union with Russia).

Kyiv appears to be a good indicator of mildly changing perceptions toward national identity and pride since independence. Most Kyivans are politically moderate as opposed to staunchly nationalistic. In Yaroslav's day, Kyiv was considered too valuable to split between east and west factions; now its physical location and political stance provide a good keel for the nation. (Its 450-member Rada is populated with centrists, nationalists, and communists of varying intensities.) Historically, most Kyivans spoke and still prefer Russian, but today many are relinquishing their former strong opposition to Ukrainian, which is good since it is now the language of government and schools. More Ukrainian is heard today in the streets than a couple of years ago, and some are embracing the national language, although Russian remains the dominant language for business.

It is nonetheless necessary to differentiate Kyiv when assessing Ukraine as a whole. While it is true that the cities were more successfully Russified (and Sovietized) than Ukraine's rural counterparts (again with the exception of Lviv), the capital and third largest Soviet city stands apart. To the visiting foreigner, the city has verve, albeit nothing like the frenetic energy of Moscow or the stateliness and grandeur (and dark, bone-chilling winters) of St. Petersburg. Kyiv is large, yet retains its provincial feel. Granted, most foreigners spend more time outside of Kyiv than in exploring the capital's farthest regions, which will surely remind them that they are indeed in the FSU. But Kyiv is an eminently liveable city. Expatriates here have almost always selected it over Moscow's chaos, preferring Kyiv's history and architecture against the steady flow of the Dnipro.

Ukrainians outside of Kyiv often dream of moving to the capital to find better jobs. Foreigners in Ukraine also typically choose Kyiv because of job opportunities (and governmental access). The major reasons that most expatriates prefer Kyiv, although few really say it, are food and community. Indeed, while Kyiv's restaurants are mostly pricey (sometimes outrageously so), their quality and variety are improving steadily, and this has more to do with expatriate than local demand. Likewise, Kyiv's "Western grocery stores," most of which are on the scale of mom-and-pop enterprises, are filled with foods imported from Western Europe and sold at Western prices. Locals generally cannot afford to pay these high prices, but neither are they spending their cash on outrageous rents or in your favorite pricey restaurant. Kyiv is not different from the rest of Ukraine just because of food, but foreigners talk a lot about food here and spend a lot of time in restaurants; not only is this the social thing to do, sometimes it's the only thing to do. Contrast this with the smaller Ukrainian towns whose shelves are not well stocked—and never with imported foodstuffs—and where Western-styled restaurants have not arrived.

The good news for the foreign visitor is that, whatever your location, you will surely not spend a lot of money on clothes in Ukraine (unless you shop exclusively at Benetton). Wealthy Ukrainians travel abroad to buy clothes.

Odesa is similarly adapting to accommodate the Britons, Germans, and other Westerners arriving there. The second largest port in the Soviet Union has long been regarded as Ukraine's most international city, with a reputation all its own for humor. Also, its milder climate makes it especially attractive.

The three other cities boasting populations of over one million (Kharkiv, Dnipropetrovsk, and Donetsk) are less Westerner-friendly, which has its own reward. Take, for example, the case of the popular expat hangout in Kyiv, the Arizona Barbecue where you can order Corona and American "ice" beers, plus the Kyiv staples of Tuborg, Carlsberg, Guinness, and locally-brewed Obolon. Pitchers of margaritas are also popular (if expensive) accompaniments to overpriced cheeseburgers, nachos, tacos, and similar fare. Arizona's great success led to the opening of a second restaurant in Donetsk. Its walls were decorated with the same 1950s Americana and license plates that had made the Kyiv location a success (even if the taped American music is not on a long-enough loop). The Donetsk locals liked it. Still, it didn't take the owners (and chef) long to change the menu to focus on Ukrainian staples like *varenyky* (dumplings) and borshch since the clientele is overwhelmingly Ukrainian. Also, Ukrainians like to have their own vodka bottle on their table. They never eat and run, partly because dining out is a rarity and should be savored among friends; this affects the turnover in a given evening.

THE SOVIET LEGACY

Popular accounts of Soviet life made frequent reference to shortages and queues, excessive alcohol intake, and communal living, all of which were valid generalizations. Today, the shortages and queues seem largely a thing of the past in the larger cities, except when adverse financial news in Ukraine or from Russia creates a run at money exchange points. This point is not to be taken lightly, as deteriorating economic conditions in Russia and Ukraine bode poorly for these and other FSU countries. Serious setbacks in the wake of the

August 1998 financial crisis are clearly in evidence and suggest that things may get worse before they get better.

Within the foreign community, some say that now you can find anything in Ukraine that you want—as long as the price is right. I say, if you find something today that you think you might want tomorrow, don't wait to buy it. Shipments are irregular and mercurial.

Outside the larger cities, the shelves are never well stocked, and the local residents can't afford to buy the products if they were. Yet Ukrainians are survivalists and exemplify the concept of "getting by." For most, the *dacha* (country cottage) is more necessity than luxury. The idea that Ukrainians escape to their village sounds like a great weekend getaway, but there is much work to be done at the *dacha*. Under Brezhnev, each family was entitled to one hundredth of a hectare for private use. This strip of land, or *sotka*, continues to grow many of the vegetables that will tide the family over during harsh winters and often harsher economic times.

Problems stemming from excessive alcohol intake continue to plague Ukraine and indeed have risen in the last decade. Alcohol, specifically vodka, is very much a part of Ukrainian culture. It is a source of both pride and embarrassment. Chapter Four discusses vodka and its associated traditions in detail. Suffice it to say here that people coming to Ukraine for an extended period should be prepared to drink toasts; if you have an alcohol problem before you arrive, you should reconsider your decision to come at all.

Ukrainians are accustomed to communal living. Private owner-ship of apartments is a distinguishing feature of independent Ukraine, yet for economic and practical reasons, communal living remains very much a part of Ukrainian culture. Communal living exacts a high price on family relations and marriages. Living in cramped quarters is not conducive to easy relationships, and the divorce rate in Ukraine is high. Some divorced couples continue to live together out of necessity. Alcohol-related problems disrupt home life as well.

PUBLIC DISPLAYS OF AFFECTION

Often Ukrainian couples are more outwardly affectionate than Americans. They enjoy holding hands and kissing in public. For young couples whose communal apartments provide no privacy, park benches may be the best alternative. The street is often their only space; while not private, it is away from their cramped living quarters. None of this means, however, that their elders approve.

Cold weather does not drive people from the streets; many bundle up and continue to stroll, their clothes as somber as their expressions. Nevertheless, when the chestnut trees lining Kreshchatyk Avenue bloom in the spring, Kyiv takes on a different feel. The streets are far more lively, smiles are evident, and brighter colors and miniskirts return. Molded white plastic chairs and tables sprout alongside kiosks, with Coca-Cola and Pepsi umbrellas competing for visibility.

A typical scene along Kyiv's Kreshchatyk. (Photo courtesy of Catherine Isabel Dalton.)

Women stroll together arm-in-arm or holding hands, as do men to a lesser degree—sometimes in the spirit of camaraderie, sometimes hanging onto each other after too many toasts.

Except for the New Rich, dining out is reserved for special occasions. Ukrainians share with other Europeans their love of dancing, which is often a part of an evening out on the town. In hotel dining rooms there is a dance floor, often next to large, blown-out speakers that play sentimental music such as *Kakaya Zhenshchina* entirely too loudly for those trying to have a dinner conversation. Synthesizers are popular instruments for live music in the hotels.

Flower vendors were among the first privatized businesses in Ukraine and are commonly situated near metro entrances and in the underground passageways. Women buy flowers for themselves, or men buy flowers for them. Watch out for even numbers! They signify death. Often you will see couples strolling or sharing an alcoholic drink on a public bench; the woman in each case holds a single rose.

PRIVACY AND PERSONAL SPACE

During the Soviet era, the unspoken idea was that if you needed privacy you were hiding something. There were no phone books to locate those lucky enough to have phones installed, so these people were also lucky in having privacy. There are still no pages for residential numbers, while the waiting list for a new phone remains tremendous. The popularity of cellular phones is understandable, even if those who have them often sport them in obnoxious ways. (A sign outside Kyiv's Studio Restaurant asks patrons to kindly turn off their phones before entering.) Now as in Soviet times, you need to keep track of your friends and their phone numbers—and addresses, for it seems as if people are always changing apartments here!

Dark and dingy entrances to apartment buildings are overwhelmingly the norm; this tends to discourage people from wandering where they aren't invited, but it isn't the reason. In the Soviet days there was often a *babushka* (an old woman who wears a *babushka* or scarf) posted near the elevator (the *lift*—say *leeft*—and pay attention to whether it breaks down often); her job was to watch the comings and goings of people in the building. Today no one stands guard, and hallway lights burn out (or are stolen) and are not replaced. Sometimes, in the hallways, you can't escape the smell of urine. (See Respect for Elders below for more about *babushka.*)

Front doors to apartments often hide a second door inside. The ones you'll see may be padded brown nawgahide and covered with buttons resembling a vertical mattress pad; others are wooden or steel. Most are uninviting. In noting down addresses, always ask your friends not only for their apartment and floor numbers, but also which building entrance to use, and whether there is a (working) front door code. Wandering in the dark can be creepy.

Another interesting phenomenon pertains, I can only surmise, to crowd control. Building entrances often have several sets of double doors. Naturally, in winter these should be closed to retain the heat. (Sometimes many windows are then opened because the heat is cranked too high and can't be adjusted.) But even at other times only one set of doors will be operable, and only one of the double doors will open. Traffic in both directions will thus use the same door. Even McDonald's on Kreshchatyk is guilty of this.

Metro stations stand apart with their separate entrance and exits; their heavy, dangerous swinging doors have been called "widow-makers." Still, you rarely get the sense of people rushing to catch the metro, although there is shoving when standing in a line for something. Maybe this is because they know a very long escalator ride (or two) separates them from the next train. It's much harder to pass through the tight crowds of people with their shopping bags in tow.

The invasion of personal space seizes the attention of many foreigners. First, there is the practice of standing close in lines or standing a bit too close when speaking to you. Cutting in lines and even shoving in crowds, while never personal, is common. Moreover, no one would ever apologize for this. (If you happen to, they'll know

71

right away that you are foreign, but they probably already know.) For those with claustrophobic tendencies, the Kyiv and Kharkiv metros can be a harrowing experience. I personally dislike the metro when people start shopping for the holidays.

In Ukraine, I am most reminded of the luxury of privacy when the loudspeakers on Kreshchatyk fire up for holiday celebrations or a bit of political grandstanding (which is really the same thing). Both were part and parcel of the Soviet propaganda machine, and these loud-speakers never fail to transport me to another place in time. On overnight trains, too, if you're not already awake, a loud piped-in radio will serve as your alarm for the last hour before arrival.

One cold December night in 1995, I returned to the Hotel Rus after an exhausting trip. Once installed in my new room, I discovered that I was unable to turn off (or down) the hidden radio—the one which I heretofore didn't know existed. Exasperated, I tried unsuccessfully to pry it from behind the heater. I muffled it with an extra pillow and bedspread and even my overcoat but to no avail. Miserable, I conceded defeat and rode the elevator to the lobby where I demanded a change of room. The Soviet-schooled receptionist replied dispassionately that all the rooms were the same: they were testing the fire alarm and I needed to wait … for as many hours as it took.

This story seems foolishly minor in retrospect, but it is times like these—especially when you are as exhausted as I was (or maybe homesick)—that will test your ability to live in Ukraine. You will be assaulted frequently by things that seem incredible or inane. You will also hear expatriates ranting about Ukrainians and everyday absurdities. Heed my warning above: Ukraine is not for the meek. That includes us.

Another cultural surprise for me were the screaming matches, replete with profanities, between Ukrainians in our office. Emotional outbursts and florid excesses (as in compliments, flowers, hospitality, and drinking) are not uncommon, while self-expression and alternative lifestyles are not accepted. In Ukraine, you also need to be prepared for those times when racism or anti-Semitism rears its ugly head. Virulent stereotypes are ingrained, and this is where outside observers may wish to impose their world views. When provoked, remember that your views are not welcomed, and in any case, patronizing attitudes never help.

Many foreigners observe an abruptness in Ukrainian behavior. Cards are slammed on the table during a friendly card game, and *nyet* (meaning *no*) or the Ukrainian *ni* (say *nee*) is more emphatic than in English. Again, according to Western standards, people appear less courteous and less appreciative in part because niceties like "thank you," "you're welcome," and "please" are not spoken with the same frequency. It is not unusual when mis-dialing a residence to have the person hang up on you without a word, simply because he or she was not the person you were calling. (There are the occasional others who will want to talk even after you've discovered your error.) Service-without-a-smile is the norm, not the exception, although we are seeing a gradual change, in particular with businesses that are trying to adapt to Western models.

STARING IS NOT IMPOLITE

Staring is culturally acceptable in Ukraine, and foreigners are often recipients of such unwanted attention. I experienced it mostly from elderly Ukrainians or in places away from city centers where foreigners were less common, and consequently more visible, in the community.

In general, while younger Ukrainians are attracted to the West and want to see Western business practices adopted, by contrast, today's elderly were taught throughout their lives to mistrust all foreigners. Those few foreigners who visited during Soviet times were an oddity, and their movements were both limited and highly scrutinized. Separate apartment houses were formerly designated for foreigners, and Soviet citizens were explicitly warned not to mingle with expatriates. To some Ukrainians, the expatriate population represents capitalism's evils that Soviet propaganda had railed so hard against.

It is difficult, if not impossible, to comprehend the vast changes Ukraine has undergone since the days of *glasnost* and *perestroika*. Today's pensioners are financially and psychologically exhausted, having lived their whole lives under a regime with certain known quantities. They worked, not necessarily too hard since the Soviet system did not reward those who worked hardest; but they played by rules that guaranteed a pension upon retirement. What they expected, of course, was that it would provide for their needs, as opposed to the practically worthless pensions that are the reality today.

While foreigners are by no means credited with destroying the pension system, their increased presence in Ukraine coincided with changed attitudes. It is no wonder that a percentage of Ukraine's population, especially elderly citizens with their inadequate pensions, yearn for the glory days of communism. Some argue that things weren't especially good then, but at least they knew what to expect.

RESPECT FOR ELDERS

English dictionaries give "a woman's scarf" as one definition for *babushka* (say *BAbooshka*). When you hear the term, in all probability the speaker is talking about "grandmother" or simply the ubiquitous older woman who often wears such a scarf knotted below her chin. *Babushky* (plural of *babushka*) often come across as humorless and dour. (I generally assume that most are widows and struggling to survive on paltry pensions.) They view themselves as a mouthpiece for morality and have no qualms about scolding a stranger. For example, Ukrainian babies are well wrapped, even suffocatingly so, despite the heat. Lo and behold the mother whose baby's legs are exposed to a passing *babushka*!

Respect for elders is very much a part of Ukrainian life. My Ukrainian assistant once told me that we could not easily reprimand the office housekeeper for poor performance, as she was older than we were. I had to politely disagree with this. (For the record, this housekeeper was not a pensioner nor especially old.)

My assistant voiced similar concerns when I complained to my landlady that removing furniture from my apartment without giving me prior notice was not acceptable. I certainly had no intention of being disrespectful, but I also wanted to make a point that we had a signed contract, including clauses about what furniture would be provided and how much advance warning (72 hours according to our lease) the landlady would give me before entering the premises. The larger issue for me was that any unplanned disappearance of furniture from my apartment might be construed as theft.

CONTACTS, NOT CONTRACTS

Ukraine is very much a society based on relationships rather than contracts. As elsewhere, the coexistence of relationships and contracts is hardly mutually exclusive, but in Ukraine the relationship always takes precedence.

Now as in the Soviet era, people are heavily reliant upon friends and family to provide them with food and other necessities during difficult times. Similarly, you will often—without asking—be offered the names of cousins and friends who can provide whatever service you may be needing. Westerners tend to be more cautious in

recommending an individual in case the latter's poor performance damages their own credibility. This is not the case in Ukraine, where doing a favor for a friend, or even bringing two new parties together, is the primary consideration.

For your part, you need to make certain about the person with whom you are dealing. The law does not provide adequately for contract compliance, and many view a contract as simply another piece of paper. Clearly, for those looking to do business in Ukraine, it is imperative to understand that you cannot simply fly into town, meet some folks, sign a deal, shake hands, and hop back on a plane. You need to be prepared for a long-term investment in time and relationship-building. The relationship is the linchpin in all business transactions, never the contract.

Similarly, you will find that as soon as you land in Ukraine you will need to link up with a good translator and driver, and probably a lawyer and accountant who can assist you through the byzantine Ukrainian business world. Expats will also provide you with a wealth of knowledge, suggestions, and shortcuts. I highly recommend an early trip to O'Brien's Irish Pub, the Arizona Barbecue, or whatever the latest hot spot is—it won't be hard to find out—for a beer and some relationship-building. Contacts, both foreign and local, can often provide shortcuts along the miles of red tape that you will inevitably encounter during an extended stay in Ukraine.

Greasing Palms

Ukrainians also need a technique for surviving their country's red tape, in addition to the bribery, corruption, and crime that were rising during the late Brezhnev era and have escalated since independence. (Only during Stalin's reign was bribery less of a problem, and that was out of fear.) The Soviet concept of *blat* roughly translates as "access, pull, or connections" that is always more powerful than currency, which in any case you can only spend once. A related term is *svyazy* meaning "connections and strings," which is not the same as *vzyatka*, meaning "kickback or bribe." Today, *blat* and *svyazy* remain enormously valuable and *vzyatka,* enormously pervasive.

Ukrainians have a strong tradition of helping friends and family. Skeptics argue that even family members can never be fully trusted, but this is a perception from Stalinist days when the system encouraged people to turn in family and friends for actions against the state. There is the famous story of Pavlik Morozov, the 14-year-old Ukrainian who denounced his own father for hoarding grain in the early 1930s. Many Soviet monuments were erected to this little hero-martyr whom the villagers had killed for his betrayal. Recent evidence shows that Stalin privately thought him "a little swine" for denouncing his father, but turned his example into a useful political weapon. Today it is comforting to be able to rely on others to help you get what you need, information or otherwise. Even more so than in Soviet times, many Ukrainians remain perpetually financially strapped while their costs for food and apartments have rocketed.

Although, unlike *vzyatka*, *blat* and *svyazy* do not involve the exchange of money or bribes, small gifts may be given. *Blat* is what I sometimes call "tipping in advance." People talk about the value of a bottle of beer or a box of chocolates in easing a sticky relationship, or as a show of kindness or gratitude. (An old folk saying: "If you don't oil, you cannot start your journey.") One English friend in Moscow remarked that the occasional packet of cigarettes to the parking attendant meant his car didn't get nicks—in contrast to the unhappy experiences of his friend, who assiduously refused to play the game. There's a joke that when *blat* dies there will be no funeral; where would we find the coffin or nails?

While younger and good bureaucrats have largely jumped ship, the older bureaucrats in place tend to abuse their position and demand bribes to supplement their paltry income. The old Soviet curse, "May he live on his salary!" applied equally to governmental officials and ordinary citizens, only the latter opted to moonlight to supplement their incomes. (You will find that many of the kiosk vendors and street sellers of books and postcards were trained as engineers or earned doctorates; they turned to selling because they needed more money.) Some argue that in another decade these corrupt officials will be retired, and a younger generation, eager to emulate the West, will not tolerate the current rampant abuses in the system.

Sometimes Europeans single out Americans for their "puritanical" views toward petty corruption, but none will dismiss the detrimental impact of coming into contact with Ukraine's mafia. The world is clearly watching to see how the Ukrainian government will rein in this accelerating problem. The allegation that the police is involved with the mafia's activities is especially disheartening to ordinary, law-abiding citizens.

BARTER

Barter has long been a way of life for Ukrainians. The increased number of items available for barter since independence has, if anything, strengthened this practice. Naturally, barter has its greatest appeal when you genuinely want what is bartered. Yet learning to barter has become a survival necessity, as there are endless stories of people being paid in potatoes and used car tires. While they can eat potatoes, they might not need tires.

One advantage to those who barter is that these transactions are not taxed. This has repercussions for the state, which is in dire need of tax revenue. Reforming the tax code is a constant discussion in the Rada. Inadequate tax collection means that preventative maintenance of infrastructure is mostly postponed until a crisis occurs. We've all heard stories about miners striking because they hadn't been paid in months, and factory wages in arrears is hardly unusual. A Ukrainian in our office quit the army because he hadn't been paid for months; he is the lucky exception because he jumped into a high-paying job.

The corporate worlds in Ukraine and Russia have embraced bartering on a grand scale, both out of necessity and the desire to avoid heavy taxation. It was estimated that in 1992, 6% of corporate revenues in Russia came in the form of barter. In 1998, that figure had mushroomed to 70% or 80%, according to current sources. Ukraine's figures are presumed to be in line with Russia's. Not surprisingly, good barter negotiators command high salaries today.

The tradition of barter, like the *dacha*, exemplifies Ukrainian flexibility, industriousness, and creativity. I am reminded of a joke about two Ukrainians who meet to strike a business deal. The first wants a cartload of sugar, for which the second demands a fair price. The deal is settled and off they go in opposite directions: the first to locate some cash, and the second to locate some sugar.

Make no mistake: Ukrainians are survivalists, and their ability to "get by" is a distinguishing feature of the Ukrainian personality.

NEKULTURNI

What does it mean to be *nekulturniy* (say *neecoolTOURnee*)? Literally, it means uncultured, and this is quite derogatory. An egregious error is not checking your coat at restaurants, nightclubs, or the opera. As they won't admit your coat inside the opera and most restaurants, you can generally avoid that damnation. If you worry about being cold in the restaurant, just remember that the other guests won't have their coats either. The travesty of centralized heating is that chances are just as likely that the heat will be higher than you'd like.

Many coats do not have loops for hanging them sewn into their lining. If you own such a coat, you may hear sighs of frustration when you check it at restaurants. With the increase of foreigners, coat-checkers will probably become better psychologically equipped to deal with the absence of loops. But beware the opera houses. The coat-checkers there can be downright mean! I've even read suggestions that international students traveling to the FSU sew in these loops in advance of a winter visit!

Other *nekulturniy* behavior includes sprawling or slumping in a chair. Sitting with your ankles crossed is a sign of unnecessary assertiveness or hostility, especially to older people.

SUPERSTITIONS GALORE

Ukraine is marked (as elsewhere) by its own blend of superstitions, health concerns, home remedies, and rules of etiquette. For example, sitting on cold stone steps is considered bad for one's health and also inappropriate behavior. As a rule of thumb, follow the example of locals in unknown situations. The phrase "when in Rome ..." tells only part of the story; the Slavic spin is the accurate one here; "In private do as you wish but in public do as you are told."

An open window in my office was often an invitation for unsolicited comments from staff members: that the window was open explained why my back hurt or I had the remnant of a cold. There are strong beliefs that sitting on cold surfaces or drinking from cold cans will cause colds. Leaving the house with wet hair or exposure to any sort of draft (including close proximity to an open window) is considered an invitation to catch colds. If you already have one, you will be reminded endlessly not to touch a glass of cold juice, for example. Tea, never coffee, is imperative in the recuperative stage. Garlic is well known for its magical and medicinal values; it has even earned the nickname "Russian (or Ukrainian) penicillin."

According to some, superstitions help to explain life's inequalities and unpredictability, including the randomness and capriciousness that marked the Soviet era, particularly under Stalin. Yet the superstitious nature of the Eastern Slavs was entrenched long before the communists arrived; rural communities have long been marked by the popularity of folk wisdom, home remedies, and superstitions. The popular Russian saying, *"Khuzhe bivaet,"* translates as "It (or things) could be worse." There is a resigned quality to Ukrainians that boggles and frustrates foreigners, but this too is about survival.

One popular superstition pertains to women sitting at the corner of the table (I must have done this too many times): it means not getting married for seven years. Whistle inside a building, and you will whistle away your money. Knocking on wood for good luck (or as a preventative) appears universal, just as a black cat crossing your path never bodes well. Ukrainians will also symbolically spit over their left shoulder, the same one over which they will toss three pinches of salt if they spill some. This is because the devil sits over your left shoulder, an angel over your right.

Borshch made on a Thursday signals that the devil himself will bathe in it, and a pot left unattended on the stove can mean trouble for your whole family. If you count *varenyky* (dumplings) as you make them, they will overcook and their fillings will seep out. An empty bottle on the table could mean depleted food reserves, so move it just to be safe. If a knife falls to the floor, a male will visit; a spoon, a female; and if a coal falls from the stove, expect a guest from far away. If you want to catch a witch, wrap a piece of cheese in a cloth and tie it to your shirt during Lent. On the Saturday before Easter, witches will appear and beg for the cheese.

The cat must be the first to enter a new house, so death will take the cat and not your grandmother. If you put your clothes on wrong, adjust them immediately or people will beat you. A cultural statement could be inferred from this last one, but it's probably better not to read too much into superstitions.

If you leave something behind unintentionally, this means you will come back. For example, a foreigner who leaves a pair of shoes will eventually return. For shorter journeys, one should sit awhile before leaving the house. If you forget something when you leave, you should not go back for it. However, if you must, look into the mirror (or don't). If some superstitions sound a bit contradictory, they are. This is the great thing about them!

ON GENEROSITY AND ETIQUETTE

As stated above, Ukrainians are very generous and hospitable. (Chapter Four explores the nature of Ukrainian hospitality and discusses traditional foods and drinking customs.) General rules of etiquette dictate that you should always offer to share snacks and cigarettes with those around you, including strangers. You'll find that fellow travelers in your train compartment will offer you bread, sausages, bottled water, and vodka—whatever they have with them. Sometimes it's hard to refuse. An elderly woman on the train absolutely insisted on making my bed for me; she then instructed that a man in our compartment, a high-ranking military official whose driver was meeting him, give me a ride once we reached our destination. He was on a tight schedule, but she was his elder, so he said *yes*.

Like whistling indoors, standing with your hands in your pockets when meeting someone is impolite, because you are supposed to shake hands. Keeping your hands in your pockets is a form of disrespect, although close friends won't mind.

In Orthodox churches, skirts are more appropriate for women, but traditions are changing. Women should at least cover their head with a scarf or hat, and men should remove their hat. I once made the mistake of forgetting my scarf when throngs of people congregated for the all-night Easter service bearing baskets of foods to be blessed. Traditionally, even non-practicing Ukrainians attend this service, and everyone carries a white candle. Like all Orthodox services, there is standing room only, and the scent of incense is pervasive. Imagine my surprise when I discovered that a foul burning smell was actually my hair on fire!

Never shake hands across the threshold of a door; this is very bad luck as it forecasts a quarrel. Remember this in all business and personal introductions. Also, always take off your gloves before shaking hands. Expect to check your coat, umbrella, briefcase, and baggage at the entrance of upscale restaurants and the like.

Universal rules of etiquette dictate that on public transportation you should give your seat to the elderly and handicapped, as well as to pregnant women and mothers with small children. Never place your feet on train seats or on tables. Chewing gum in public is not considered polite, but neither is spitting, which is nonetheless more common than you are probably used to seeing.

GESTURES

Ukrainians are not particularly known for their hand gestures. But there are a few worth mentioning. One is the way in which Ukrainians count using their fingers. A clever story, surely apocryphal, was that one way to catch spies in the old days was to watch their use of fingers.

My favorite gesture is that of flicking one's neck for a drink. There is the story about a man who saved Peter the Great's life (or did some great favor for him). In return, the tsar gave the man a document that stipulated free drinks for life. The man needed only to present this at a tavern or inn to receive his drink. Perhaps after a night of excessive booze, the document was misplaced, whereupon the man had his neck tattooed with the tsar's decree. Thereafter, when he desired a drink, he merely flicked this tattoo. Today, minus tattoo, the gesture of flicking one's neck is still related to drinking. Often it is the response to a question; for example, in response to "Where were you last night?" a flick would mean "I was out drinking" or "I drank too much." Flicking one's neck can also mean, "Let's go have a drink."

A Swede once asked me the meaning of a Russian painting entitled "Waiting for a Third." It showed two men on a park bench with a bottle of vodka. While the subject was Russian, it could have been Ukrainian. The title refers to the tradition that vodka be drunk in groups. *Na TROikh* means "for three." A gesture that relates to this entails holding the middle and index fingers together horizontally. This indicates that the person is waiting (or looking) for a third.

Two fingers over your shoulder (indicating military stripes) means a KGB man. Pointing to an imaginary chandelier means this room is bugged. A curved index finger as eyebrow symbolized Brezhnev, noted for his bushy brows.

Finally, don't put your thumb between your index and middle fingers. This is a particularly rude gesture.

BEAUTY'S CURSE: THE WOMEN IN UKRAINE

Ukrainian women are quite good-looking. Expatriate men certainly comment on this a lot, and even the Beatles sang their praises in *Back in the USSR*: "Well, the Ukraine girls really knock me out. They leave the West behind."

Ukraine is prime hunting ground for discovering female models these days. Long legs, Slavic cheekbones, beautiful blondes à la Poland, and stunning brunettes attract the good, the bad, and the ugly. The good include expatriate men who come to Ukraine in search of young, beautiful wives; many Ukrainian women are also eager to land a green card. (I've heard that this is more prevalent in Kyiv than elsewhere.) The question is, at what price?

Throughout Ukraine, people are trying to improve their lot. This is a great thing and should be universal. Ukrainians from the small cities hope to move to the larger cities in search of better jobs. This is not particularly easy because the draconian *propiska* persists in free Ukraine. The *propiska*—the stamp in the Ukrainian's internal passport (a carryover from the Soviet era)—designates where the holder must live and effectively places a cap on the official populations of the larger cities. (Kyiv, then Kiev, was the third largest city in the USSR with a population in 1990 of 2.6 million.)

Today, even those lucky enough to live in the larger cities are often looking to emigrate. The intellectual Jewish community has been especially hard hit in recent years in light of mass emigrations. Ukraine's brain drain is a problem, but more disturbing still are human watch reports that cite Ukraine as the leader in the female slave trade. An education campaign is under way to protect Ukrainian women from bogus advertisements offering good jobs abroad for dancers and would-be restaurant workers. Documented cases include young girls who found themselves in a new country (Israel and Turkey are not uncommon) where they were beaten and forced into prostitution; some saw their Ukrainian passports burned.

That said, Ukrainian women do take much better care of themselves than Ukrainian men. Roughly 12% of the women smoke vs. more than 80% of the men. Women also strive to dress well and wear makeup. They also wear heels, which especially impresses me since people walk so much and often on uneven surfaces. They travel great distances from the suburbs, which means that both in the city and the outskirts they walk to meet the metro, trolleybuses, trams, and buses. Or they simply walk.

Women also drink less alcohol than men and live significantly longer. The average mortality for Ukrainian men is now 56 years (vs. 57 in Russia). This statistic may be somewhat skewed due to the number of World War II deaths, but it has dropped by nearly five years since independence, which is a precipitous drop in such a short period. Alcohol is an enormous factor contributing to this decline, aggravated further by malnutrition, unvaried diets, stress, fear, work, or unemployment.

Ukrainian society is sexist. The old Soviet statistics regarding equal pay for equal jobs were overstated like so many other statistics, and today this is clearly not the case. There are few women in high positions in the government; women are more likely than men to be laid off; and they are excluded from some of the higher-paying jobs because of the physical strength required. Why then is it that so many women work like beasts of burden, for example, hauling wheel-barrows of gravel and stone? Some Ukrainians admit that this embarrasses them, but others accept it as business as usual.

The concept of "sexual harassment" is far removed from the Ukrainian mindset, which is to say it exists but is taken for granted, and sexual favors for bosses are not unheard of. Many newspaper ads are discriminatory, specifying an age range and gender for applicants (such as "female aged 23 to 29 ..."). The age issue, according to some, is necessary because older applicants cannot be trained properly. On the other hand, some foreign men have admitted they like working here because they can hire whom they want and don't have to deal with the strict hiring practices encountered in their own country.

An American man told a Ukrainian friend that Ukrainian women are so pretty but don't smile enough. She replied that Ukrainian women never have any rest. She argued that they work as hard as the men, or harder, and are expected to be the responsible ones. Not only do they drink and smoke less, they also tend to the children, buy the groceries, mend the clothes, prepare all the meals, and clean the house. They carry a far greater burden in family responsibilities, and these divisions of labor don't appear to be changing with the times, as in the West. Wages for women have actually dropped since independence, while female unemployment has risen. Thus, while the Soviet stigma of not working has changed in the last decade, for many women paid employment is rarely achievable.

For those fortunate enough to be employed, maternity leave in Ukraine allows for up to one year, usually with six months' pay.

FASHION SENSE

While Ukrainian women strive to dress well, their business attire is not always appropriate by Western standards. For example, they may wear jeans and a nice sweater to a meeting where a skirt or dress (you won't see many local women in suits or tailored pants) would have been a better choice. On other occasions, someone will select a dress more befitting a cocktail party. Youthful inexperience or limited wardrobes may account for such choices. Among young Ukrainian women, however, there is an appreciation for current fashions that is generally neglected by the older women.

Business attire for Ukrainian males ranges from fancy, Western-tailored suits to modest, mouse-colored suits, and from standard, military uniforms to jeans and casual attire. For some, flashy colors are favored, with burgundy blazers especially popular. Shiny, nylon running suits are also popular, with open collars revealing gold chains and a little chest hair. Men huddle on street corners, in entrances, and at restaurant tables; sometimes hiding behind sunglasses, they dangle cigarettes from their lips, and look dour. You will wonder at times who is an entrepreneur and who is mafia. Still, you won't find all the men with the bodyguards that populate Moscow, yet there are plenty of fancy, Western cars driven by personal drivers; this is a necessity in Ukraine where there is zero tolerance for drinking and driving. Parking and having someone to watch your car are other issues.

Men sporting mustaches, and big bushy ones at that, are documented as a Ukrainian folk type. Hetman Bohdan Khmelnytsky and Taras Shevchenko were both mustachioed. In the old days, spectacles frequently distinguished the wearer as a foreigner, but this is beginning to change as the number of *optika* stores rise. Some swear by shoes, just as surely as the man wearing socks with his sandals is more likely German or Ukrainian than American. Also, men here rarely wear shorts, whereas foreign men might when the weather warms up.

Gold teeth were once viewed as a sign of status, and gold crosses are increasingly worn by Ukrainians rediscovering religion. (Crosses and religious symbols dangling from rear-view mirrors are also common.) Although attitudes may be changing, tattoos to most Ukrainians are considered in poor taste and often an indication that the wearer spent time in prison. Their designs certainly look crude. Wearing cologne is rising in popularity with the younger and entre-preneurial set, whereas deodorant is used sparingly. I am reminded of a story about a woman trying to buy bread, tampax, and deodorant in a hyper-inflationary environment. Deodorant was the first to go.

Far more offensive to me is the combined smell of domestic cigarettes and alcohol. Most Ukrainian smokers prefer imported cigarettes to so-called domestic (i.e., Russian) ones, which are high in tar and produced from Russian or Zimbabwean tobacco. These are decidedly foul-smelling and an unmistakable affront to fresh air.

FAMILIES AND FAMILY PLANNING

One solution for people wanting to move to the cities, but prohibited due to their *propiska*, has been to marry someone living in that city. This has led to marriages contracted on financial arrangements. There was even the occasional, if apocryphal, story of a rural couple that had married then divorced so they could remarry to move to the city, whereupon they were divorced in order to once again marry their original spouse. Along similar lines, I know of a medical doctor now living in the United States who wanted out of his marriage but was unable to get a separate apartment. He chose to take on a second job sweeping the streets for two hours each day; this was in addition to his medical post and lengthy commute. Yet the street-sweeping job entitled him to a separate apartment, and this is how he was finally able to move out.

Stories of birth control in the FSU are not pretty. Access to reliable and safe birth control has largely been denied to Ukrainian women. Abortions remain a common form of birth control, and I have heard both jokes and actual accounts where Soviet, industrial-strength condoms were rinsed and reused. The bigger issue is that men often refuse to wear condoms, and their partners have shrugged this off.

A Ukrainian now living in London tells the story of visiting her gynecologist who asked how many abortions she had undergone. When the woman said there had been none—that in twenty years she had given birth to only one child—the doctor chastised her for being dishonest with him about her medical history. In fact, there are accounts of women who have had as many as a dozen abortions; the Soviet average according to many sources was seven per woman during her child-bearing years!

One cynical view maintains that doctors have unethically perpetuated the practice of numerous abortions despite adverse effects to the woman's health. This was because abortions were technically illegal, and hence a higher fee could be charged. It is true that medical salaries are pitifully low. It is also true that the majority of doctors in Ukraine is female.

Ukraine currently has a negative birth rate, and people express fear of having children in the wake of Chornobyl and other environmental hazards.

An unwed mother is considered a disgrace, whereas a divorced mother raising children is almost expected. (As elsewhere, grandmothers play a significant role in raising their grandchildren.)

Couples living together but not married are common and accepted; the woman is often referred to as the *zhena*, meaning "wife" in Russian. In Ukrainian, *zhynka* means both "woman" and "wife." Until recently, marriage ceremonies were performed in "wedding palaces" in light of the Soviet dismissal and disapproval of religion. (Divorces were also easily obtained.) Today's so-called "church weddings" are increasing in popularity, just as attendance at church services is rising sharply.

An old Russian wedding tradition was that guests shouted *"Gorko!"*—meaning bitter, a reminder that life is hard; so the couple should kiss and make life easier.

One change in independent Ukraine is the increased difficulty in marrying a non-Ukrainian. One friend nearly abandoned the paperwork process for his Moldovan fiancée; obtaining proof that she was single turned out to be a bureaucratic nightmare. One irony is that the couple met while she was working (legally) in Ukraine. Now married, the wife is required to stay in Ukraine or the FSU for five years before she can obtain Ukrainian citizenship. Travel abroad is prohibited.

Outside a cat exhibition in Kyiv. (Photo courtesy of Meredith Dalton.)

CITY ANIMALS

Pets are popular with Ukrainians, and you will come across a number of large dogs being walked throughout Kyiv. Kyiv is lovely with lots of green space, including small and large parks. Cats are less visible.

A few years ago a news story described a horrific place on the outskirts of Kyiv where stray dogs were killed for their hides. Certainly if you own dogs, take care that they do not stray.

There is a new city tax for owning dogs. Specifically, on a resident's utilities bill, in addition to heating and water, there is a new item called *sobaka*, meaning "dog." This is yet another attempt to impose unreasonable taxes because the state's coffers are empty. Unfortunately, both citizens and their pets lose since this tax contributes to abandonment of pets.

HOMOSEXUALITY

In December 1991, homosexuality was legalized in Ukraine. Most argue that it is still not accepted and its legalization was merely an attempt to appear more progressive in the eyes of the West. Ukrainians enjoy making gays the butt of many jokes, although some say attitudes are improving. An American friend, who is gay and Jewish, says that in his experience accounts of Ukrainian prejudice against both these groups are exaggerated.

Nevertheless, the gay movement is only just beginning, and its most vocal spokespersons tend to be very young. In Ukraine's macho culture, most older gay men remain closeted. More than likely, they describe themselves as bisexual and often indicate that they still intend to marry one day. Russian slang for "gay" is *goluboi* (say *gahlooBOY*), which is derived from the word for "light blue." ("Dark blue" is *siny*, say *SEEnee*.)

A gay and lesbian association called Ganymede was founded in 1991 but has not received adequate support within the gay community; one explanation is that the founder, despite good intentions, is a straight woman. A gay publication introduced in 1997 (*Odin C Nas* or *One of Us*) has been well received within the gay community. The Internet has helped draw together the younger computer-literate generation, on a broad spectrum of issues ranging from gay activism to environmentalist issues.

Kyiv's gay scene, like much of the capital's nightlife, is constantly changing venue. Until recently, gay discos and bars operated on an infrequent basis and were criticized by some as seedy and sometimes unsafe. This is beginning to change; for example, a gay disco close to the metro line and operating regularly on Saturdays has pleased members of the gay community.

Ignoring larger issues of prejudice, the privacy problem for young gay couples is essentially the same as for straight ones. Where can they go to find privacy? A lot of gay sex reportedly goes on in public parks but removed from public view. Most gay sex is unprotected, and recent figures regarding HIV infection are patently disturbing. Ukraine in 1998 distinguished itself for the fastest growth of HIV in Europe. The Ukrainian acronym for AIDS is SNID (say *sneed*); in Russian, it's SPID (say *speed*). Seventy per cent of Ukraine's current cases are due to drug use.

Gay friends noted that gay bath houses do not exist in Ukraine despite the popularity and long tradition of bath houses in this region. Gay men visiting the *banya* (or sauna) should know that sex does not take place there, and the actions of the man wielding the traditional birch branches should not be interpreted as any sort of sexual advance.

JEWS AND PASSPORTS

Several years ago, I blurted to a recent emigré to America, "I didn't know you were Ukrainian." He had just told me he was raised in Kyiv, not Russia where he was educated. "I am not Ukrainian," he said politely. "I am a Jew."

The internal passport with *propiska* continues to be used in Ukraine but what has changed since independence is the infamous fifth line (or fifth point) of the passport, reserved for nationality; in Soviet times Jews were considered a separate nationality. They still are, but not for passport identification. Today the fifth line is for citizenship, and the reference to Jews has been dropped. It's no longer quite as easy to discriminate against Jews, although historically last names often identified a person's nationality.

The history of Jews in Ukraine incontrovertibly affected the Ukrainian people, Jews and non-Jews alike. Like Russification measures aimed at stamping out Ukrainian and other ethnic identity, the Jews were discriminated against in their own country. Babi Yar and its gruesome history were cited in Chapter One. Stalin's visceral hatred of Jews is well documented, and his death in 1953 probably prevented a flagrant backlash against all Jews in the Soviet Union.

Non-Jewish Ukrainian friends have told me that discrimination against Jews is exaggerated or even unfounded. Some report that

The site where the Jewish synagogue stood before its destruction in World War II, Lviv. (Photo courtesy of Meredith Dalton.)

Jews discriminate against them; you'll notice that Jews work together, and they cite that two of Ukraine's wealthiest men are Jews. So this is proof that there is no discrimination! Jewish friends tell a very different story, and many of them remain interested in emigrating abroad. There is also jealousy on the part of non-Jews since, historically, it was easier for Jews than non-Jews to emigrate.

RACISM AND DISCRIMINATION

On several occasions, I overheard staff members voice prejudices against Jews without batting an eye. Racism against dark-skinned individuals appears equally ingrained. A common claim is that much of the current criminal element hails from Central Asia, where skin color is darker than in Ukraine. Other Asians also tend to be suspect.

Technically speaking, Ukrainians must carry their documents with them at all times. Likewise, foreigners are advised to have their passports on them, although I would suggest a xeroxed copy is safer than the passport itself. The following anecdotes seem to indicate that it is a good idea to carry a copy of your passport with you at all times.

A US Army recruit told me about spending three weeks in Kyiv on a training course. Because he is African-American, he was repeatedly stopped by the transit police demanding to see his documents. In a single day, he was stopped three times in precisely the same spot, just as he was entering or leaving a central metro station. A friend had advised him only to show his passport but never to hand it over, or he might be forced to pay a bribe to get it back.

One night a very close friend, a bronze-skinned Englishman whose father is from Delhi, was harassed by the police. He didn't have his documents on him, so they took him to the station where they detained him for some twenty minutes. One officer even hit him in the face for no apparent reason. It is not surprising that he is always skittish around *militsia* after this.

Finally, another close friend, a man from Ecuador with a proud Inca heritage, came to study at the University of Kyiv on full scholarship at age 17. I met him after he had finished his bachelor's and master's equivalents, but he remained in Ukraine, in part because he had a young son there. The son had asthma problems. Also the marriage had failed. Willie's dark skin presented him with challenges, but none was insuperable. There was a brief period when his Ukrainian visa wasn't in order, and he was between student and business visas. His solution during this period was to walk about the streets wearing only business suits; he said he was less likely to be stopped if he dressed professionally. That he is fluent in Russian was a valuable, even necessary, skill for his long-term success. (He has also learned to drop the names of powerful allies when necessary—a useful technique in this society where connections truly matter.)

I cite the above stories about these expat friends because foreigners need to recognize that some will have a harder time than others. For some it will not be worth the hassle.

ATTITUDES TOWARD WESTERNERS

One overwhelming perception is that all Westerners are rich. Some Ukrainians will try to exploit and overcharge them, for example. There are also those gracious souls who would never overcharge because they honor Westerners as guests in their homeland. Most Ukrainians lie somewhere in between; some are looking for green cards, some for English tutors and friends, and some simply want Western business contacts. Westerners need to be prepared for those who aim to exploit them and be worthy of those who honor them.

An Englishman in Kyiv ventured provocatively that the British (as well as the Dutch) were probably better suited for living in Ukraine than Americans because of the Empire's colonial traditions, including recent experiences in Africa and India. It's an interesting concept to Americans, and one that might easily make Ukrainians chomp at the bit, given their recent break from centuries of outside domination.

Americans do have cultural traits that can be exploited as weaknesses, especially in situations abroad. Americans tend to be sociable, and they place high importance on candor and trust. They often exhibit a superior attitude toward others, and their emphasis on money and materialism as a measure of one's success is at variance with Ukrainians who regard spirituality as the more noble pursuit. The need for professional recognition and ambition is a common American trait; contrast their individualism with the collective mentality of Ukrainians who never truly appreciated the free thinking encouraged by the Renaissance.

For all foreigners abroad, the absence of friends and family can lead to isolation and loneliness; Americans are especially vulnerable to people offering friendship and flattery, whereas Europeans are considered more reserved.

SOVIET AND POST-INDEPENDENCE STEREOTYPES

Old Soviet stereotypes included the *nomenklatura*, Communist Party *apparatchiky*, bureaucrats, the military, the proletariat, the intelligentsia, dissidents, *babushky,* and pensioners. Newer stereotypes emerging in the post-Soviet era include the New Rich, the mafia, entrepreneurs, and an emerging middle class.

In simplistic terms, the Soviets could be divided into the haves and have-nots. The *nomenklatura* or *apparatchiky* were the minority (some say 20%, but this seems generous) and clearly on the winning side; the proletariat (or working class) was a catchall for the rest. Only the highest ranking military officials fell into the privileged class. While these terms are used less today, for some the primary change is that many former communists are today's strongest advocates for democracy. This is because they were best poised to take advantage of so-called market reforms. While the West watched eagerly to see if and how reforms were being implemented, the Communist Party bosses managed to line their pockets by breaking up state monopolies and selling off chunks among themselves at fire-sale prices. The consensus today is that the super-rich in both Russia and Ukraine did not add any value when they usurped their present wealth; they merely redistributed their country's mineral resources among a select group of friends. To the have-nots, this talk of democracy is little more than perpetuating the glaring inequities of the totalitarian regime. Pessimistic observers remark that they have only succeeded in rearranging the deck chairs on the Titanic.

There are also diehard communists who are attempting to make a comeback. They are playing to the nostalgic sympathies of older voters who have been left behind and whose lives are so diminished. But these communists, like the voters they attract, are mostly older generation, in a country where youth has a decided advantage.

The intelligentsia of yore is largely disillusioned by society's reforms, and their struggles to survive are nearly as acute as for the pensioners. Some have turned to more entrepreneurial, if less palatable, professions by default rather than desire; sadly, others have turned more to the bottle.

Where are the Soviet dissidents? Most dissidents were Jews, and because of Soviet and Ukrainian discriminatory practices, they continue to emigrate in record numbers. One American Jew reported that half of her Jewish Ukrainian friends had left in the last three years.

The lives of pensioners and *babushky* have been irrevocably altered due to the devaluation of their pensions amidst society's vast changes. Likewise, aging Soviet military heroes sometimes wear their uniforms and medals of honor, their stoic pride now tinged with sadness. The military no longer holds the prestige of the Soviet era, and in fact is racked today with brutal hazing rituals, bad morale, and stories of obsolete (or nonexistent) equipment and insufficient fuel supplies. Formerly the Cossack tradition was cited as good training ground for the military and contributed to very high percentages of Ukrainian officers in the Russian Army. Today, sons of career military are choosing career paths different from those of their fathers. This proud Cossack tradition may be permanently displaced by nostalgia.

Bureaucracy has expanded greatly since independence, in part because the power base has shifted (for Ukrainians) from Moscow to Kyiv. However, younger generations are much more likely to turn their backs on governmental careers, including military ones. Only time will tell how Ukrainian society will adapt during the next decade; some claim optimistically that the situation will improve once the current wave of bureaucrats retires.

The greater concern is the powerful grip of the mafia in post-Soviet countries. The New Rich, or New Russians, refers to the new breed of moneyed businessmen whose most defining characteristic is ostentatious spending habits. Many will tell you that the New Rich and the mafia are one and the same. You may hear the term *krisha* (say *KREEsha*), meaning "roof", the slang for mafia protection.

LIAR, LIAR

It is hard for many Westerners to grasp the state of corruption and bribery in Ukraine; it is equally difficult to truly understand Ukrainian attitudes toward democracy and capitalism. For over seventy years, the Soviet system infected most of its citizens with the notion that capitalism is about grabbing, cheating, and wheeling and dealing. Today the actions of the mafia and top government officials support this premise. According to many, this group is both the main product and sole beneficiary of capitalism in Ukraine, whereas for the average citizen, democracy is marked primarily by free elections, increasing hardship, and *tufta* (say *toofTA*) as usual.

Tufta roughly translates as "institutionalized b.s."—for example, inflated harvest figures and tourist-speak of yore, that were intended not only to sanitize but to paint a rosier picture to citizens and outside observers. In large measure, *tufta* is an affront to the intelligence of ordinary Ukrainians. (*Tufta* can also mean just "b.s.") Two related words are *vranyo* vs. *lozh*. Both essentially refer to lying, but the first resembles a fib or white lie or even blarney, told to avoid offending someone. It's non-vindictive rubbish. *Lozh* i ı harsh, deliberate lie.

SNAPSHOTS OF TRANSITION: CORRUPTION AND CUSTOMER SERVICE

Petty corruption and bribery go hand in hand in Ukraine. For some, bribery is merely one cost of doing business, just as reliance upon personal connections (*svyazy* or *blat*) is obligatory.

Visibility in Ukraine attracts unwanted attention. Some foreign investors avoid types of businesses requiring storefronts, for example restaurants. One prominent European entrepreneur (in the true sense of the word) announced in late 1998 that he was throwing in the towel after seven strong years in Ukraine. Relentless corruption had finally exhausted his patience.

Visibility invites the tax inspectorates in search of trumped up fines and bribes. One friend who sells used car parts was fined because the time stamped on his cash register receipts was not adjusted for daylight savings time. The $200 fine was intended to discourage further "defrauding" his customers. There was a second, trumped-up, but less expensive, fine. The irony is that when they dropped the cash register fine, he felt like he was getting away with something although he still had one bogus fine to pay! Be prepared for this common psychological ploy.

Also common is a range of fines wherein an official will offer you the lower one as if he's doing you a favor. For example, when I was recently stopped for jaywalking, the policeman said that the fines ranged from two to nine UAH (then $1 to $4.50). He gave me the lesser fine, which made sense since there was absolutely no traffic nearby, but I had been at fault. A friend joked that it's harder to understand the range of fines for not putting on your seatbelt; either it's fastened or it's not!

Some foreigners skirt the issue of bribery with talk of finding a "common language" with the different parties. Others will tell you that a necessary trait for survival and sanity in Ukraine is flexible ethics, which is essentially the same thing. One important point always to remember is that Westerners are perceived as wealthy (and thus money should be no object to them), but if Westerners give in too easily, they will assuredly drown. Your best first approach should be manners; after that, you might try the "common language" approach.

Attitudes toward customer service are improving. Restaurants catering to Western clients recognize and want this business, and all businesses can see that Ukrainians now have choices. Customers appreciate and can often demand courteous behavior. In Kyiv's expat hangouts, some waitresses seem to smile too much, as if that is part of the training. Smaller establishments also seem to be emulating McDonald's successes. To see how much progress has been made, you merely need to visit a state hotel in a smaller town where they are not accustomed to dealing with foreigners. Even in the big cities, many of the old state hotels perpetuate Soviet practices of general unhelpfulness. Even if rooms are available, you may be turned down without an advance reservation. They're not in business to make money, so they don't care.

Several stories provide recent snapshots of Ukraine in transition:

I went with friends to the movies where the projectionist had started the film early, so it would finish early and he could go home. He started the film without any audience! We made him restart the reel. A couple weeks later, I boarded a plane from Crimea to Kyiv, and the plane likewise took off twenty minutes early. I was shocked, as not all the seats were filled.

In a poker game with expatriates and locals playing, a Ukrainian turned his cards over and excused himself for the restroom. When he returned a few minutes later, his face was ashen; he openly panicked that he was spending too much time "around foreigners." When he had excused himself from the table, he had walked off without taking his cards with him; he had failed to consider that someone at the table might try to cheat him.

There was also collusion: that very evening, the same Ukrainian proposed that he and another player remaining in the hand simply split the kitty. Rules against collusion were foreign to him.

An American friend ordered tea in a hotel restaurant. The waiter offered him the standard choice of black tea or one of several imported specialty teas. After hearing the choices, my friend still selected the standard tea. When his colleague requested one of the imported teas, the waiter retracted his offer. The colleague was flustered and then became insistent, but the waiter wouldn't budge and excused himself. A second waiter brought the tea and explained that the original waiter was trying to sell teas from his personal stash, but he had panicked that his boss might find out.

One of my favorite stories happened in the Hotel Rus dining room. At the end of the meal, I asked the waiter for separate checks. I explained that I was sorry, but my boss required this for accounting purposes. The waiter cordially smiled and disappeared for a long time. When he returned he had six checks for the three of us, which he laid out very carefully on the table. "This is for you; this is for your boss." In each case, the boss's receipt was roughly three times the actual amount of the meal. What the waiter didn't know was that my boss was at the table!

Foreigners should be wary of being overcharged. One friend discovered that his check for dinner trebled one night. When he complained, the waiter said that chicken was sold according to grams and that the menu's price was for 100 grams. My friend argued that this was not the case in the past and demanded to see a manager. The manager explained that this was a mix-up and apologized, but clearly the waiter (or the establishment) had been hoping to over-charge.

Once in Lviv I complained that I was being overcharged for my *shashlik*; however, it turned out the menu price was for 100 grams whereas the serving portion was 150 grams. Also be aware that menus often show the price of wine, like vodka, in 50-gram or 50-ml measures. A standard wine glass, however, is three to four times this. Without this knowledge, you'll think someone is trying to stiff you when the bill arrives.

EXPAT COMMUNITY

Ukraine's expatriate community boasts its share of personalities ranging from do-gooders to bottom-feeders. Most prominent are members of the donor community and their contractors, diplomatic personnel, volunteers, representatives of big business, entrepreneurs, journalists, and missionaries.

The Ukrainian diaspora stand apart within the larger expat community. The diaspora community is unique in that their parents and grandparents fled Ukraine for America and Canada. (Often the parents cannot understand how the children could possibly want to return.) The diaspora comes with its own set of issues and agendas; I've heard locals criticize this group for its tendency to proselytize.

The nature of expatriate work attracts singles, including many men in search of Ukrainian girlfriends or wives. Fortunately for them there are lots of especially attractive Ukrainian women, who genuinely appreciate the way that most foreigners treat them.

The expatriate community, here as elsewhere, also attracts its share of misfits. Some are married but have problems at home with their wives or children. Others come to Ukraine hoping to avoid an alcohol problem or the stigma that accompanies it, but they are choosing the wrong country—alcohol is a key element of Slavic culture and a large factor in expatriate social life. Still others had trouble with work at home; maybe jobs were hard to find (or keep), or maybe life was just too boring. There's a small group that gets addicted to being big fish in the overseas community, even if it is essentially a fishbowl.

Many foreigners working in Ukraine chose to come because of professional background and the search for an intellectual challenge. Some get addicted to the lifestyle and say that the status quo back home is at best stifling. One young consultant described America now as high energy and stasis; Ukraine as lethargy and motion.

Finally, there is a growing number of younger expatriates arriving in Ukraine. They are not the flannel-plaid and nose-ring set found in other parts of Europe, Latin America, or Southeast Asia, partly because visa restrictions don't make it easy to enter Ukraine, and many young travelers are far more attracted to the Czech Republic, Hungary, and other places. But Ukraine has an off-the-beaten-track allure. And more Russian majors are making their way to the FSU: Ukraine offers a glimpse of the edge without the free fall of Russia.

The Donor Community and Embassy Personnel
Among the donor community's most visible members are employees of USAID (United States Agency for International Development) and TACIS (Technical Assistance to the CIS, which is the EU's equivalent), and their many contractors. Also present are EBRD (European Bank for Reconstruction and Development), the World Bank, the British Know How Fund, Soros in various manifestations, Canadian aid organizations, and others. In overall terms, the EU is Ukraine's largest aid donor, and Ukraine wants EU membership. (It also says that the EU discriminates against it, unlike its neighbors to the west.)

Foreign aid and embassy direct hires should probably be differentiated from both their contractors and from the community at large. For example, most aid workers and embassy folks live in truly Western apartments surrounded by modern appliances and the rugs and trinkets accumulated during previous assignments in Africa and Latin America. The fact that their cars display diplomatic plates means that they won't be hassled by the dreaded traffic police, known by the acronym GAI. Also, they get to shop in the commissary and have periodic shipments of food from home which translates into stockpiling Doritos and Diet Dr. Pepper.

Another central distinction between the diplomatic personnel and aid employees vs. the rest of the expatriate crowd is that the former groups have access to cash through internal mechanisms. Consequently, they don't tend to understand the money woes which only a couple years ago could be described as hell on earth; fortunately, this situation is beginning to improve. Cash machines appeared in 1998, and some of them work. A lot of people take cash advances from credit cards and pay high fees in Ukraine (3% is common) as well as the bank's originating fee; also, money can be wired via Western Union. Visa, MasterCard, and Eurocard are increasingly accepted at hotels, upscale restaurants, and shops, but don't expect to cash traveler's checks anywhere. A new location advertising Thomas Cook Traveler's Cheques may provide alternatives in the near future. As of early 1999 there is still no American Express office.

Aid contractors—unlike aid employees—still have (sometimes significant) cash problems, but they do have other perks. While they don't get diplomatic license plates like embassy and aid workers, they may successfully divert traffic fines by flashing the green cards issued by their embassy. These cards suggest diplomatic immunity for the holders, but don't rely on them in a real pinch. These cards are also passed out capriciously and technically only to foreign contractors staying in Ukraine for over one year.

Just remember this: capriciousness, or arbitrary application of policies, is something you will come to accept more in Ukraine, or you just might not make it here. There is real diplomatic immunity for real diplomats; and while these green dip cards (if you hold one—and many contractors do) can be of assistance, my advice is, don't abuse your privilege. There are many arrogant foreigners and probably more Ukrainians who would like to snag them for it. However frustrating aspects of Ukraine's laws, customs, and culture may seem to you, your challenge is to work within that system. It will require creativity, guts, and sometimes tolerance verging on madness. Did I forget to mention patience?

Volunteer Organizations

Volunteer organizations such as the Peace Corps and the MBA Enterprise Corps, together with the missionary community, deserve highest kudos as the altruists in the larger expatriate community. Other volunteer groups including the International Executive Service

Corps (IESC) and VOCA also provide a tremendous service; however, because their assignments are generally short-term, their presence is less visible within the expat community at large.

The Peace Corps's largest mission worldwide in 1998 was in Ukraine with 170 volunteers. Tragically, one volunteer was murdered in his Chernihiv apartment in September 1998 during an apparent robbery. While conceding that violence can occur anywhere, another volunteer remarked that he generally felt safer in Ukraine than at home, in Chicago. (For the record, most Peace Corps deaths worldwide are the result of auto accidents, not violent crime. Ukraine had had no previous problems.)

Most expatriates in Ukraine still stand out in their community—probably more so outside of Kyiv—and it is important to recognize this. On the other hand, Peace Corps volunteers are dispersed throughout Ukraine and are not necessarily strongly visible in Kyiv's expatriate community. They also tend to live a more local lifestyle, both in terms of income and functional language skills. Specifically, Peace Corps volunteers are expected to speak Russian or Ukrainian depending on the location of the assignment; similarly, current policy is that MBA Enterprise volunteers communicate at work in Russian. Also, while the MBA Corps offers larger monthly stipends than Peace Corps, neither group of volunteers is flush.

Contrast this with VOCA and IESC volunteers who have comfortable, though not luxurious, apartments provided by their host organizations. These apartments are most often near the city center. The farther one ventures from downtown Kyiv, the more affordable the rents become and the better your language skills need to be. Because VOCA and IESC assignments are typically for shorter periods, these volunteers can hardly be expected to speak Russian or Ukrainian. Moreover, these volunteers generally provide specialized expertise; often, the high level of their positions at home cannot allow for extended tours abroad.

The Missionary Community

Ukraine's missionary community has been steadily growing in recent years, even if its presence tends to be less visible within the expatriate community at large. One reason is that the missionaries, like some of the volunteers above, tend to live farther from the city center where there is more affordable housing. Usually, their housing is not paid for, or there are considerable financial constraints. One missionary wife with children suggested that embassy staff, aid workers, and their contractors had driven the rents up so high and that they don't really care since they don't pay their own rents; rather, their taxpayers do. (This is true for so many companies whose overseas packages include rent and other perks; otherwise, they could not attract the proper talent needed for the overseas positions.)

Many missionary families are united in this tightly knit community, separate from the larger expatriate community. The missionaries have even started their own school called New Hope Christian School. Non-missionary children may be admitted according to a higher tuition scale; naturally, all will be following the religious instruction. Still, tuition will cost significantly less than the other private schools available in Kyiv, including the Kiev International School (KIS), the Pechersk School, and a French-Ukrainian school.

Finally, the missionaries are somewhat isolated from other expats, because they are not part of the bar scene which is so popular, especially among the singles set. (Certainly, not all expats are heavy drinkers, but the majority drank before they arrived and often report drinking more in Ukraine than they used to at home.)

Turf Wars

While aid direct hires and embassy personnel must pay taxes in their home country, some aid contractors are currently exempt from taxes in both their home country and Ukraine. (The argument against this practice is that bilateral agreements were developed to avoid double taxation, not to avoid taxation altogether.) The Ukrainian government periodically steps up its talk about taxing all foreigners, which gets the donor community up in arms. My advice is to research any revisions to the Ukrainian tax code that might apply to you and your company *before* you depart for Ukraine.

It should come as little surprise that the private sector resents this loophole, since it is not exempt from paying taxes. The private sector also does not have access to embassy checking, diplomatic plates, or the green card cited above.

In spite of these differences, it is wrong to assume that there are many camps and lots of resentments among the expatriate community. There are separate camps and sometimes strong opinions, but the community at large remains both cliquish and tight despite its differences. The most vociferous critics tend to come from the private sector, who often views its work as superior to that of the donor community and embassies.

Without all the perks, some members of the private sector suggest that theirs is a more authentic experience, i.e., they are dealing with the Ukrainian bureaucracy as Ukrainians do. For example, one friend complained of the arduous paperwork process required for bringing pets in and out of the country. Like the traffic fines cited above, she stated that simply flashing one of the green "diplomatic" cards could have eliminated the hassle.

Probably those who hold the green cards do a disservice to those who don't. A valid point is that the green cards perpetuate discriminatory pricing practices against foreigners. For example, in Ukraine there are currently three hotel rates—although I hear ministers stay for free in certain hotels, which would make four. The three rates I know well are for locals, expats, and expats at diplomatic rates; the last falls somewhere between standard expatriate and local rates. Holders of the green card receive the diplomatic hotel rate, not the standard overpriced expat rate. As an example, if our local staff paid $12 for a hotel room, I usually paid closer to $48, and the expats who weren't holders of green cards paid closer to $100. The argument, then, is that some of the people who are in a position to influence standardized pricing do nothing to help those outside of the beloved perks system. It's much like the apartment rent issue; people don't care how much their rent is as long as their paycheck isn't involved.

For me, a six-month bureaucratic nightmare opened my eyes to accepting some perks as gift horses. My goal was to open a company bank account. Many firms circumvent corporate accounts by having an employee open a personal account where the paperwork is vastly simplified, but I was advised for tax reasons not to do so. The problem lay not with the bank itself but with Ukraine's complicated banking laws. In the end, the insufferable process was obviated because my employer was a USAID contractor. It turned out that an earlier document prepared by USAID existed but had not been updated to include our name among authorized companies and projects. Once the bank recognized this, our problems were easily rectified. The bank was delighted to help us find a way out of our morass; we were happy to learn that the document existed and, once revised, would enable us to easily open our account.

In my case as a USAID contractor, I could never legally register my company, although I was technically required to. There was a problem because of conflicting legal codes. While I wanted to be compliant, there was not yet a vehicle for our doing so.

All I can (lamely) say is that every situation is different, and there are no pat answers. With that said, the private sector's periodic whining about lack of special treatment is generally valid.

The Private Sector

Within the private sector group, two generalized personality types emerge. You might call them the Big Boys vs. The Rest. The big boys include the consultants and accountants from the Big Five accounting firms. While many of these firms first came to Ukraine to implement aid energy projects, they now have separate corporate structures to handle non-aid work. The multinational consumer products companies have also arrived. McDonald's, Procter & Gamble, Pepsi, and Coca-Cola are all ready to pounce on the 50 million plus population living in Ukraine. Cargill, Monsanto, and John Deere, among others, have a vested interest in the country's grain production.

The expatriate employees of these large companies live well, often in Western-style apartments with Western appliances, if they're lucky, while the majority of the expat population lives in furnished apartments of the so-called modern local style. (You may notice the difference when you wash your first load of clothes and wonder if the small and finicky machine was designed by the makers of the Easy Bake Oven. And there won't be a dryer, only a clothesline.)

More families with children are now arriving, especially in Kyiv, where there are several established international schools available. Many of the larger companies have minimal expatriate staff, in part because their costs to the company are so much higher than for local staff. Also, other companies with long-term goals don't necessarily need a large expatriate staff; their goal is to establish a presence for future Ukrainian business activities. A long-term commitment means laying a lot of groundwork over time; personal and business connections are the key, but this doesn't have to mean a large staff.

Let us turn to the second set. This includes both smaller companies interested in establishing a presence here as well as the maverick entrepreneurial set. They are all mavericks and probably all entrepreneurs; it's just that some are more reckless than others. There are cautionary, if interesting, tales about Western businessmen going astray, or at least trying to play by Ukrainian rules and hiring their own mafia security to play hard ball and level the playing field. Of course, the field isn't level, whether you're diaspora, a fearless (or feckless) maverick, or even Ukrainian. The Californian bar-owner who jumped into bed with the Chechen mafia to avoid some Kyiv thugs was lucky to go home with his life. The Pennsylvanian who several years ago opened the luxurious Grand Hotel in Lviv pulled out of that joint venture the way others have before and since: either someone you know gets deep-sixed and you reconsider, or one day you learn that you are no longer part of a joint venture.

On Dating and Aging

If you're female, your coat will be removed for you, your cigarette will be lit for you (and you won't be treated as a pariah for this nasty habit), and frequently your bar tab will be paid for you. If you're single, you'll probably date some of the expatriate men and then become bitter because they prefer to date the local women. One young man explained, "It's weird, it's like dating your mother or someone from the 1950s, but Ukrainian women are really supportive in what you do." Along these lines, young Ukrainian girls, when asked what they want to be when they grow up, often respond, "I want to be really beautiful so I can marry a rich man."

Ukrainian women are extremely attractive and many have stolen a Westerner's heart. You rarely see the converse: few expatriate women date local men, although one of them talked of women she knew who came to Ukraine in search of men. A distinguishing feature here is fluency. Those who speak the language have a very different experience; they also tend to survive longer in Ukraine.

Age is highly appreciated in Slavic cultures. A lot of middle-aged foreign men come to Ukraine and attract younger, beautiful, and devoted wives. A cynical joke reads: "A foreigner is not just a future spouse, but a means of transportation."

A 67-year-old consultant told me one reason that he lives in Ukraine now is ageism in America. At his age, he couldn't find a challenging job in America, whereas in Ukraine he is appreciated for his age and expertise. Graying hair is a positive attribute. The average Ukrainian bureaucrat these days is around 50, or so it seems, since the younger generation jumped ship. These bureaucrats prefer to work with someone closer to their own age when possible, as opposed to the 20- and 30-somethings offered especially by the larger consulting firms.

Along these lines, a former Peace Corps volunteer said the Corps most heavily scrutinizes recruits in their 30s and 40s, because often they are running away from something, whereas younger or older volunteers typically have other motivations.

THE EXPATRIATE EXPERIENCE

Living abroad expands your way of looking at the world. Living in Ukraine encouraged me to examine how different cultures approach negotiations and problem-solving and how they view and treat diversity and conformity. Individuals continually reshaped my cultural stereotypes, not just of Ukrainians but of the North Americans and Europeans whose paths I also crossed. Living in Ukraine also made me treasure the bounties I had left behind. Overall, despite the occasional bout of pettiness, Ukraine's expatriate community is close-knit and welcoming. One of its greatest aspects is that it is easy to make friends of many ages, nationalities, and professions.

What bothers me most within this community are basic concerns about arrogance and limited cultural sensitivity. An "us vs. them" mentality arises, and is even natural, because of cultural differences and economic considerations. For example, Kyiv's restaurant choices are still limited and on average quite expensive. It is not unusual to spend $75-100 on a dinner for two and quite possible to spend significantly more. The average monthly wage in Ukraine is less than the cost of that dinner, although expatriate companies often pay substantially more for their bilingual staffs.

Expatriates clearly need to make greater efforts to improve their foreign language skills. One expat said that foreigners who don't learn the local language will spend their time abroad essentially trapped behind a glass wall. Homesickness or loneliness are also more likely. So study, take classes with a tutor, and by all means learn the alphabet before you arrive! Buy a pocket phrasebook now so that you can learn the basic pleasantries. If you can speak Ukrainian or Russian, be proud of your foreign language skills and use them.

It's really presumptuous to blurt out English in a restaurant, although you won't believe how common it is. Unfortunately, more often than you would like, if you try to order a beer and butcher the Russian or Ukrainian language, the server will respond in English. But give it a whirl first. You need to practice for all those other daily encounters where possibly no English is spoken. This might include buying vegetables at the *rynok*, hailing a cab across town, or negotiating a better price for tourist items on Andriyivsky Uzviz (okay, some vendors do speak some English). Still, if you leave the confines of the major cities, the rest of Ukraine speaks only pidgin English.

Refrain from criticizing Ukraine in English in front of Ukrainians, who in most cases will understand English far better than you understand Russian or Ukrainian.

FINAL THOUGHTS:
UKRAINIANS ON EXPAT EXPERTS

Many Ukrainians are skeptical about the many foreign consultants who come to advise them, often in areas which, even without advice, Ukrainians will eventually come to decide for themselves. As an example, let me tell you about a Ukrainian-American colleague who proved unwilling or unable to handle Ukraine after 17 years in America. I recall an occasion when he tried to give a waiter a lesson on proper service. After making the waiter sit in his own chair, he draped his napkin over his forearm. His air was condescending and inappropriate. The fact is that this man felt that all Ukrainians who hadn't left Ukraine, as he had done, were cowards. (It is relevant that he was Jewish and never felt fully Ukrainian.) It is no wonder Ukrainians tire of outsiders telling them how to live their lives differently.

These same Ukrainians watch how foreigners spend money, on projects and in restaurants, and you'd be amazed at what they know about our salaries. (If they don't, they are likely to ask.) Ukrainians have openly observed that the expatriate community holds more than its share of marital, extramarital, and alcohol problems; they recognize those people who are running away from home, often because they'd like to themselves.

At times I too find myself among the harsher critics of the donor community: the way it spends money and the work that its contractors sometimes do. Yet I recognize that some of the loftier projects—which are also among the most challenging and interesting—would not receive any support at all if it weren't for foreign aid. There are not that many foreign businesses ready for the plunge, and Ukrainian firms and the state itself lack the financial resources for the changes to infrastructure that are so needed today.

Chapter Three

HUMOR AND LANGUAGE

HUMOR AS "LITERAL" ICE BREAKER

Bohdan, Ihor, and Vasily went fishing one cold winter day. Alongside its banks the Dnipro was starting to freeze, but it was still easy to navigate the small boat through the water. The three men were clearly more interested in drinking vodka than in fishing, and all three became drunk quite quickly.

"Pass the bottle, Bohdan," said Ihor. Bohdan thrust the bottle toward his friend, but his abrupt movement threw the boat off balance. In an effort to steady himself and the boat, Bohdan stood up. In his woozy state he toppled into the ice-cold water. Ihor and Vasily panicked as they watched their friend sink below the water's surface.

Being drunk themselves, each hoped the other would make the first move. At last Ihor exclaimed, "Well, we have to do something." So he dipped his arms into the icy water, and shrieking from the cold, he flailed around trying to catch his friend's arm or leg. Vasily followed and with great relief he yelled, "I've got his jacket; help me drag him aboard." The men hoisted the body into the boat with great effort, whereupon it became clear the man was not breathing. Ihor knew again that Vasily wouldn't make the first move, so he started to perform mouth-to-mouth resuscitation. "Good God," Ihor announced, "I didn't know what bad breath he had." Vasily looked at the man's feet and said, "Yeah, and I didn't know he was wearing skates."

Some contend that the best test of a foreigner's fluency in a given language is the ability to understand jokes and local humor. Few foreigners spending time in Ukraine will achieve the fluency or language skills necessary to comprehend fully or communicate via humor. Foreigners coming to Ukraine are mostly business people who do not have the time (or interest) to devote to language studies. But we are seeing increasing numbers of recent college graduates, many of whom majored in Russian, choosing to live abroad and use their skills. Entry-level jobs for them, if they are lucky enough to find them, typically don't pay well, but their language skills can partially make up for this. They can find cheaper housing away from the city center where there tend to be fewer English-speaking Ukrainians, and they can use the Russian they have studied.

Taking language lessons upon arrival in a foreign country is a good idea. However, for many of us, to achieve fluency might well take several years. You will have to weigh the practicality of studying Ukrainian or Russian depending on your personal circumstances. You should start with the basic niceties in both languages, then concentrate on learning one language better. Whichever language you decide to learn, exposure to local humor is always a good means toward understanding some of the subtleties of a different culture.

COMMON THEMES

Regional humor often reinforces, even perpetuates, cultural stereotypes. Today jokes pertaining to excessive alcohol intake, bureaucratic inefficiencies and nonsense, the "New Rich," and the increasing roles of the mafia and corruption in post-communist life are among the most prevalent themes in Ukraine. While each of these will be addressed below, one of the remarkable features of humor in this post-communist era is, of course, the relaxed climate for jokes. Some argue that the characteristic biting sarcasm of the dissident era is no longer possible in the present (democratic-leaning) situation. Parallel arguments are sometimes advanced regarding the effects of these newly found freedoms in the realms of literature and the visual and performing arts.

1. Vodka

Jokes about vodka are legion and certainly not unique to Ukraine and Russia. (It also follows that some Ukrainians tell these jokes about Russians and vice versa, rather than simply about themselves.) Within the FSU, many countries share strong vodka traditions, although customs may be influenced regionally by Muslim traditions, for example in Kyrgyzstan, or by the celebrated viniculture of Georgia and Moldova. Crimea is also celebrated for its wines.

Outside the FSU, Scandinavia and Poland are leading vodka producers and share many of the Slavic traditions and, consequently, many of the jokes about overindulgence. Certainly, none of these places can claim exclusive rights on jokes about vodka—or alcohol in general. The following, for example, has been told as an Irish joke, substituting whiskey as the drink of choice:

A man was staggering home with a bottle of vodka in his pocket. He slipped and fell to the ground with a hard thud. Struggling to his feet, he felt something wet running down his leg. "Please, God," he begged, "let it be blood!"

In contrast to the deep sarcasm of the dissident jokes treated separately below, a host of silly, sometimes slapstick, jokes abound pertaining to excessive alcohol intake:

—Excuse me, what time is it?
—You know, I could use a drink too.

Alcohol often masks other issues or problems; below, we see the strained relationship between a (nagging) wife and her husband:

Wife: You promised me you'd become a different man.
Husband: I know, but he drinks too.

This contemporary (post-communist) joke evinces the bitter-sweet realities of inflation and hardships incurred as a result:

—With the rising cost of vodka, Daddy, it looks like you'll have less to drink.
—No, sonny, that's where you're wrong. You're going to have less to eat.

A final joke in this category assumes knowledge of the reference to 50 grams as a standard measurement for vodka.

—They say that life begins at 50.
—Yeah, but it's even better after a hundred or two.

While kiosks sell a variety of imported and domestic vodkas, local brands are often sealed with non-reusable caps made of thick foil. The Slavic tradition is that these bottles are drunk in one sitting. Hence, the hangover remedy calling for "the hair of the dog that bit you" takes on a different meaning here. Another drink as a hangover cure on the morning after implies that a new bottle must be opened and then finished. In this way, the hangover and its cure will be perpetuated.

2. Marriage, Infidelity, and In-laws

Common joke themes revolve around marriage difficulties and infidelity. While neither is uniquely Ukrainian (or Soviet), the popularity of these themes is telling. Below is a sampling of these jokes:

—Honey, when we get married, I'll be there to share all your troubles and sorrows.

—But I don't have any, my love.

—I said, when we get married...

—Masha! I didn't know you smoked. When did you start?

—That night my husband came home early and found a cigarette butt in the ashtray.

A woman is admiring a fur coat in front of the mirror.

"Mother, did Daddy buy that new coat for you?" asked her son.

"No, my dear, if I relied on your father, I wouldn't have you, let alone this nice fur coat."

The rest of the world has its in-law jokes, but in the former Soviet Union these jokes are especially popular. Similar in many respects to the jokes about strained marriages, in-law jokes are often attributed to many years of severely cramped living quarters, often shared by multiple generations and extended family members.

—Mr. Gorsky, do you have any children?

—Yes, I have three daughters.

—Do they live at home?

—No, they aren't married yet.

A mother tells her daughter, "Your boyfriend is such a jerk, I would be delighted to be his mother-in-law!" (Contrast this with the traditional Christmas toast to a man's mother-in-law: that her throat never becomes dry.)

A young woman tells her husband the bad news—that her once rich father is now bankrupt. The young man exclaims, "I knew that old miser would find some way to separate us!"

3. Everyday Life and Minor Hassles

While the above jokes about vodka, strained relationships, and in-laws are not unique to the FSU, the following jokes address aspects of everyday life as lived and handled in Ukraine. Although the division is somewhat arbitrary, I am separating minor hassles here as distinct from major hassles and the dissident jokes.

Lada

Like the jokes about Aeroflot (which seem equally popular outside of the FSU), Lada (aka the Soviet Fiat) jokes remain quite popular:

—Why does the Lada Samara have a heated rear window?
—So that your hands won't freeze when you push it.

Queuing

One of the many negative images of the Soviet era was the notorious shopping queue. For former Soviet citizens, it remains a pervasive memory that is occasionally revived. These jokes are examples:

The plural of man: "queue"

—Grandma, what was the biggest road catastrophe of all time?
—My dear, it was when the Kyiv queue crashed with the Moscow queue.

SHE SUDDENLY
BECAME NOSTALGIC
FOR THE QUEUES

119

Shopping

Since independence, shopping has taken on a new dimension, and there are many jokes now about the outrageous spending habits of the New Rich. One real frustration for the average Ukrainian is that he is visually assaulted by what he cannot afford.

The following joke makes sense when you understand that most Ukrainians carry their own plastic bags whenever they go grocery shopping. These bags are widely available for sale in kiosks, or you will see a lot of mostly elderly women selling these at the farmer's market, or *rynok*. Only in some of the Western-style grocery stores, with their uniformed guards watching the doorways, are bags provided at no charge.

Soviet dementia: A man stands in front of a grocery store with an empty bag and cannot remember if he was going into the store or coming out.

Mushroom collecting

This joke plays on the popularity of mushroom collecting—and the occasional tales of poisonous mushrooms:

—Doctor! Which mushrooms can you eat?

—All of them. There are just some that you can only eat once.

Taxes

Given the prohibitive tax structure, there is rampant tax evasion.

A doctor says to his patient, "You say that you're happy to pay your taxes ... And when exactly did this start?"

Changing borders

Lviv, the so-called capital of western Ukraine, is often cited for its changing political borders. Lviv entered the 20th century under the rule of the Austro-Hungarian Empire until the Hapsburg Empire collapsed at the end of World War I. Following the Russian Revolution, Lviv was very briefly the seat of an independent government but was quickly restored to Polish rule. It remained under Poland (except for a brief period in 1920 under Soviet rule) until 1939, when Moscow seized control. From 1941 to 1944, Lviv was occupied by German forces and subsequently liberated by the Red Army. In 1991, when Ukraine declared independence, Lviv was at the forefront of the nationalist movement. This staunchly Ukrainian-speaking region never fully succumbed to the dominance of repressive Moscow.

This is a long-winded history lesson as lead-up to a one-liner joke, but it demonstrates how complicated shifting borders can be:

An old lady upon hearing that her home is now in Ukraine, not Poland, responded: "Thank God, I don't think I could have handled another of those cold Polish winters."

Poking fun at other former Soviet nationalities

Like America's Polish, Irish, and Aggie jokes, Ukraine has its penchant for regional humor, and certain Soviet nationalities were primary targets. For example, upon meeting a neighbor from Moldova, the jocular Ukrainian response is "I'll speak slowly then." Another group targeted by Ukrainians and Russians were the Chukchi. These jokes have been described as "Russian Eskimo jokes" since the Chukchi live so far away in frozen climates. While these jokes seem innocuous enough, they are probably not to the Chukchi, since the jokes poke fun not only at their clime but at their native intelligence.

A third nationality targeted especially in Soviet times were the Georgians. They were frequently the butt of jokes because of their entrepreneurial habits and desire to make money. While the term "Georgian speculator" had derogatory implications (since speculating, or profiteering, was illegal), these jokes portrayed Georgians as crafty as opposed to unintelligent.

A plane flying to Moscow was hijacked by a man wielding a loaded gun. "Take me to London!" he demanded. A second hijacker burst into the cockpit with two guns, demanding, "No, fly this plane to Paris!" A Georgian entered the cockpit with a bomb. He announced, "This plane is going to land in Moscow as scheduled."

After the plane landed, the first two hijackers were carted off to jail. The Georgian was honored in a special ceremony. "We honor you today as a state hero. What made you so bold as to demand that the plane fly to Moscow?"

The Georgian replied, "What was I going to do with 5000 carnations in Paris?"

4. Dissident Wit

Whereas jokes describing minor hassles of everyday life provide for good humor, they lack the creative edge and biting sarcasm of the dissident jokes. There is even a poignancy in dissident jokes and their treatment of the harsher realities of Soviet life.

Dissident wit reached its pinnacle during the twilight years of the Brezhnev era, reflecting a growing cynicism in the USSR. The propaganda machine was weakening, corruption was on the rise, and Pioneer camps were losing their once-powerful grip upon youth through communist indoctrination. However, to disregard the danger inherent in dissident jokes is a naive simplification of a tense, political environment. A carefully selected audience was paramount, but there was still an element of Russian roulette in the telling. That a person could be sent to the gulag for an improper joke redefined the art of joke-telling; the very nature of dissident humor was always improper by Soviet canon. Still, the themes of these jokes were a fair yardstick of the concerns of Soviet citizens.

Among these themes were the difficulties of Jewish (and Soviet) emigration, communist propaganda and Soviet leaders' exaggerated claims, political repression, chronic shortages, corruption, the KGB, the neutron bomb, Chornobyl, an i Brezhnev, who was quite senile at the end of his life. Alcohol abuse, changing political borders, and Georgian speculators also remained popular themes.

Visas

The term Soviet dissident conjures up several images for me: one is of those anonymous (to me) Soviet citizens seeking against odds to emigrate from the USSR.

Most dissidents were Jews, reports Rabbi Telushkin in his book, *Jewish Humor: What the Best Jewish Jokes Say about the Jews,* further noting that Robert Toth, former *Los Angeles Times* Moscow correspondent, is certain that Jews created the majority of dissident jokes. Telushkin's book is insightful as he presents jokes as a form of instruction. Some of the more popular ones are repeated here.

The following is a reflection of the anti-Semitism felt both during the Soviet era and today. OVIR is the Office of Registration and Immigration that issues internal passports with the *propiska,* the registration stamp that states where the holder is entitled to live. Also, Soviet passports recorded the nationality of the holder, with Jews being treated as a nationality distinct from Ukrainian or Russian. This practice facilitated discrimination against potential job applicants, university students, and other matriculants.

A Ukrainian Jew paid a visit to OVIR. The OVIR official sat at his desk, shuffling papers without bothering to look up at his visitor. The bureaucrat began with the usual questions: "Why, specifically, would you like to emigrate from the Soviet Union?" The Jew began, "There are two reasons, really. The first is that, every time my neighbor gets drunk, he bangs on the wall and shouts, 'When the Soviet Union falls, we're going to expel all you Jews!'" At this point, the official looked up at his visitor and interrupted, "Well, I don't think you should worry about that. I'm quite confident that the Soviet Union will be around for many years to come." The Jew replied, "That's the second reason."

This joke has a bittersweet aftertaste in that both Jews and non-Jews wanted to emigrate from the Soviet Union. However, in the case of Soviet Jews—Ukrainian, Russian, or other "nationality,"—they recognized that the end of communism would not solve the problem of anti-Semitism. In fact, given the statistics on Jewish emigrations since independence, this joke was somewhat prophetic.

Soviet leadership and propaganda

Rabinowich is a common Jewish character in Soviet jokes.

"Rabinowich," a friend asked, "do you read communist news-papers?"

"Yes, of course!" he responded. "How else could I know what a happy life I lead?"

A similar joke recounts that Soviets know the future; it's the past they're not sure of. This is, of course, poking fun at communism with all its promises for the future and at the same time its revision of the past. The phrase "Shining Future" referred to a standard piece of communist rhetoric (like *tufta* above) designed to win popular support.

—What was the nationality of Adam and Eve?

—Russian, of course. Why else would they think they were in paradise when they were homeless, naked, and just had one apple for the both of them?

The next two jokes were circulating during Brezhnev's time. I've heard several variants on the first one (later updated to accommodate new leadership), but the gist is as follows:

All the Soviet premiers were assembled on a train. The train stopped in the middle of Siberia. The locomotive driver announced, "This is how far the tracks have been built."

Stalin shouted, "Kill the driver!"

Khrushchev said, "Let's disassemble the track behind us and use the supplies to build the track ahead of us." (Alternatively, "Let's pardon the crew and bring in a new one.")

Brezhnev said, "Let's close the curtains and imagine the train is moving."

Andropov was asleep and didn't notice anything.

Gorbachev ran out and started shouting, "This train isn't moving! This train isn't moving!"

Jimmy Carter and Leonid Brezhnev died and were preserved in ice. In 1995 they were revived.

Brezhnev opened the Pravda *newspaper and laughed: "Top U.S. communist leaders meeting tomorrow."*

Carter opened The Washington Post *and laughed: "Border dispute between Finland and China."*

This one I have heard told of Western politicians as well:

A famous politician decided to throw a dollar bill out the window of his private plane.

"Why are you doing that?" his aide asked.

"I wanted to make the person who catches this happy today."

The politician drifted into reverie, then interrupted himself.

"But now I have a better idea," said the politician excitedly. "Why not throw out a stack of bills and please lots of people?"

"Actually," the pilot interjected from the cockpit, "you could please everyone in the country if you threw yourself out."

A placard near the coat check inside the Rada, the Ukrainian Parliament building, reads: Hooks are intended for the express use of Members of Parliament (or their coats).

Here are examples of the intentionally misunderstood:

A young man is asked, "Why didn't you attend the last communist meeting?"

"Oh, I would surely have come if I had known it was to be the last!"

Three young Pioneers were asked what good things they had done to help their fellow citizens.

The first boy, Oleh, replied, "I helped an old lady cross the street this morning."

The second boy, Andrey, replied, "I helped Oleh help her across."

The third child answered, "And I helped Andrey and Oleh."

The teacher smiled approvingly but felt obliged to ask, "Now why did it take three strong boys to help one old lady cross the street?"

"Oh," replied the third child, "she didn't want to cross."

Outrageous promises, exaggerated claims

The communists were known for their exaggerated claims, ranging from overstated production figures to outright denial of poverty. Some of the wittiest jokes stem from the outrageous promises made by the Soviet leaders. One of the better-known jokes about Brezhnev's absurd and grandiose claims is worth repeating here:

At a press conference Brezhnev boldly announced, "By the year 2000, every Soviet citizen will have his own airplane."

A heckler in the crowd interrupted, "What do we all need airplanes for?"

Visibly irritated, the Soviet premier replied, "Idiot! Suppose you are in Moscow and you hear that in Kyiv they have potatoes!"

Rabbi Telushkin offered a variant of the above joke:

Brezhnev was boasting about the Soviet Union's supremacy in space, going so far as to propose that one day every Soviet citizen would receive a ticket to Mars. A heckler in the audience exclaimed, "But I just want one to Vienna."

Finally, a third variant poked fun at Brezhnev's dim wit when he announced that the Soviets would outdistance America's space program: the Politburo had voted to send a team to the sun.

"But we will be burned alive," pleaded one cosmonaut.

"And you think we know nothing?" barked Brezhnev. "We are arranging the details so that you will land at night."

Ultimately, it was the deliberate fabrication of history that was one of the distinguishing features of the Soviet Union:

Lenin was planning his first trip to Poland. In the final weeks before departure, it was decided that the greatest gift to the Polish hosts would be a painting of Lenin in Poland. At a Central Committee meeting, much concern was expressed about locating an appropriate artist quickly. The Artists Union was notified, and an emergency meeting was held to select the best artist. The artists assembled as instructed, but the artist selected for the assignment was visibly concerned: he told the chairman that while he was appreciative of the honor, he felt that he had inadequate time to do the subject justice. The chairman disagreed and told him that, if necessary, he should not sleep until this important assignment was completed.

Three weeks passed. Twenty-four hours before Lenin's departure, the Central Committee summoned the artist to bring his masterpiece straight away to headquarters. The artist arrived, carrying under his arm a large canvas. When the painting was unveiled, the committee members were aghast to see a nude woman and man in a compromising position. "Who is this woman?" the chairman thundered. "Why, Comrade, that is Mrs. Lenin," the artist replied. "And who is this man?" demanded the chairman. "That is Trotsky," the artist replied. "And where is Lenin?" the chairman roared.

"Lenin is in Poland."

This is a great joke on two levels. Trotsky, of course, was the revolutionary leader later vilified as traitor, and Lenin never visited Poland. This joke makes fun of the communist manipulation of history to continually support its agenda.

From the outset, the communists set out to create historical precedent where there was none. Lenin's Plan of Monumental Propaganda of 1918 called for artists to decorate the streets with the busts and sculptures of communist heroes. The most likely precursors were found in Marx and Engels of the 19th century, but this was not enough. Consequently, to the historic bloodline of communism were added 18th century heroes of the French Revolution along with international figures such as Beethoven and Bach! In this way continuity with an artificial communist past was fabricated.

There is also the famous 18th century story of the so-called Potemkin villages, fake fronts set up by Count Potemkin in the countryside to deceive (and impress) Catherine the Great during her travels to Crimea. Both during the Russian Empire and the Soviet Union that followed, the tradition of deception has generally gone both ways, from the top-down and from the bottom-up. *Pokazukha*, which means "show," is the common term for this. This is related to the *tufta* examples of falsified production figures in the factories and on the farms—which were the norm, not the exception. (Moreover, grain production was measured in the field prior to harvest; thus, grain lost to spoilage and theft was considered part of the total yield.)

In the Stalinist era, the falsification of history ranged from doctoring photographs to grossly manipulating and falsifying statistics to rewriting textbooks to exclude all but a communist interpretation of history. Socialist Realist paintings beginning in the 1930s often illustrated historic events that never happened. Many paintings placed Lenin and Stalin in places that they had never visited (for example Poland) and doing things that never happened; for example, the famous painting of Lenin installing light bulbs in the countryside as symbolic testament to communism's technological progress.

The tenets of Socialist Realism, as applied to both literature and the visual arts, were surrealistic in form: specifically, Socialist Realism stipulated generic worker-heroes, not individuals. With their preference for blond and athletic types—not the typical Soviet profile —these paintings are reminiscent of Nazi art of the same period. The women are buxom and the men virile, but they are nonetheless sexless stereotypes. They are smiling and happy, often engaged in sport or installing electrical lines, a symbol of the bright future ahead of them.

Gorbachev, for one, stringently resented the caricatures of happy Soviets working on the *kolkhozy*, or collective farms, as shown, for example, in the Stalinist film *Cossacks of the Cuban*. Gorbachev's family came from peasant stock, and he knew such depictions were antithetical to life on the *kolkhoz*. As much as these paintings and film were pure artifice, Stalin's revisionist history that expunged real people from photographs, paintings, and history books once they had fallen into disfavor marked the pinnacle of spin-doctor abuse.

In the Soviet Union, and now in Russia and Ukraine, the telling of history continues to be tweaked. Many revolutionary street names are being replaced by their former, pre-revolutionary ones. In Russia, the statue of secret-police head Feliks Dzerzhinsky stood in front of Lubyanka Square and KGB headquarters until it was toppled in mass protests in 1991. At the end of 1998, Parliament's communist sympathizers outnumbered its liberals when they voted to resurrect the statue on the square. Presumably the communists hoped to make a statement about the rise in Russian criminal activity. The recent fanfare surrounding the proper burial for the Tsar's family is another case in point. Everyone's guess is that the pendulum of historical interpretation will continue to sway for some time.

Environment

One occasionally hears jokes about irradiated Chicken Kiev or Chornobyl. These are tasteless at best (no pun intended). The actual extent of environmental damage, fostered through years of the catch-phrase "production at all costs," is far from known.

The following joke is poignant for its black humor:

—*Why did Stalin wear knee boots while Lenin's were much shorter?*

—*Because during Lenin's time, Russia was polluted only up to the ankle.*

Internal security

The Hermitage Museum was hosting a grand exhibition. One of the prize Egyptian mummies from the museum's permanent collection was to be included. Unfortunately, this mummy had never been properly dated. The curators met with a team of art historians and archeologists in an effort to decide how best to label this fine specimen. An unannounced visitor arrived late to the meeting and said that he could ascertain the age. He asked for no interruptions for thirty minutes or so. The team of scholars was perplexed but followed instructions; once the stranger disappeared into the vault, they began asking one another in hushed tones who knew anything about this visitor. There was silence.

Two hours passed and the man finally emerged; he appeared tired and cross. "This mummy is 3200 years old."

"How did you determine that?" the curators asked in unison.

"Let's just say that, initially, he was not very forthcoming ..." *announced the KGB officer.*

Chronic shortages and absurd inefficiencies

For years, Westerners heard the tales of long queues, chronic shortages, and absurd inefficiencies of the Soviet system. Here is one of my favorite jokes:

A man is at last able to order a refrigerator, and the clerk tells him that it will be delivered to his apartment in ten years.

"Will that be in the morning or afternoon?" he asked politely.

"How could it possibly matter? This is ten years from now!" *bellowed the clerk.*

"Well, it's just that I have the plumber scheduled for that morning."

A similar joke stresses the absurdities of the communist era:

—Is it true that under communism people could order food by phone?

—Yes, but the delivery was by TV.

Corruption and theft

Tales of corruption and crime have soared in the post-independence era, but the Soviet era had its share. Here's a well-known joke:

A man leaves the factory one day slowly pushing a wheelbarrow covered with a piece of cloth. The guard stops him at the gate, lifts up the piece of cloth and seeing nothing, shrugs and lets the worker pass. The following day the same worker is stopped, and again the guard waves him through. The third day this happens, the guard can no longer contain his curiosity. "I don't get it, Comrade. Every day you leave and I know you are stealing something. What is it?" "Wheelbarrows," replies the worker.

5. Current Jokes: The New Russians

A new category of jokes has emerged since independence. The New Rich, or New Russians are the wealthy citizens prevalent in Russia and Ukraine who have scads of money and revel in flaunting it. The New Rich and the mafia are considered one and the same by most, and their money is considered tainted in origin.

In the communist system, two worlds coexisted: the *nomenklatura* and the rest. The difference then was that, while the rest knew of the *nomenklatura*'s excesses, they didn't have to examine it daily and in fact were largely shielded from it. In today's economic environment, there exist only the embryonic vestiges of a middle class; Ukraine is, for the most part, divided between the haves—primarily the New Rich (who are ostentatious)—and the have-nots (who are not).

Like the terms "yuppies" or "Generation Xers" and the images that they convey, "New Russians" conjure up the newly moneyed class in Russia and Ukraine who send their children to private schools abroad and toss their money out of planes and around the French Riviera. They are conspicuous in their extravagant spending habits and outrageous lifestyles. The women wear the finest furs, and the men, the very best in imported clothing. Mercedes, Lexus, and Range Rover vehicles confer the proper status. A popular joke goes:

Two New Russians were strolling down the street. The first one turned to his friend and said, "What good taste you have; your lovely designer tie is just like mine— and how much did you pay for yours?"

The friend coolly boasted, "$1200."

The first man gloated, "Why, you fool, you can buy that same tie down the street for $2000!"

Jennifer Gould, in her 1996 book *Vodka, Tears and Lenin's Angel*, recounts the joke of two New Russians who travel to Spain to locate a birthday gift for another friend back home:

Outside the Prado Museum, the two encountered a huge line. They knew that this queue meant something of great importance was

131

available. An exhibition of Salvador Dali, including some works for sale, was the source of the queue and excitement. Once inside, the New Russians happily located a Dali painting for which they paid $1 million. As they left, one of them turned to his friend and said, "Now we've got the card, let's find the present."

My little sister heard this one in St. Petersburg. It says a lot about how ordinary people view the New Rich:

A New Russian was asking his friend about a good place to take a vacation. The friend suggested that an African safari might be a good idea.

The first replied, "It doesn't sound all that relaxing to me, but maybe I don't know enough about it. What exactly do you do on a safari?"

"Well, first you get to buy a new wardrobe, and then you'll buy a new Jeep. As you drive around, you'll look out the windows on your left side and shoot; then you'll look to the right and shoot."

The first one said, "No, I want to relax on my vacation. You just described my job."

New Russian jokes poke fun at not only the nouveaux riches' lack of good taste but also their defamation of things sacred:

A New Russian rushed into a jewelry shop and said, "Look here, brother, I need a cross—a good golden cross, about a kilo in weight— on a heavy gold chain. And I need it quick!"

The shopkeeper was alarmed by the man's behavior, fearing that the New Russian might pull out a gun and start shooting. The shopkeeper asked the man to please wait while he went to the vault to locate an appropriate cross.

"Let me show you this lovely cross, sir. It is gold, with diamond and emerald inlay, from the 16th century, weighing 650 grams. It formerly belonged to Archbishop ..."

The New Russian looked at the cross with disgust and said, "Damn, couldn't you find one without a gymnast?"

Themes of corruption accompanied the dissident jokes about bureaucratic inefficiencies. These problems persist today, and so do the jokes, albeit with modern twists:

A Russian businessman met a genie who promised to grant his three wishes.

—I want five million dollars, U.S., in cash.

—You've got it.

—And the top-of-the-line Mercedes sedan, royal blue, tan leather interior ...

—Easily done.

—And rid me of the Solntsev mob "protection."

—Are you crazy? I pay the Solntsevs myself!

Finally:

—Are you aware of what will happen if you present false evidence in court?

—Sure. I'll be driving a new car.

LANGUAGE: UKRAINIAN VS. RUSSIAN

It has often been said that, just a few years ago, only peasants and intellectuals spoke Ukrainian. This is clearly changing, and Ukrainian is now the official language of Ukraine. However, the business language of Ukraine remains Russian, and in Ukraine's eastern and more populous half, Russian is more commonly spoken in homes. This is true even in the capital, although the city's preferred Western spelling has been changed to Kyiv (rather than the more familiar Russian "Kiev") to reflect its proper transliteration from Ukrainian.

The Ukrainian language is not a dialect of the Russian language as Soviets wanted the outside world to believe. Rather, each language penetrated and interacted with the other's syntax and vocabulary. Moreover, a mixed idiom is not uncommon.

Their similarities have been compared to those between German and Dutch, although there are considerably different dialects within the Ukrainian language, especially around Galicia (the capital of which is Lviv) and Volhyn. These are almost incomprehensible to heartland Russians. In the Western oblasts ethnic Russians are truly a minority: in Galicia, Volhyn, Rivne, and Transcarpathia, there are fewer than 350,000 ethnic Russians.

Compare this with Left-Bank Ukraine, where the majority of Crimea's population is Russian, as are one million of Kharkiv's 1.6 million residents. Another 4.5 million in Dnipropetrovsk, Donetsk, and Luhansk are Russian, with an additional million Russians in Odesa and Mykolayiv. Consequently, you will find that Left-Bank Ukrainian and Russian speakers understand each other. As stated earlier, a mixed idiom is quite common today in many parts.

Ukrainian is the more lyrical language; it is softer and less guttural than Russian. You'll notice that *tak* means "yes" in Ukrainian, while *da* is Russian; "no" is pronounced *nee* in Ukrainian in contrast to the world-familiar, and often emphatic, *nyet*. Even the untrained ear can reasonably distinguish Ukrainian and Russian, on television for example. Ukrainian also shares more similarities with Polish, a West Slavic language. The months are especially poetic; my favorite example is *lystopad* ("leaves are falling"), for November, although it would be more appropriate for October. Regardless, Ukrainian months are named for flowers, grasses, ice, and other seasonal features. Russian names for months are much closer to our Latin equivalents, for example *Yanvar, Fevral, Mart*, and easier to memorize.

The Eastern Slavic languages (Russian, Ukrainian, and Belorussian) are written in Cyrillic script in contrast to the Western Slavic tongues (Polish, Czech, Slovak, and Sorbian), which are written in Latin script. The Southern Slavic languages are split, reflecting the historic differences between Eastern Orthodoxy and Catholicism. Thus, Croatian and Slovenian are in Latin, whereas Serbian, Bulgarian, and Macedonian are in Cyrillic, as is Old Church Slavonic.

English speakers notice that several Russian or Ukrainian block letters resemble English ones, while some in script form resemble others; for example, *d* and *t* in script resemble Latin *g* and *m* (generally drawn with a line over it). The River Prut is one such example. In Cyrillic, it looks like Прут and in cursive, it is closer to *прут.* While students are expected to exhibit good penmanship, there is little appreciation or tolerance for adding unconventional flourishes. Ukrainians also don't tend to use block letters much; cursive script is the norm.

In both languages, one can see influences from French, which was at one point the preference of the Imperial family and other nobles. Here's a sampling of these influences: *bagazh* (luggage or baggage); *bilet* (ticket); *buro* (bureau or office); *dush* (shower); *passazh* (passageway); *magazin* (store); *pliazh* (beach); *etazh* (floor, level, or story). In *biznes* (say *BEEZnes*), you will recognize a lot of terms derived from their English equivalents. From German, there are fewer words. *Buterbrod*, meaning sandwich (or simply *sandvich*), is one of the more common ones.

Basic Grammar

The articles "the" and "a" do not exist in Ukrainian or Russian. It is therefore necessary, and not difficult, to determine out of context whether someone is referring to "a" table, for example, or "the" table. (This partially helps to explain why native Russian and Ukrainian speakers speaking English often delete and misuse articles.)

In both languages words have gender: masculine, feminine, and neuter. Fortunately, it is almost always possible to identify the gender by the word's ending. It is nonetheless necessary to ensure that adjectives agree in gender and case with the noun they are modifying. In Russian and Ukrainian, there are six cases, and the case ending of a particular word will indicate whether it is the subject, the direct object, or indirect object of a particular sentence. In this sense, word order is not as important as it is in English, for example. (Think of, "I threw John the ball." You can't replace "I" with "John" or "the ball" without altering the verb or changing the meaning of the sentence.)

To foreigners, verbs of motion are difficult to grasp, since these verbs differentiate between foot and vehicular travel and whether the action of the verb is uni- or bidirectional. Another characteristic feature of Slavic grammar is the division of verbs according to aspects: perfective forms (often with a prefix) indicate a completed action whereas imperfective indicates an incomplete one.

Finally, Slavic languages have a reputation for being hard to pronounce. Since the Cyrillic alphabet is easily mastered, the main source of this frustration may be the unfamiliar consonant clusters as well as the soft and palatalized consonants, marked by raising the tongue to the roof of the mouth. What is nice about Ukrainian and Russian is that the rules of pronunciation are quite simple (much like Spanish). In Russian, unstressed vowels are short whereas in Ukrainian they are not. Thus, the word for "beer" in both languages is *pivo*, with the first syllable stressed. In Russian, it sounds like *PEEva*, in Ukrainian, *PEEvo*.

Learning any foreign language is a noble, time-consuming goal, and certainly not everyone is capable of doing it well. On the other hand, learning the basics is often not as complicated as some people fear. In Ukraine, it's a matter of practical necessity, and your painstaking efforts to speak the local language will be greatly appreciated, especially since many foreigners fail to go beyond the bare minimum.

Basic Greetings

I recommend that all visitors bring with them Russian and Ukrainian phrasebooks. For Russian, there are many options—I like *Barron's Russian at a Glance*. For Ukrainian, both Lonely Planet and the Rough Guide have good phrasebooks. All are inexpensive, fit easily into a pocket, and handy to have with you wherever you go.

The following list of greetings is essentially provided as an introduction to the very basics and to show similarities and differences in the two languages.

Ukrainian	Pronunciation	Russian	Pronunciation	English
Так	*tak*	Да	*da*	Yes
Ні	*nee*	Нет	*nyet*	No
Ъудь ласка	*BoodLASka*	Пожалуйста	*paZHALoosta*	Please; You're welcome
Дякую	*DYAkooyoo*	Спасибо	*spaSEEba*	Thank you
Доброго ранку	*DOBroho RANkoo*	Добрый утро	*DObree OOtra*	Good morning
Добрий день	*DOBriy den*	Добрый день	*DObree dyen*	Good afternoon
Добрий вечір	*DOBriy VEcheer*	Добрый вечер	*DObree VYEchir*	Good evening
Добридень	*doBRIden*	Здравствуйте	*ZDRASTvuytye*	Hello; Good day (general greeting)
До побачення	*dopoBAchennya*	Досвидания	*dasveeDAneeya*	Goodbye
До зустрічі	*doZoostreechee*			
Привіт	*preeVEET*	Привет	*preeVYET*	Hi

137

Як справи?	*yak SPRAvi*	Как поживаете	*KAK pazhiVAyitye*	How are you?
Добре	*DOBray*	Хорошо	*kharaSHO*	Fine; good
Я знаю	*YA ZNAyoo*	Я знаю	*YA ZNAyoo*	I know
Я не знаю	*YA NE ZNAyoo*	Я не знаю	*YA NEE ZNAyoo*	I don't know
Я розумію	*YA pozooMEEyoo*	Я понимаю	*YA paneeMAyoo*	I understand
Я не розумію	*YA NE pozooMEEyoo*	Я не понимаю	*YA NEE paneeMYoo*	I don't understand
Скільки коштує?	*SKEELkeeKOSH-tooye*	Сколко стоит?	*SKOLka STOeet*	How much does it cost?

The familiar Russian *do svidaniya* (say *dasveeDaneeya*) and the Ukrainian *do zustrychy* (say *doZOOstreechee*) and *do pobachennya* all mean "until we meet again." *Privyt* or *privyet*, meaning "Hi," is reserved for friends, not strangers.

General Advice on Language

Learn the alphabet, and this means before you go. You can learn it on the plane if you like. It is really not as hard as you think. Most people learn Russian first, then Ukrainian.

There are a few hitches, so start with the ones you already know:
A is A
K is K
M is M
E is E or Ye
Ë is Yo (and is always the stressed syllable)
O is O
T is T

These are a bit tricky:
B is V
И is ee as in *meet*
Й is y as in *yes*
P is R (and it's rolled—rumor has it that Stalin couldn't trill his very well)

C is S as in *Siberia*
H is N as in *no* or *nyet*
У is oo as in *boot*

These are the easy weird ones; some have Greek influences:
Б is B as in *borshch*
Г is G as in *girl* (H in Ukrainian)
Д is D as in *doctor*
Л is L as in *lamp*
П is P as in *Paul* or *Pavel*
Ф is F as in *football*
Я is Ya

At last, the weird ones:
X is kh, like the ch in Scottish *loch* or German *ich bin* …
Ц is ts as in *tsar*
Ч is ch
Ш is sh
Щ is shch as in *cash check, fresh cheese*
Э is e, used only as the initial letter in words
Ю is Yoo

In Russian there are two silent signs; Ukrainian has only the soft
sign:
Ъ is the hard sign
ь is the soft sign

Then, put them in order:
А Б В Г Д Е Ё Ж З И Й К Л М Н О П Р С Т У Ф Х Ц Ч Ш Щ **Ъ Ы** ь **Э** Ю Я
(The highlighted letters don't appear in the Ukrainian alphabet.)

Finally, Ukrainian variants:
А Б В Г **Г** Д Е **Є** Ж З И **І Ї** Й К Л М Н О П Р С Т У Ф Х Ц Ч Ш Щ Ю Я ь
(The highlighted letters aren't in the Russian alphabet.)

A Few Notes on Ukrainian Variants

The difference between the Ukrainian Г and Ґ is that the former is more like an h, the latter (which is far less common) like a g.

И, І, Ї and Й are pronounced as follows:

И is like i in *bit*

І is like ee in *beet*

Ї is like yea in *yeast*

Й is like y in *yet* (and always pronounced strongly, even at the end of a word). Hence, for the English name Andrew, we hear *ahnDREE* in Ukrainian and *ahnDRAY* in Russian.

In E and Є, the former is like e in *yes*, the latter like ye in *yes*.

Common Signs

Once in Ukraine, you will find that even a basic ability to read the alphabet will help you with common signs. You will frequently encounter these basic words:

метро

This is the metro. Kyiv and Kharkiv both have one. Once inside, you'll notice that the entrances have signs designating вхід (or вход in Russian); the exits will be designated by ыхід (or ыход in Russian).

ресторан

Restoran (the famous Pectopah to non-Cyrillic readers).

ремонт

Remont (say *rayMONT*) is a general word for repair or renovation that you will frequently encounter. If you ask why something is closed, this is the likely answer. Like *rynok* below, this word is used by many foreigners in English conversation to discuss the ongoing reconstruction of roads and apartments.

рінок (or рынок in Russian)

The *rynok* (say *REEnok*) is the farmer's market. Discussions on food and shopping in Chapters Four and Five will describe the *rynok* in better detail.

Learning to read only a few basic words will make your life easier from the start. You'll recognize these words in the signs around town designating a particular establishment. One thing many foreigners new to these Slavic languages appreciate is that, in Ukraine, you won't be overwhelmed by signs such as "Try our fresh loaves, baked daily." If you can read the word for "bread," you're in good shape. Other useful words to learn early on include: coffee, milk, juice, vegetables, fruit, flowers, shoe or watch repair, key (as in "Keys made here"), university, institute, hospital, hotel, and church. (Some of these listed are similar to their English equivalents, which makes them easier to recognize if you are just starting out.)

Today you won't hear a lot about the *berioshka* (literally, birch) stores; these were the hard currency stores designed for foreign visitors to the Soviet Union. Soviet citizens were excluded from shopping here, as foreign currency transactions were illegal. In Ukraine these stores were called *kashtan* (literally, chestnut) stores, and they no longer exist, although a state store has retained the name. (Again, see the Shopping Section in Chapter Five for more details.)

A Digression: Anthony Burgess

Did you ever wonder where Anthony Burgess got his *Clockwork Orange* slang? He adapted it from Russian, so that the slang wouldn't date or localize the book to a particular era or region. Maybe you recall the words droog, bog (say *boag*), moloko, kravvy, horrorshow, or grazny. They are from Russian words for friend, God, milk, blood, good, and dirty. "Good," however, isn't *horrorshow*. It's more like *kharashow*, the initial *kh* pronounced like *ch* in the Scots *loch*.

A Handful of Useful Words

можна/можно (say *MOzhna*)

Mozhna means "possible," as in "Is it possible?" This word is used a

141

lot for "Please" as in "*Mozhna sche pivo*?" (May I have another beer?) The division of what is allowable versus what is forbidden is an important cultural distinction. For example, Westerners often believe that anything not forbidden is allowed—the proverbial glass is half full. For Ukrainians anything not explicitly allowed is probably forbidden. *Nemozhna* should be learned alongside *mozhna*. This means "it is forbidden or impossible."

Pivo is "beer." It's Пiвo (say *PEEvo* with a long "o") in Ukrainian, and Пиво (say *PEEva*) in Russian.

Similarly, вода, meaning "water" in both languages, is pronounced *voDA* in Ukrainian and *vaDA* in Russian.

Сiк (say *seek* in Ukrainian) and сок (*sok* in Russian) mean "juice."

Хлiб (say *khleeb* in Ukrainian) and Хлеб (*khleb* in Russian) mean "bread."

A mixture of Russian and Ukrainian words or phrases you are likely to hear include пашли (say *pashLEE*) or поэкали (say *paYEKalee*), both used for "Let's go." The first is on foot, the second by vehicle.

Пока (say *paKA*) is slang for "See you later."

Ладно (pronounced *LADna*) is slang for "Okay."

Нормално (say *NORmalna*) or ничего (say *neecheVO*, literally meaning "nothing") is also common.

Иди суда or идите суда (say *eeDEE suDA* or *eeDEEtye suDA* for the plural form) means "Come here."

Понятно (*PaNYATna*) means "(It is) understood." Male speakers may say понял (*PONyel*) for "I understood," while female speakers will say поняла (*panYALa*). The "a" at the end of a verb indicates both past tense and that the subject is female.

In Ukrainian, Що це (say *Shcho tse*?) means "What's this (or that)?"—and is often said while pointing. In Russian, for Чмо эмо?, say *Shto eta?* These are always handy to know in any language. In both Ukrainian and Russian, there is no present tense of the verb "to be." Since there are no articles, the response you get will begin with *Tse* or *Eta* meaning "This is ..." and followed by the noun, for example *telefon*. You also might hear the more emphatic Что это такое? (with *takoye* at the end). It is translated as "What the heck is this?"

In Ukrainian, the words for "red" and "black" may be confusing at first; чорний (say *CHORnee*) is black; червоний (*cherVOnee*) is red. In Russian, чёрный (*CHORny*) is black and красный (*KRASny*) is red. Thus, Red Army Street (not yet renamed) is *Chervonoarmyiska vulytsia* in Ukrainian and *Krasnoarmeiskaya ulitsa* in Russian.

Finally, there may be days when you have to deal with a кошмар (say *kashMAR*). This means "nightmare." But don't dwell on it.

ADDRESSING PEOPLE

The old days of *tovarish* (say *taVARish*) meaning "Comrade" are over. Don't revert to it; it's considered rude now.

Gospidin and *Gospozha* are Russian for Mr. and Ms. Ukrainian equivalents are *Pan* and *Pana*. *Gospidini* and *Pany*, the plural forms of Mr., are used for Ladies and Gentlemen or, simply, Gentlemen.

In written correspondence, "Dear Mr. Chomiak" is not used. You will instead write "Respected Mr. Chomiak."

The Use of Patronymics

Tradition has been to use the first name and patronymic in work situations to show respect, but without the formality of saying, for example, Ms. Marchuk. At the same time, this practice wasn't as informal as simply calling her by her first name.

Ukrainians are quick to correct outsiders who make reference to their patronymics as middle names. The patronymic is derived from their father's first name; it is placed behind their own first name. The *ovich* or *evich* in a man's patronymic is loosely translated as "son of," whereas *evna* or *ovna* for women indicates "daughter of."

In this way, my friend Pavel, the son of Valentin, becomes Pavel Valentinovich Ustimenko; his sister is Olga Valentinovna Ustimenko. (If their grandfather's first name was Konstantin, their father would be named Valentin Konstantinovich Ustimenko.) Ustimenko is the family name or surname.

Patronymics are tricky for foreigners and they don't tend to use them much. Ukrainians know that we have no equivalent form, but it's a gesture that will be appreciated if you use it.

Ukrainian and Russian Name Equivalents

The following list includes a selection of common first names in Ukrainian, followed by their Russian variants. Be aware, however, that there are different transliteration systems in English, and since both the Russian and Ukrainian alphabets have more letters than English, there isn't a one-to-one correlation, despite certain Cyrillic letters which translate as two letters and Щ which is transliterated as *shch*. (Throughout this text I have omitted soft signs, whereas other sources may indicate them with the symbol '.)

For the name Andrew, you will find many transliterations such as Andriy, Andrii, Andrei, Andrey, and even Andrij in English. The real difference between the two languages in this case is in pronunciation, not transliteration. For example, Ukrainian approximates *AhnDREE*, whereas Russian is *AhnDRAY*.

Some i's in Russian (but not all) are transliterated as y's from the Ukrainian, for example, Borys, Iosyf, Maksym, Nykyta, and Osyp are Ukrainian variants for the names Boris, Iosif, Maksim, Nikita, and Osip. The Russian variants are far more common to English readers. Similarly, g's in Russian are h's in Ukrainian. Thus you will see Ukrainian/Russian variants, such as Bohdan/Bogdan, Ihor/Igor, Oleh/Oleg, and Olha/ Olga.

Finally, note that there is an "o" more often in Ukrainian names than in Russian:

Oleksiy, Aleksei

Oleksandr, Aleksandr
Oleksandra, Aleksandra
Olena, Elena
Dmytro, Dmitry
Evhen, Evgeny (pronounced and sometimes transliterated as Yevgeny, Yevgenii.)
Hryhoriy, Georgy
Mykhailo, Mikhail
Mykola, Nikolai
Pavlo, Pavel
Petro, Petr (pronounced Pyotr)
Serhiy, Sergei
Vasyl, Vasily
Volodymyr, Vladimir

Refrain from addressing Ukrainians by their English equivalents, for example, Petro as Peter, or Olena as Elaine, and so on unless they prefer it and tell you to.

Ukrainian and Russian Surnames

Traditionally, the ending of one's surname indicated one's nationality. Many Ukrainian surnames end in *-enko*, including the most celebrated Ukrainian poet and artist, Taras Shevchenko.

Many Georgian names end in *-vili*, Armenian in *-ian*, and Russian in *-ov* (transliterated as *-off* or *-ow* in French and German spellings). Names ending in *-sky* or *-y* (with their various alternates) are also Russian names. An *-a* at the end of the name designates the person is female, for example Goncharova. But not all names change to the feminine form, for example those ending in *-enko*.

Other common endings for surnames are *-uk* or *-iuk*, such as Kravchuk, the surname of independent Ukraine's first president, and the Burliuk brothers, who were famous Ukrainian artists around World War I.

you and You

Both Ukrainian and Russian (like other European languages) have two forms for "you." The familiar *ti* or *ty* is always singular, and *vi* or *vy* is both the formal and the plural form.

Foreigners need to be aware of these distinctions; to be on the safe side, use the formal "you" for all business dealings unless instructed otherwise. When you slip up, don't worry. Ukrainians will understand, just as they appreciate sensitivity to their cultural traditions.

Diminutives as a Form of Affection

Pick up a copy of *Anna Karenina,* and you will see that diminutives are exceedingly common for family and friends. Aleksandr or Aleksandra becomes Sasha; Alla, Allochka; Evgeny, Zhenia; Olena, Olenka; and Pavel, Pasha. But this is just a start. I've seen as many as twenty variants for the name Maria.

Ukrainians don't seem to object to foreigners calling them by their diminutives, since after all these are an indication of affection. My sisters Catherine and Elizabeth have never had English nicknames, but Ukrainian friends have no qualms about calling them Cathy and Betsy. Ukrainians don't view calling friends by their nicknames or diminutives as presumptuous, as long as the form is used in their native language. Remember though not to address Ukrainians by the English equivalents of their names.

In addition to first names, diminutives for some nouns often designate a smaller version; *stol*, or table, becomes *stolik*. *Dochka*, derived from *doch*, means "little daughter," but in a particularly affectionate way. (The Spanish language has similar diminutives for degrees of size and affection: for example "very small," and "very, very small," are endearing forms of "small.") The word for "water" in both Ukrainian and Russian is *voda*; the diminutive becomes *vodka*. But *vodichka*, not *vodka*, is the term commonly used to indicate "a little water" as in "I'll have a little water." The next chapter will discuss drinking traditions in detail.

— *Chapter Four* —

SOCIALIZING, FOOD, AND DRINK

UKRAINIAN HOSPITALITY

Ukrainians are generous people and gracious hosts. It is a real treat to be invited into a Ukrainian home where guests are treated like royalty and an even greater compliment to be invited to sit around the kitchen table. Be prepared to remove your shoes upon entering a friend's home. To keep their apartments clean, most hosts will provide you with a pair of slippers called *tapochky*.

When invited to dinner in someone's house, casual attire is generally accepted. For your part, bringing a gift is traditional and, in my opinion, mandatory. Customary gifts include alcohol (or juice), chocolates, cake, or a bouquet of flowers. If you bring flowers, make sure that the number is odd; even numbers are reserved for funerals. It is also entirely appropriate to give flowers to other men's wives, just don't get carried away. If there is a child, it is customary to bring a small gift as well. Gum or candy is generally appropriate; by all means if you have a trinket from your own country, this will be well received.

On certain occasions, you may want to give a small gift other than food, drink, or flowers. This small token of your friendship doesn't have to be expensive, and probably should not be. For example, in the old days foreign cigarettes were welcomed; now Western brands are available everywhere and outsell domestic tar. Instead of giving something that is available in Ukraine, souvenirs from your home state or country, such as postcards, pins, and keychains, are always a good idea. Likewise, in business settings, a pen or other trinket with your company's insignia is always appreciated. (I carried with me a stash of lapel pins displaying American and Ukrainian flags, which I doubt were worn much but were well received. Indian arrowheads are always a hit and especially appropriate since my home state was Indian Territory until 1907; Ukrainians love to hear this history.)

One thing I've always enjoyed about Ukraine is that you won't find many homes, or even some parts of homes, that you might call unliveable. Homes that I've visited are eminently liveable, lived-in, comfortable, and often a bit disorderly. Furnishings vary; the luckier homes may have a piano, and bookshelves are generally prominent and well stocked. I've encountered several homes with a wall-sized photograph resembling the backdrop of a late-night talk show that never changes regardless of the season. Rugs hanging on walls are both decorative and serve as insulation. I especially love that the furniture and space have multiple purposes: the living room or den becomes a bedroom, thanks to all those amazing chairs—to say nothing of the couches—that convert into beds; the writing table is also the dining table, and so on.

Ukrainian homes reflect the personalities of their owners, which is to say that they are unpretentious, practical, and adaptive. Your hosts, or more likely hostesses, are generally unapologetic that their floors are less well-scrubbed than Westerners might be accustomed to; Americans would at least try to give excuses. The grooming habits of Ukrainian men reflect an unpretentiousness as well, and foreigners frequently observe the limited use of deodorant. While women take far greater pride in their personal grooming, they had neither access to nor money for toiletries and household cleaning products under the Soviet system. Today, still constrained by money (and always by time since it is the women who both cook and clean the home), a gift bar of soap makes a real treat for your hostess.

In the Ukrainian kitchen, guests are treated like family—or at the very least as intimate friends. This point should not be taken lightly; in a culture accustomed to communal living, privacy and trust are at a premium. In the Soviet era, one learned to be very selective in choosing friends; only with your most trusted friends could you sit in the kitchen and speak a little more openly if you dared.

When visiting friends, you should be prepared to accept all food and drink that is offered. Flatly turning down food may be considered rude. Ukrainians don't seem to understand vegetarians, dieters, or alcoholics, so if any of these applies to you, you will need to proceed gingerly. Sometimes people get around this by saying that they have an allergic reaction. The Ukrainians do understand the concept of *vranyo*, described above as a white lie. They are known to fib under certain circumstances so as not to offend their guests.

At the dinner table, take small helpings as you will be encouraged to take more later. Leaving a small amount of food on your plate is considered good manners as it shows you are satiated. Also, be careful when complimenting your hosts' belongings as they just might offer the admired object to you.

When you are invited into someone's home, amateur entertainment is sometimes part of the evening's festivities; occasionally your hosts will ask you to sing something, but it is more likely that they will perform for you.

Let us turn now to the food and drink that you'll most likely be sampling while you're in Ukraine.

DRINKING CHOICES

Water Safety

I recommend drinking bottled water, but this can be expensive and heavy to carry; if you live in a multi-story walk-up and try hauling a box of bottles once a week, you may start to consider boiling water or filtering systems. There are various purification systems available, including hand-held pumps; some but not all of these can remove the parasite giardia in addition to other impurities.

If you drink or cook with tap water, it is recommended that you boil it for ten or more minutes. It is highly improbable that you can fully avoid tap water, since your friends will offer you tea or you will have food and drink from a restaurant. (As far back as the 15th century people were worried about water quality in Kyiv, one of the reasons cited for the growing consumption of beer.)

People often ask about present levels of radiation and residual safety issues related to Chornobyl's tragedy. For most of the country, the larger concern now is that the Dnipro and other water sources were contaminated by the wanton disregard for environmental pollution during the Soviet era. Many radioactive pollutants have been leached out of the soil and have now contaminated water sources. Obviously, growing crops in some regions is extremely hazardous. (As for air purity, foreign embassies monitor changes in radioactive levels and regularly perform tests for their foreign personnel living in Ukraine. Air quality continues to test within acceptable ranges.)

If you are dining out, you may wish to order water. Specify *mineralna voda bez gazy*, meaning "mineral water without gas," if you mean "still," like Evian. Or say *mineralna voda gazovana*, meaning "with gas," if you want fizzy water like Perrier. You might ask for Evian or Perrier by name, and the waiter can recommend an equivalent European substitute, not of local or FSU origin.

If you are attending a Ukrainian dinner, more than likely the water placed on the table will be one of the mineral waters produced in the FSU. These are gassy, and some have a decidedly salty taste. Georgia is reputed to have the best mineral water, and there are many spas there. (*Gruzia* is the name for Georgia.) Within Ukraine, the Carpathian spas also produce sulfurized mineral water. Among the best waters are Lavtusa, Morshenka, and Hutsulschina.

People frequently warn against drinks with ice cubes since the water used to make the ice is suspect, although iced drinks still aren't common; the few cubes you get in a McDonald's drink are fine since they use purified water. You can ask for drinks without ice if you think the cubes are frozen tap water. Also watch for unwashed fruit and vegetables, including lettuce; don't eat them unless you are confident that they were properly cleaned.

When in doubt, remember the saying, "Boil it, cook it, peel it, or forget it."

Milk or Moloko: Local or UHT

When I lived in Moscow and bought local pasteurized milk, it always soured within 48 hours or so. I later learned that when you buy milk, even so-called pasteurized milk, you must boil it first. In Ukraine you can buy milk from a *hastronom* or milk store. *Hastronom* (*gastronom* in Russian) means a state grocery store, which differentiates it from a Western-styled grocery store. A milk store is really a dairy store since they also sell farmer's cheese, hard cheese, eggs, and *kefir* (a tasty yogurt drink). One drawback is that milk stores smell like soured milk upon entering. You will also see milk for sale in the streets from time to time. It is sold in plastic bags, and I know of no foreigner who buys it. If you choose to, I would recommend boiling it first thing.

Not surprisingly, some advise viewing all dairy products as suspect. I usually purchased the ultra-pasteurized milk because it was widely available and had a long shelf life (about six months if unopened), but I bought my eggs, cheese, and sour cream at the *rynok,* which also carries a wide selection of fruit, vegetables, meats, honey, and cut flowers.

UHT milk (ultra-pasteurized at high temperatures) is now common throughout Europe and in the larger Ukrainian cities. It is great to keep on hand for cooking, cereal, and coffee, as it tastes so much better than powdered milk. Parmalat is a common brand name; this Dutch-Ukrainian joint venture also produces many of the fruit juices in cartons. The only problem is that low-fat milk can be hard to find; but what can one expect in a country that doesn't like Diet Coke?

Smetana is a lightly soured cream. It is commonly used in sweet and savory soups, in sauces, dressings, marinades, and desserts. It is used as a filling in both soft dough dumplings and fritters.

When you buy eggs, you will typically ask for ten eggs (*desyatok yaiyets,* which is how you say "ten eggs"), even though the plastic egg crates that you'll buy at TSUM (see the Shopping Section in Chapter Five) hold six, twelve, or eighteen eggs!

If you want to buy cheese (*sir*—say *sear*), ask for a kilo or a *polkilo* (say *POLE-kilo*) if you want half. You can also ask for several hundred grams. This also applies to buying sausages at the *rynok*.

In the *rynok*, you can always sample items before you buy. Simply ask, *Chy mozhna sprobuvatu*? (Is it possible for me to sample?)

Tea

Chai appears to be a universal term for tea in much of the world, and tea is quite popular in Ukraine, especially Georgian tea. The Carpathians are known for their *chornika* tea made from bilberries or huckleberries grown in the mountains.

The samovar (literally, self-boiler) has Russian origins, and while they seem most common today on trains, you will see them available for sale, for example on Andriyivskiy Uzviz (more in Chapter Five about shopping for souvenirs). Do be aware that any items from periods earlier than 1945 are not permitted to leave the country. One friend who left two years ago still has two samovars in Ukraine!

The electric samovar speaks for itself, but otherwise the samovar is filled with coals. Very strong tea is steeped, then diluted with water. The teapot is placed on top and kept warm, and hot water is dispensed through the spigot. The metal tea-glass holder, called a *pidstakannik* (*podstakannik* in Russian), meaning "under the glass," is generally made of silver and holds a simple glass, a *stakan*, filled with tea; you will find such teapots on the trains.

Tea with lemon and lots of sugar is most common, but preserves are also a popular sweetener. Tea is never served with milk. Tea is served not during but after a meal. If you want it served during a meal, you must specify: *seichas i potom.* This is Russian for "now (literally, right away) and later."

Kofe and Kava

These are the Russian (say *KOFyeh*) and Ukrainian (say *KAva*) terms for coffee. Much coffee in this country is Nescafé or some similar powder. If you buy instant coffee for home or your office, be forewarned: not all instant coffees are created equal. Coffee is typically served very sweet (and without milk) in demitasse cups.

In almost all business meetings, you will be served instant coffee; sometimes you will be asked to choose between coffee and tea. Cookies or chocolates will very likely be served; other occasions may call for open-faced sandwiches of cheese, sausage (*kovbasa* in Ukrainian or *kolbasa* in Russian), or salmon roe. Vodka or *konyak* (which is brandy) are frequently paired with these sandwiches.

For your part, it's a sign of good hospitality to offer at least a few cookies when serving coffee or tea.

Soft Drink Competition and Boxes of Juice

Coca-Cola and Pepsi have battled it out here as elsewhere, and most outdoor umbrellas seem to advertise one or the other. Pepsi came to Russia early and arranged a business deal with Stolichnaya (meaning "Capital") Vodka, but Coca-Cola is stronger in Ukraine today. The soft-drink company has recently built a large bottling plant outside Kyiv, and Coca-Cola, Sprite, and Fanta (orange) are widely available.

What about Diet Coke? Early 1997 saw the last of a dependable supply of diet drinks. These came out of Hungary and other European bottling plants, but now that Coca-Cola bottles its own drinks, there is little need for diet drinks since Ukrainians don't drink them.

In 1996 when Diet Coke was available in select grocery stores, a Ukrainian co-worker said that it was difficult to find diet drinks in Kyiv because they weren't popular. My capitalist colleague argued that no, it was difficult to find in the stores precisely because it was popular and sold out quickly; this was all about supply and demand. Who was right? They both were—one held the expat view and the other, the Ukrainian.

Parmalat produces a variety of juices in paper cartons. They are pricey but very good. Apple, orange, peach, pear, cherry, banana, pineapple, strawberry-kiwi, passion fruit, mango, and blackberry are among the flavors available. In restaurants or bars, you will ask for *sik* or *sok* (juice); are you ready for the choices? Learn your favorites (and the most common choices):

apelsinoviy is orange, not apple!

yablochniy is apple.

ananasoviy is pineapple (like *ananas* in French).

tomatniy is tomato, even though the word for "tomato" is *pomidor*.

vinogradniy is grape.

Zero Tolerance

Whatever you may have heard about excessive drinking and alcoholism in Ukraine, don't even think about drinking and driving here. There is zero tolerance, meaning that just one drink before driving is too much. As in other parts of Europe, this credo is taken very seriously in Ukraine. Professional drivers will not touch a drop of liquor during work hours, and foreigners must designate a driver if drinking is to be part of the evening's entertainment. Locals and expatriates alike use drivers, official and gypsy cabs, and public transport after any drinking they have indulged in.

A deputy's son once remarked, after being arrested for drinking and driving, that the arresting police were less easy to bribe than in the old days. He got off easily nonetheless; he was only detained for three hours. As we had earlier attended the same party, every one of us recalled that he had drunk very little. But that isn't the point: Zero Tolerance is Zero Tolerance.

The traffic police in Ukraine do not need a reason to pull you over. They are notoriously corrupt and unpleasant. If you're a foreign visitor in this country, don't risk getting randomly stopped after drinking even a small amount of alcohol.

A rare thing happened when some friends hailed a gypsy cab in Odesa late one night and discovered very quickly that the cabdriver was drunk. Luckily the cab ran out of gas whereupon my friends escaped on foot! (If you opt to hail a gypsy cab, it is standard procedure to negotiate the price in advance. More on gypsy cabs and other transport in Chapter Five.)

Vodka and Horilka Origins

No cultural assessment of Ukraine can be complete without an examination of the role that vodka has played throughout history. Both Polish and Russian historians have asserted that their respective homeland was the birthplace of vodka; their argument is essentially academic. More interesting is William Pokhlebkin's thorough *History of Vodka*, wherein the author examines vodka's historical role from a Marxist perspective; he is essentially speaking of Russia and the Russian Empire in this book.

In Russia the origins of vodka date back to the Middle Ages, and by 1478 an official monopoly on the production of grain spirits had been established. While there were numerous names for alcoholic beverages, the term "vodka" was not in usage until significantly later. In its earliest usage, vodka as a generic term referred to medicinal remedies and fragrances; this is one of the reasons cited for drinking vodka neat and in small gulps. One would never sip medicine or dilute it with water. The term "vodka" in the sense of drink presumably did not appear in Russia until the late 19th century, and then it was the lower classes who popularized its usage. Vodka (in this word the *d* is pronounced more like a *t* and the *o* is long) is actually a diminutive for *voda*, meaning "water." *Vodka*, then, is "a little water," and the diminutive form implies an improved version of one of life's staples.

Wine and mead were well documented early on, and wine in many cases was a catchall for both traditional wine and grain spirits. Both grain wine and burning wine, among others, referred to vodka. The adjective "burning" refers to the distillation process and to the fact that the alcohol could be set alight. The Ukrainian word for "vodka" is *horilka* (say *horEELka* or *gorEELka* in Russian), meaning "flaming." In Ukraine you will hear both *horilka* and vodka.

Vodka in Russia was primarily distilled from rye. Pokhlebkin and other apologists for Russian vodka maintain that anything else is inferior and can lead to drunkenness, alcoholism, and hangovers. Nevertheless, the starch used need not be grain; hence in Poland and Ukraine, depending on local availability, we find vodkas also made from wheat, sugar beet, or potatoes.

A (Marxist) Snapshot of Vodka

Gorbachev's well-publicized attempts to reduce Soviet alcoholism failed. His error was in attacking vodka as the source of alcoholism, when it was merely a scapegoat. The difficulty, of course, is that the causes for excess alcohol consumption were many—and far more elusive than vodka. Rampant alcohol abuse reflected deep-rooted ills of society: among them, mass disillusionment and demoralization, the Party's diminished focus on education, and a contradictory, even hypocritical, stance toward alcohol usage. A popular joke around this time described the plight of a man who had finally lost all patience with Gorbachev. He announced to his friends that he was off to kill

Gorby; his friends applauded the boldness of his gesture. But he quickly returned to them with a very sad face. Alas, the queue had been too long.

By attacking drunkenness in standard top-down, Communist Party fashion, the social and economic roots of alcoholism were essentially driven underground during this period. The production of *samohon* (moonshine; *samagoan* in Russian) rose; this was dangerous since improper distillation always contributes substantially to alcohol-related deaths. After Gorbachev's campaign got under way there was a run on sugar which is used in many home brews. The only good news of his campaign was that violent crime dropped; it quickly rose after the campaign was abandoned.

Evidence suggests that proper alcohol distilling in Russia arose in the monasteries, as it had in Catholic Europe. The Church probably wanted the vodka monopoly, just as in Kyivan Rus the salt monopoly was held by the Church, specifically by Kyiv's Monastery of the Caves. By the late 15th century, however, vodka distilling quickly became concentrated in the hands of a secular state monopoly. This no doubt contributed to the Church's negative attitudes toward the "devil's poison."

In the 16th century, "tsar's taverns" were introduced. Tavern-keepers were responsible for both the production and sale of vodka. Essentially, they rented the monopoly. Annual receipts were handed over to the government, but the tavern-keepers were otherwise free of controls. Large-scale corruption, bribery, theft, and drunkenness arose from the unholy union of production and sale. Historians argue that these traits—often considered "Russian"—were not characteristic before the advent of vodka distilling. Selling vodka on credit also led people into debt and semi-enslavement. At the same time, this system drove up prices without improving quality. "Tavern revolts" erupted in the mid-17th century, and this system was soon abolished.

In 1705 Peter the Great (Peter I) decided that the state's priority during the Northern War was to obtain the highest possible profit from vodka sales. His solution was to reintroduce the earlier system despite its ruinous consequences. He also required that innkeepers pay in advance, thus obtaining money to fund his fleet regardless of revenues, which he anticipated would rise. The system only lasted ten years because Peter feared the people couldn't tolerate more.

Peter the Great was also known for the drinking punishments he enforced in which the offender had to publicly drink more than a liter of vodka; vomiting, alcohol poisoning, and public mockery were the desired results. Peter waged a war against the Old Believers in the Orthodox Church who espoused sobriety; he also handed out free vodka to soldiers, sailors, shipyard and road workers, and builders. His rule serves as an example of the ways in which the government's manipulation of vodka policy and reliance upon vodka sales effected significant social change.

By the late 19th century, vodka consumption distinguished Russia's social classes. For the Russian peasant, who often received free vodka, little had improved since the Middle Ages. The problem then as now involved the manner of consumption (cups of vodka gulped while standing and without food) and inferior quality.

After the October Revolution of 1917, the new regime banned alcohol altogether. This was in response to the frightening degree of drunkenness witnessed during the revolution and in the years before.

After 1924, a new state monopoly limited the alcoholic strength of vodka to 20% (abv). During World War II, Stalin issued vodka as part of the troops' regular rations. He had observed that vodka appeared to diminish the sensitivities of his terrified subjects during the Great Terror; now he hoped to bolster confidence during wartime. After the war, massive alcoholism surfaced, primarily among the working class. Stalin continued to maintain very low vodka prices as a bribe to his workers. A delicate balance was needed to deaden their consciousness without destroying their ability to work. (It's especially desirable to have sober armed forces.) Further, vodka sales then as now were a critical source of state revenues.

Between 1917 and 1937, disapproval of drunkenness marked a true communist. After World War II, official opposition to drunkenness was maintained; yet the government was attacking the consequences of the nation's moral decay and never its underlying causes. Similarly, the government periodically raised wages for dangerous work rather than improved adverse work conditions. (A recent example is the doubling of salaries for Chornobyl's liquidators.)

In the wake of Gorbachev's failed anti-alcoholism campaign, Pokhlebkin argues that what is needed today is comprehensive alcohol education. Drinking without eating and drinking adulterated products, especially *samohon*, is deleterious and potentially suicidal. Genuine help must be available for those who need or request it, and product quality must be maintained as high as possible by the state. If it does not, the populace is at risk. Further, if prices are too high, people will make their own illicit home brews, which is even more dangerous. Without these measures, the prophetic wisdom of the popular saying, "More people are drowned in a glass than in the ocean," is inescapable.

Vodka Traditions and Toasts

Vodka traditions are an irrefutable part of Slavic culture. Vodka serves as the ideal complement to the salty, spicy, and fatty cuisines of northern and eastern Europe. Nevertheless, Russia and Ukraine share mixed attitudes toward vodka: there is both pride in their drinking traditions and embarrassment due to excess consumption.

Ukrainian and Russian vodkas are widely available throughout Ukraine; prices are quite cheap by world standards and quality varies. One of the reputedly best brands in its signature squared-off, green glass bottle is Ancient Kyiv brand; I prefer other brands as this one imparts a strong aftertaste. New, high-quality vodkas have been appearing in the last couple years; these are intended to compete with the best foreign labels. Some vodkas, such as Poland's recent export called Belvedere, have fancy designs etched on the back of the bottle, that are visible through the glass (and clear liquid).

Be aware that bottles may be sealed with a foil cap, a standard bottle cap, or screw top. Some people say not to touch any but the screw-tops. In all cases, pay especial attention if you buy vodka from kiosks; I've heard of cases where bottles were tampered with and refilled with alcohol of inferior quality. Further, lower grades of Soviet grain alcohol contain trace amounts of ether; in cases of excess consumption, this impurity can lead to blindness. Given the above hazards, some people prefer to buy, at higher prices, imported vodkas from Finland, Sweden, and Poland, widely available in Ukraine. When you are invited to Ukrainian banquets, however, you will be drinking Ukrainian *horilka* (or Russian vodka).

In Ukraine, *horilka* (and sometimes *konyak*) is typically served throughout the duration of the meal. A Cossack tradition was to sometimes serve warm brandies and vodkas; nowadays, however, vodka is chilled and drunk neat in small clear glasses.

Flavored vodkas are also popular in Ukraine. *Nalivka* is alcohol infused with fruit; because it's so sweet, its potency can creep up on you. Some say these first appeared to mask the impurities. Regardless, Ukraine's specialty is *horilka z pertsem* (pepper-flavored vodka).

There are many traditions associated with vodka drinking; some of them approximate superstitions. For example, some say you must leave your glass resting on the table while another person refills it. To lift the glass then or before all glasses are poured is considered bad luck. Others say it's less bad luck than bad manners, when I thought bringing the glass closer to the server was the polite thing to do!

Also, filling the glass more than two-thirds full is the mark of boorishness. You should not refill your own glass, and never pour from a bottle backhanded—this is very insulting. It is also mandatory to serve at least a bite of food when serving alcohol. Serving only drinks without a bite is a serious breach of etiquette.

When toasts are being made, you cannot piggyback a second toast on someone else's. Two toasts means two separate shots of vodka, not one. Along these lines, guests are often asked (or expected) to give toasts at dinner, so you should be prepared to do so. This applies to both business and personal situations.

Many foreigners know that *na zdorovya* means "to health," but this is really more appropriate for food. *Za vashe zdorovya* (UKR) or *Na vashe zdarovye* (RUS) literally means "to your health," and this is considered the better toast where alcohol is involved.

Below is a smattering of common toasts:

Smachnoho—Bon appétit! Very Ukrainian!

Za druziv—To friends.

Za vas—To you.

Remember *dyakuyu* and *spaciba* mean "Thanks" in Ukrainian and Russian, respectively.

Never drink before the first toast is made. Typically, after any toast, guests clink their glasses together, then drink their shot at the same time. (Don't clink your glass if your drink is non-alcoholic.) The first shot is usually drunk all in one gulp, although women can get by with nursing their glass from the very start. A whistling sound, a loud breath, or even the smelling of one's sleeve are common immediate reactions followed by the salty bite of pickle, herring, or other appetizers. Subsequent shots are not necessarily downed in one gulp, which is good news if there are many toasts. (See *Zakusky* below for more on appetizers.)

If you intend to stop drinking early, you shouldn't start. This is a courtesy issue. With that said, people who don't drink are suspect. Frankly, despite the problems associated with alcohol abuse, alcoholism (like vegetarianism and dieting) is little understood in Ukraine. The key to drinking vodka is to follow the example of Ukrainians. This means eating between every two toasts. There will be plenty of foods to sample. Traditionally, the third toast is to the women present, and the men will stand up during this toast.

Aside from banquets and dinners, you should recall the tradition of drinking in groups of at least three people. The tradition is to finish the bottle, and empty bottles must not be left on the table. When drinking with Ukrainian friends, it is not uncommon to share one bottle before pouring the next.

Breaking a glass intentionally is considered good luck according to some; to others, it's a flagrant waste of a valuable commodity. If you do break a glass, expect to pay for it. Many view drinking directly out of the bottle (or flask) as utterly uncouth and not open for consideration. Only the basest of alcoholics could do this. I heard of a group of friends who, during Gorbachev's temperance campaign, drove an hour into the woods to drink vodka privately. When the men stopped in the woods, they discovered they had forgotten to bring glasses, whereupon they returned home, sober and without speaking.

Samohon

Samohon, homemade spirits, is illegal, tastes evil, and is commonly unsafe. On a farm near Cherkasy, I tasted what our hosts proudly boasted was made the day before our arrival; I tried a second taste with tomato juice, and then I vowed never to touch it again.

In late 1998 the Russian government decided to increase vodka production. The recent increase in imported vodkas and bootleg production, including *samohon*, had been cutting into state revenues. The precipitous rise in the production of *samohon* in the post-Soviet era bodes poorly for both Ukraine and Russia (for health and political reasons).

Wine, Champagne, Brandy, Beer, and Kvas

Ukraine today produces one-third of the wines in the FSU. Its principal wine-producing regions include Transcarpathia and Crimea. Its wines typically compete with those from Moldova and Georgia, the FSU's other primary wine producers, or with wines from Romania, Bulgaria, and Hungary. Other imported wines are also available in Ukraine on a limited basis.

Ukraine is the largest producer of sparkling wines in the FSU and has fine dessert wines. The Sauterne-like sweet wines of Crimea's

Massandra cellars are especially notable; this esteemed winery dates back to 1785. Ukraine also produces brandy, locally called *konyak;* the best in the FSU presumably comes from Armenia. Like vodka, Crimea's ruby and Madeira wines as well as Ukrainian *konyak* are often downed in one gulp. *Konyak* is served neat.

Under the Soviet system, farmers were paid based on the sugar content of the grape. Hence, grapes were frequently picked too late or even after they had rotted. The machines were not cleaned often enough either, and this imparted off-flavors, or the wine was simply allowed to stand too long. These problems need to be addressed and rectified if Ukrainian wine-growers ever intend to expand beyond local production and compete in world markets.

Like Moldova, Crimea produces a distinctive ruby-red champagne in addition to its traditional sparkling wines. Soviet Champagne is widely available and has kept its Soviet name, *Sovyetskoe Shampanskoe Vino;* other brands widely available include *Ukrainsky* brand and *Krim* (meaning Crimea). There are five levels of increasing sweetness, but even the driest is quite sweet by Western tastes.

This sweetness makes for nice mimosas, the traditional combination of orange juice and champagne. In fact, sweet champagne works better in mimosas than dry champagne, which should ideally be drunk on its own. The tang of passion fruit juice (*maracuya*) mixed with champagne is an excellent variation.

Pivo means beer, although in the Middle Ages it had a generic meaning of drink. Kyiv's ubiquitous Obolon beer has improved its selections and quality over the years. It is cheap and unpasteurized, so doesn't keep long. Many cities including Odesa, Lviv, and Vynnytsa have produced their own beers but apparently without Obolon's recent marketing success. Obolon's competition for the time being is Slavytich, but Obolon stays ahead by test-marketing new products. In addition to its high and low alcohol beers, Obolon also bottles its own rum and cola drink, a gin and tonic drink, and hard cider. These all have a high alcohol content and are sold in many kiosks.

163

Outside a wine shop in Crimea. (Photo courtesy of Meredith Dalton.)

In the outdoor cafés and in bars, Carlsberg, Tuborg, Guinness, and Kilkenny are often available. Bitburger and Corona are here as are the occasional American Budweiser; more often, Budweiser is the Czech pilsener like Budvar. Expect to pay Western prices for all but local beers. There are two standard sizes: literally, small (*malenkiy*) and large (*bolshoi*, like the Theater, or *velykiy* in Ukrainian), which translates into half-pints (or glasses) and pints.

Kvas is a murky, mildly alcoholic drink made from fermented brown bread. Sometimes it is flavored with currants. *Kvas* is sold only in the warmer months and is dispensed from large tanks. You should

164

bring your own empty bottle. You can also buy a glass on the spot, but like the old machines that dispensed water for kopeks, there is usually only one glass, and chances are good that it won't be well cleaned between patrons.

UKRAINIAN FOODS

Two of Ukraine's staples are wheat and sugar beet. It is no wonder that vodkas in Ukraine are produced using these crops. Regional food specialties naturally take advantage of the "breadbasket's" bounty.

Bread (*khlib* in Ukrainian; *khleb* in Russian) is considered the mainstay of the Ukrainian diet, and there are endless varieties available. White and brown bread are standard fare. They are chewy, sometimes tangy, and quite tasty when fresh; like milk they lose their freshness within a day or two of purchase. *Baton* (say *bahTONE*) is a popular white loaf; *bulka* (say *BOOLka*) is a roll; *bulochka* (say *BOOlochka*) is a small roll; and *bublyk* (say *BOObleak*) resembles a bagel with its chewy texture and hole in the middle. Pita and Georgian flat bread, *lavash,* are also available. There are also wonderful decorated breads created for special celebrations.

The combination of bread and salt is a traditional symbol of hospitality. The idea is that, even if the host has little to offer, there will always be bread and salt to share with guests. The guest should dip the bread into the pile of salt and enjoy. There was also a tradition that a guest bringing bread could not be refused entertainment.

Sweet breads are popular in Ukraine, and retain their freshness a bit longer, thanks to the honey or molasses in the dough. One of the more popular sweet loaves is poppy bread. *Mak* (say *mahk*) means "poppy," and *khlib z makom* or *makivnyk* are among the names you might hear. *Medivnyk* is a honey cake; *med* in Ukrainian (in Russian, *myod*—rhymes with "toad") means "honey" which is always available at the *rynok*. Fried pies filled with fruit and jam are also tasty.

Babka is a type of sweet bread known for the abundance of eggs in its batter. Traditional recipes called for as many as seventy eggs!

Kalach is a traditional braided bread, also rich in eggs. Ukrainian sweet breads generally have a much lower sugar to flour ratio than American breads. But some of the Austrian-influenced sweets and many Ukrainian cakes more than make up for this sugar deficit.

In Ukraine, there are certain breads associated with one particular holiday. *Paskha*, meaning "Easter," is the traditional Easter loaf, although there are many regional variations. In the east it is typically tall and iced, more like a cake; in western Ukraine, it is more bread-like and decorated with dough shapes. *Korovai* is the traditional tall wedding bread decorated with fantastic forms of flowers, animals, and sheaves of grain.

Typical Ukrainian Fare

To Western tastes, much of Ukrainian food may appear heavy and fatty just as food from America's Midwest, the so-called corn belt, is known for its stodginess. Regional cuisines reflect local climate and growing conditions. To the average Westerner, much of Ukrainian cuisine also resembles Russian, although regional variations share similarities with Polish and Hungarian cuisine. Some of the sweet breads, strudels, cheesecakes, and tortes were influenced by Viennese cuisine. To essentially lump Ukrainian and Russian cuisines is an oversimplification; it is more accurate to recognize elements adopted from the other's cuisine. For example, Ukrainians borrowed *shchi* and *solyanka*, two kinds of soups, while Russians adopted from Ukrainian cuisine, borshch, *varenyky* (filled dumplings), and cheese pastries, among other things. A Polish cookbook from circa 1900 included French and Austrian recipes, some of which were subsequently assimilated by Ukrainian households. Thirty years later, a Ukrainian cookbook included some of the same recipes.

Holubtsy (literally, little pigeons) are stuffed cabbage leaves which originated in Turkey. Today, the Black Sea cuisine exhibits a Mediterranean influence, with eggplant especially popular as well as many seafood dishes. In the Carpathians, beef and dairy cattle are raised; sheep were especially popular in the 19th century, and the region is noted for its *bryndzia*, made from ewe's milk and similar to Greek feta cheese.

Varenyky, another Ukrainian Staple

One of the most common national dishes is *varenyky* (say *vahREN-eekee*), or boiled dumplings akin to ravioli. They are often doughy and may be filled with meat, mushrooms, cottage cheese, potatoes, cabbage, or sweet cherries. Potato-filled *varenyky* smothered with mushrooms and onion sauce make a good combination. *Varenyky* are sometimes confused with *pelmeni*, which are Siberian dumplings.

Dumplings and pancakes are also common. Pancakes, called *bliny* (say *BLEEnee*), are thick and doughy like American pancakes, and quite small, or thin like French crepes, rolled and filled with caviar (*ikra*, say *eeKRAH*), berries, mushrooms, sour cream, or a sweet cheese pastry filling. *Mlintsy* are the thicker ones; *nalisniky* are the thinner ones, filled with cheese, for example.

Pirohy or *piroshky* are pies or turnovers, with sweet or savory fillings; meat-filled *pirohy* are reminiscent of Britain's meat pies.

A Penchant for Meat

Both fat and garlic are essential Ukrainian ingredients, and pork is as highly prized for the fat as for the meat. Ukraine's diet tends to include more meat than Russia's, since raising livestock was always an important feature of Ukrainian agriculture. (When meat supplies are limited, meat may be distributed at the table according to age or rank.)

Typically, Ukrainian borshch includes more meat, and also more vegetables, than Russian borshch. Also, Ukrainians have a reputation for making better and more varied kinds of sausages than the Russians. Ukrainians visiting America are appalled by the lack of good sausages and the limited varieties. Larded meats and meats in aspic are also typical Ukrainian fare.

In general, simply prepared meats are not a feature of Ukrainian cuisine. Chicken Kiev was presumably an early 20th century invention to upgrade provincial food. The food in the cities is rarely considered as good as that found in the provinces. Certainly many Ukrainian home-style dishes are not ideally suited for restaurants.

The Orthodox calendar is marked by periods of fasting (or restrictions) followed by religious feasts; during Lent and Advent, for example, only meatless dishes are served.

Kotleta Po-Kyivsky and Other Meat Dishes

Kotleta po-Kyivsky: you've heard of it as Chicken Kiev, but it's not a national dish by any stretch. It's easiest to find in the old Soviet Intourist hotel dining rooms; it's tasty, but it's plenty greasy. After all, the sign of good Chicken Kiev (I have yet to see it spelled Kyiv!) is butter spurting out when you first cut into it. That's because it's made from boneless chicken stuffed with or wrapped around butter, then seasoned, floured, and deep-fried. (See Chapter Five for more about Soviet Intourist hotels.)

A more common menu item is fried or baked chicken leg and thigh; the leg is often adorned with a miniature white-paper chef's hat.

Pork cutlets are common menu items; these include *wiener schnitzel* equivalents or breaded cutlets stuffed with mushrooms. Like Chicken Kiev, these are served with potatoes (which are only sometimes edible in the Intourist places). You might instead request a side dish of rice (*rys*).

Stroganoff, meat and mushrooms in a rich sour cream sauce, is traditionally Russian. In Ukraine it is not served on a bed of noodles, so you might request rice.

Shashlik (say *shashLEEK*) is marinated shish-kebab, typically made from pork. It is served with a sauce similar to ketchup or barbecue sauce. The grilling process is best suited for open-air restaurants. The easiest place to find *shashlik* in Kyiv is at Hidropark; you can also find it in Lviv just off Prospekt Svobody (Freedom

Avenue), near the outdoor beer places. The winning prize, for me, goes to a fantastic place that was hidden among trees, en route to Yalta, on the Crimean coast. (Many others were in view, however.)

"Ukrainian chocolate"

Ever tasted raw pork fat? It's better if it's marinated in garlic. Then you smear it on a piece of bread, and you're practically Ukrainian. Actually, it's the tradition to have *salo* when you're drinking vodka. Ukrainians say that *salo* and vodka go together because the fat helps to absorb alcohol or maybe to break it down in your system. I've even heard *salo* affectionately called "Ukrainian chocolate."

Sometime ago, I heard that Ukrainian visitors to the United States sometimes consume raw bacon as a substitute for *salo*. I didn't believe it until I witnessed it firsthand. I did not, however, participate; indeed I strongly discouraged it, but my health warnings were ignored.

Ukraine's National Soup

Kvas, a mildly alcoholic drink mentioned earlier, is made from fermented bread, from the grain itself (primarily wheat or rye), or from vegetable juices (e.g. beet or cabbage). Vegetable-based *kvas* is used extensively as stock for soups, stews, and sauces; and *kvas* from beets lends a delicious tangy flavor to Ukraine's national soup—borshch. Russia and other Soviet republics, as well as traditional Jewish cuisine, have adopted borshch, but the soup whose base is a broth of beets and other vegetables originated in Ukraine. A Ukrainian woman's cooking is often judged by her borshch.

There are endless regional variations on borshch: the broth may be clear before the customary dollop of sour cream (*smetana*) is added and muddies it; or the soup may be thick like stew and overflowing with ruby-red beets, onions, cabbage, carrots, beans, and potatoes, each depending on local availability and tastes. Some borshch has a hunk of meat tossed in for additional flavoring. There are hot and cold varieties of borshch, as well as green borshch. Garlic and dill are

especially popular seasonings in Ukraine and are used to flavor its national soup. Parsley is often added.

Borshch is a first course in Ukraine, not an entree. It may follow appetizers (see *Zakusky* below) or be served in place of them. *Pampushky* (say *pamPOOSHkee*) are often served with borshch; these are fresh rolls, sometimes resting soggily in a saucer of crushed garlic and oil. It is especially delicious when the garlic mixture is served on the side in a gravy boat. A *pampushka* can also be a jam- or fruit-filled roll.

Like beet *kvas*, fermented cabbage is another staple in Ukrainian kitchens because of its tartness, texture, and storage capability. *Kapusta* (say *kaPOOsta*) means "cabbage," and *kapusniak* is a cabbage soup with many variations. Made from fresh or brined cabbage, it might be thin like broth or thick like stew.

Wheat is concentrated in the central steppes of Ukraine, but buckwheat is especially popular in the north. *Kasha* is porridge made from buckwheat. Buckwheat is actually a fruit, but it is generally prepared like grain. In the higher-altitude Hutsul and Boiko regions, corn and barley are harvested, and they influence regional diets.

Potatoes are commonly associated with Ukrainian cooking; before the 19th century, however, the potato was scarcely used here.

Adopted from Russia, other popular soups include *solyanka*, which is typically thick and mildly spiced. *Myasna* and *ribna* (meaning "meat" and "fish," respectively) are typical *solyanky*. *Shchi* is a cabbage soup very popular in Russia. *Zharkoe* (say *zharKOYye* which means "roast") is a tasty meat and potato stew.

Caviar

Caviar is imported from the Caspian Sea region. It is available in some of the better markets (do you have a knowledgeable Ukrainian friend who can help you?) or at higher cost in the Western-styled grocery stores. The large salmon roe is tasty and quite salty; the smaller black caviar comes in different grades, ranging from so-so to magnificent.

Buying caviar with friends, Kharkiv. (Photo courtesy of Meredith Dalton.)

171

Mushrooms

Mushroom collecting is a national hobby shared by the peoples of Ukraine, Russia, and Belarus. Wild mushrooms can be found in the forests bordering northern Ukraine and Belarus (including the Chornobyl region) which were historically famous for hiding runaways from the law or foreign oppressors. Early September is reputed to be the best time for mushroom collecting.

It is best to enter the forest on a dry morning after several days of rain. There is a longstanding tradition of silence when collecting mushrooms. The mushrooms are twisted at their base or cut with a paring knife; they are not yanked from the ground. They are then laid carefully in a flat-bottomed basket.

Wild mushrooms are very perishable, and of course, not all mushrooms are edible. They are only abundant for short periods; old ones are dangerous to eat. Some mushrooms are not worth preserving, while others reconstitute well and can keep for up to three years if properly treated. Preserving methods include salting and layering in crocks; cooking and layering in pork fat, melted butter, or oil; pickling in vinegar; blanching and freezing; or sautéing and freezing.

In Ukraine mushrooms are cooked and served in a variety of dishes, but they are not eaten raw. One of my favorite dishes is called *zhulien*. The mushrooms are cooked in a very rich sauce of cream and cheese; this is an excellent first course. The word for "mushrooms" is *hriby* (say *hreeBEE*, or *greeBEE* in Russian).

Fast Food Fare

Ukrainian fast food restaurants, such as Stop or Boston Burger in Kyiv, typically serve hamburgers and fried chicken. My personal favorite is Kentucky Beirut Chicken on Shevchenko just up from Bessarabskiy Rynok; it's one of the oldest of its type, has a great name, and provides a clear plastic glove with its fried chicken. Another great fast food place is Montanya, just up the street from the university; this is a Lebanese restaurant popular with students and

My favorite fast food place, if only for the name: Beirut Kentucky Chicken. (Photo courtesy of Meredith Dalton.)

business people alike. Order the chicken schwarma with hummus platter and a side of the garlic mayonnaise.

If you need standard Western fast food, the Golden Arches arrived in 1997 with aggressive plans to expand. There are even drive-through locations. Be prepared to pay extra for ketchup—and remember, no Diet Coke—but otherwise prices are quite reasonable, even if everyone is complaining that they're higher than they used to be.

Pizza is popular and inexpensive in Ukraine. New places are always cropping up, and delivery services, while not common, were available even several years ago. Check out Vesuvio's on Reiterska for dining in or delivery, although there are now many other options for pizza lovers. Also ask your friends if Eric has a new place. This German entrepreneur deserves great credit for broadening Kyiv's dining and nightlife venues.

Zakusky

Zakuska (literally, "little taste") means hors d'oeuvre or appetizer; usually you will hear it in the plural form *zakusky* since the variety is often extensive. No self-respecting Ukrainian will drink vodka without *zakusky* on his table. These might be slices of brown bread, or bread with cheese, sausages, or even caviar. The large salmon roe—pink and salty and less expensive than black caviar—is often served on buttered bread. Smoked salmon, much of it Norwegian, is a wonderful treat and widely available in the Western grocery stores. Slice and butter a fresh *baton*, fold smoked salmon on it, add a dash of pepper, a drop of lemon juice (or simply lemon pepper; McCormick spices from Finland are widely available), and life is decidedly good.

Other *zakusky* are pickles (including remarkably crisp dills) and pickled lemon slices soaked in sugar—excellent with vodka.

There are also congealed salads and lots of fish dishes; in fact the Ukrainian love of salted herring has been attributed to the influence of the Varangians, Swedish Vikings who settled in Kyiv and along the Dnipro over 1000 years ago. Most *zakusky* are salty, fatty, and spicy—considered an ideal accompaniment to alcohol; these were traditionally served to guests who had traveled far distances to visit.

Fruit, Vegetables, Salads, and Pickles

The days of the banana queues are over; you'll see sidewalk vendors set up with fruit, vegetables, and scales. You can even find kiwis for sale in the underground passageways. In Ukraine's warm south, pumpkins and eggplants are grown. Crimea is noted for its delicious red onions unavailable elsewhere.

You will probably purchase most fruit and vegetables at the *rynok* or, for convenience's sake, in Western grocery stores. The *rynok* tests your language and haggling abilities; check around to find out who really wants your business, and taste the samples that they offer you. Bessarabskiy Rynok is not the only market, and its prices are higher than the others, but it's more convenient for people who live or work near Kreshchatyk. Find out which market is closest to you. At all of them, expect to pay higher prices than your Ukrainian friends, or ask one to come along and advise you.

When shopping for fruit or vegetables in the Western grocery stores, remember that any piece priced individually is probably very overpriced but may be worth it. Also, haggling is not acceptable in stores, only at the *rynok*.

You'll also want to take along plastic bags for shopping. For buying eggs, plastic egg crates are far more reliable than the seller's thin plastic baggie (unless you're walking only a few blocks). *Smetana*, honey, and caviar will be sold to you in glass receptacles. At the *rynok*, you can also buy cheese and all sorts of sausages and meats. For the adventurous, there are the salty, sun-dried fish that Ukrainians enjoy as snacks, and few Westerners would deign to try. Why is it that they will taste *salo*, which you can also buy here in thick slabs?

Ukrainians have mastered the fine art of pickling vegetables to preserve their bounties long after the harvest has ended. Homemade jams and fruit preserves are also very popular.

175

Ukrainian salads are varied, but traditional salad greens are rare. Most popular are salads made from chopped vegetables in a mayonnaise-based dressing. Spiced carrots are juicy and crunchy, although they (and the other salads) always struck me as odd breakfast offerings in the state hotels. In the state hotels, soggy or greasy potatoes also used to be the norm, but this is changing over time. Elsewhere they should be prepared properly.

When dining out, you might order a simple salad of cucumber and tomato slices; I advise requesting this without oil, *bez masla*, as sometimes rancid salad oil is drizzled on top. If not rancid, it tastes like vegetable oil without vinegar. Foreigners are advised to avoid lettuce (called *salat*, as are salads, to throw us off), which may not have been washed properly, except in restaurants catering to Westerners.

Garlic and Other Seasonings

Garlic (Ukrainian *chasnyk*; Russian *chesnok*) is ubiquitous in Ukrainian cooking. Garlic is known for its medicinal as well as magical powers. As an appetizer, it may be eaten raw or dipped into salt first. Like many other vegetables, it is frequently pickled—do try the tasty, pickled garlic cloves sold at the *rynok*.

Ukrainian cuisine, like American Midwest cooking, is not especially spicy. There is a definite preference for dill weed. Fresh dill is especially tasty in creamed dishes. Dill is also available in salted, dried, or frozen form. Other popular spices or seasonings include horseradish, caraway seeds, cilantro, celery root, and parsley.

Desserts

The standard dessert in restaurants is ice cream (*morozivo* in Ukrainian; *morozhenoe* in Russian). Ukrainians, like Russians, love their ice cream even when it's freezing outdoors. There are vendors selling Italian ices, Belgian-chocolate covered ice cream bars, and many local treats. However, Ukrainians complain that the local products have declined in quality.

Bon Bon in Passazh is famous for its ice creams, but you'll have to pay a deposit for the plastic bowl if you want to eat it outdoors.

Cakes are generally reserved for special occasions. People take them home for parties or serve them at banquets, but they are not generally selected from restaurant menus.

Sweet cream-filled pastries (and sometimes fried pies) are sold in busy street locations or just inside the entrance to TSUM, the state department store (see Chapter Five). An older woman generally serves her treats on a strip of coarse paper, intended to serve as a napkin or catch any excess grease. (Don't expect her to smile much.) Today the best pastries are found where the best coffee is served. Delectable pastries with custard fillings, for example Napoleans and glazed tarts (as distinct from the lovely cakes reserved for special occasions), are more widely available than just a couple years ago.

DINING OUT

Men will remove ladies' coats, light cigarettes for them, and pay for most meals. Only if a woman has called a business lunch might she be allowed to pay, but it is still a sticky matter. (See Chapter Six for more on business functions in general.)

For the most part, Ukrainians reserve dining out for special occasions as restaurant dinners are expensive. A Ukrainian banquet always entails a full meal with alcohol, appetizers, and a main course. Often the menu is set, and you won't be making selections. A variety of alcoholic and non-alcoholic drinks will be laid out; you won't have to order a thing. (Reaching across the table for something you need is okay.) These banquets are always seated affairs, sometimes with dancing to follow.

Before you are seated, sometimes you'll notice that the dinner chairs are angled. You won't need to pull your seat out; you'll just have to straighten it as you sit down. It's a clever oddity.

When dining out today in Kyiv's restaurants, it is possible to find all sorts of ethnic food: besides Ukrainian and Russian, you can find

Chinese, Vietnamese, Thai, Japanese, Indian, Mexican, Italian, Lebanese, American, Tex-Mex, Caribbean, French, Swiss, German, Austrian, and Kosher. Expect to pay for such variety. Be wary of ordering something non-Ukrainian from a Ukrainian menu; more than once an "Italian" pasta dish I ordered appeared smothered in ketchup!

A *kafeteria* typically serves coffee, alcohol, and light food and can be found in universities, for example. A *kafe* is found in the city and used to carry similar fare. Today the arrival of more European-styled cafés has expanded the traditional meaning of *kafe*. A *stolova* is our definition of a company cafeteria or private dining hall. All the old factories, institutes, and government offices had one for their employees; these were essentially mess halls subsidized by their (state) employer, where hot meals were served daily. Today the *stolova* is still an important perk for many Ukrainians, but few receive high kudos for their fine cuisine.

IT'S MY PARTY ...

If it is your birthday, you will be expected to pay for the party. Traditionally, name days were celebrated, and to some, were more important than the actual birthday; however, Soviet attitudes altered this practice. Formerly, a child at baptism was given the name of a saint, often one whose saint's day was closest to the child's birthday. It was hoped that the child would emulate the best qualities of the particular patron saint.

Birthday cards are generally reserved for people who are far away and with whom you cannot celebrate the event. Hallmark might have some trouble here. Wrapping gifts is not such an important tradition either. At birthday celebrations, the first toast is always to the honoree; the second should be to the parents.

It is never good form to congratulate someone early, and this includes bestowing birthday wishes in advance. You will be congratulated on the various holidays, including your own country's (such as American Independence Day for me), but only on or after the day has passed. Along these lines, never ask expectant parents if they have a name selected for the baby.

TIPPING

The word for "tip" (in Ukrainian and Russian) comes from *chai,* meaning "tea." In the past a tip was nominal—the idea was that it covered the price of a cup of tea for the waiter. Today tipping is expected, especially of foreigners; people tend to tip better in the expat hangouts, and the servers in the local places might benefit even more from your generosity.

Always check first to see if a service charge was included in your bill. (Useful words for receipt, bill, or check are *kvitansiya, schot, rakhunok,* or *chek,* respectively.) A standard tip is 10% to 15%; again, remember to check to see that you weren't overcharged. Note that the cost of bread is often added to your bill, even if you didn't eat the bread that you didn't order that was brought to you. If you don't want it, refuse it when they bring it to you, not when the bill arrives.

In the Soviet era, people had to request a *chisty stol* (literally, "clean table") when they dined out; otherwise, an assortment of *zakusky* were brought to the table—and naturally added to the bill.

If you pay by credit card, leave the tip on the table in cash, or your server will never see it.

DINING ETIQUETTE

It's patently obvious, but wait to eat with your host. (On the other hand, in restaurants, sometimes it's best for people to eat when their dish arrives, since not all dishes will arrive at the same time.) You should not leave until the guest of honor has, and if you are lucky enough to be that guest, don't linger too long. The oldest or the honored guest may be seated at the head of the table. Ukrainians strive hard to live up to the tradition of gracious hospitality as expressed in the Ukrainian saying, "Guest in the home, God in the home."

In serving yourself, take moderate portions. Again, obvious? Yes, but there is also the tradition that the hostess will offer you more helpings several times during the meal. It is your duty to praise the food and its variety, and to compliment the hosts on their graciousness, as stinginess or carelessness convey a disregard for hospitality. The hostess will nonetheless humbly apologize for the meager presentation. You may honor your hostess by leaving a small portion of food on your plate, indicating that your hunger was satisfied.

It's not considered polite at a formal dinner to pick over an assorted platter to get only the items you want. It is acceptable to reach across in front of others.

Eating is continental style: this means, hold your fork in your left hand and your knife in your right. When you have finished, place your knife and fork, tines up and side by side, on your plate at a clock position of 5:25. Sweets are eaten with a spoon.

UKRAINIAN CELEBRATIONS

Because of Soviet attitudes toward religion, Ukraine's centuries-long tradition of religious feasts was ignored or forbidden for many years. Instead, Labor Day (May 1) and October Revolution Day (November 7) were celebrated in place of church holidays. Further, Ukrainian folk rites were suppressed because they presumably encouraged nationalism and separatism. Some traditions were therefore better preserved in Ukrainian emigré communities.

Pagan rites were observed before the arrival of Christianity more than one thousand years ago; later these were often adopted or incorporated into Christian celebrations and folk traditions. For example, Ukrainians traditionally celebrated Christmas with *kutia*, a pudding made from wholewheat kernels, poppy seeds, and honey, a custom that dated to ancient times. Christmas was the only time of year that this dish was served. Easter was marked by the tradition of *pysanky*, intricately decorated eggs (which you can buy at reasonable prices on Andriyivskiy Uzviz; see Chapter Five for more information) and *krashanky*, dyed cooked eggs; these decorated eggs predated Christianity in Ukraine. Along the Black Sea coast, ancient Ukraine was exposed to Roman and Hellenic culture, and the traditional singing of *koliady*, or carols, may be traced to the Roman calendar.

Festive Ukrainian Cooking by Marta Pisetska Farley is an excellent source for traditional holiday recipes, but it is far more than a traditional cookbook. The author places the cuisine in the context of religious and folk traditions and shows how these have been preserved in emigré communities.

For centuries the church had called for fasting and abstinence at times, and both Advent and Lent limited meat and dairy intake. On Christmas Eve, an elaborate holy supper broke the fast from the previous day. Usually, twelve dishes were served as this number symbolized Christ's disciples. (On other feast occasions, the numbers nine and seven were chosen for their magical properties.) Underneath the white tablecloth lay hidden hay, preferably the first hay from the summer's harvest; this symbolized the manger. Garlic cloves were also included to bring good health to the family in the coming year. There was no Christmas tree, although wheat or rye sheaves were placed under the icon of the Virgin and Child. A church service beginning at midnight ended around 2 a.m. Men would wear their traditional embroidered shirts. The Ukrainian Christmas symbol of Grandfather Frost (say *Deed Moroz*) is a carryover from the pre-

Christian era. In Soviet times, Grandfather Frost brought his gifts on New Year's Eve in the anti-religious holiday spirit.

Easter Day was likewise a huge celebration including meats and sausages that were restricted until the last week of Lent, called Masliana. A folk proverb wished for seven Sundays of Masliana and one of Lent, instead of the reverse. During this last week, all work outside the home ceased. Exchanging Easter eggs was also the tradition. People attend the all-night Easter service carrying baskets of foods to be blessed for the celebratory meal.

Opportunities were made for young village people to meet in proper social settings after the hard work of the harvests. There were rituals and divining practices to help reveal the future. For the Feast of Saint Catherine (around December 7), girls would cut boughs from fruit trees to place in water. If they sprouted by New Year's, the girl would be blessed with a bright future and much happiness. And if they dried up, you know the rest. There was also a tradition of listening for dogs' barking or a rooster's first crow of the day which were believed to herald the direction from which a future husband would arrive.

The marriage ritual as described by Farley was intricate and also guided to prevent uneven matches. A boy who wanted to marry would tell his parents, who invited two respected older males to act as emissaries on the family's behalf. The emissaries (or *starosty,* from *starost*, meaning old age) would visit the girl's parents to propose the idea. They brought bread and vodka, which would be offered if the contract was sealed. It was considered rude to be forward so they expressed humble surprise and joy if the parents agreed to the union. If the parents weren't interested they would tell the *starosty* that the girl was too young. This was *vranyo* intended to avoid insult. An old joke still heard today makes reference to the consolation prize: if a man was refused, all he got was a lousy pumpkin.

If the parents agreed, the *starosty* shared bread and vodka with the girl's family, and embroidered ritual cloths (*rushnyky*) were exchanged to symbolize the agreement.

The *starosty* were also responsible for negotiating the dowry. Both sets of parents gave equally to help the couple's new start. A formal dinner was held, wherein the wedding date was set. A special bread, baked with two eggs symbolizing fertility, was served. The fiancée received a beautiful scarf and the man, an embroidered shirt.

Many customs are associated with the wedding process, including the exchange of ritual gifts, blessings, and breads. The day before the marriage, a special evening for maidens was held. Advice was dispensed, and games played. The groom arrived late and gave gifts to all the guests. The following day, the parents blessed their children before the wedding ceremony but did not attend the service. Rather, the couple gave themselves away. They dined with the groom's parents, then went to the bride's house for the reception. At both houses, they were greeted with bread and salt.

At the bride's house, the table was decorated with the *korovai*, the traditional wedding bread, two *rushnyky,* and a large pine bough, a fertility symbol. More ritual cloths and gifts were exchanged, and toasts made by every male adult relative. The newlyweds did not eat their own cake. Today, a miniature *korovai* is made for the couple to keep. It is common for close women friends to contribute tortes, and, instead of the groom, it is the guests who now give the gifts.

In addition to religious and folk celebrations, the most important life events were celebrated; these included births, christenings, betrothals, weddings, and burials.

Traditionally, mirrors were covered for nine days or turned around after a death in the family. Death anniversaries were commemorated, and twice a year special grave site services were held. Both food and *pysanky* were shared with the dead. A third ceremony for the dead was held in the home.

Ukrainians believed that the souls of dead ancestors sometimes returned to earth in the form of unfortunates, such as orphans, beggars, the homeless, or infirm. They also believed that the souls of the departed would help to preserve the family's fortunes. This

183

partially explains the tradition of setting an extra place at the Christmas table or inviting a guest in from the street. It was also a tradition to leave a bowl of food in the window sill.

Deference to dead ancestors was one of the primary tenets of Ukrainian belief. The other important tenets were reverence to God and supplication to the elements of nature. For example, the Feast of the Epiphany or the Feast of Jordan, which commemorated Christ's baptism on or around January 19, or 12 days after Christmas, was also a time for appeasing the forces of nature. Specifically, river water was blessed in an effort to protect the villages from floods.

It is sad yet understandable that so many colorful folk traditions are dying or have disappeared altogether. It is our good fortune that a book such as *Festive Ukrainian Cooking* is available as it captures a rich part of Ukraine's cultural (and gastronomical) heritage.

A FEW MORE USEFUL WORDS

Vkusny (say *fKOOsnee*) means "tasty" in Russian. *Ochen vkusny* means "very tasty." In Ukrainian, you will say *smachniy*. It's always polite to compliment your hostess on a *vkusny* or *smachniy* meal.

Pyaniy means "drunk." Don't compliment your hostess this way.

Sche (*yeshcho* in Russian) means "again," "still," or "more." You'll hear *Yeshcho raz* ("one more time"), or *Yeshcho pivo, pozhalusta* in Russian and *Sche pivo, bud laska* in Ukrainian, which means "Another beer, please."

Dyevushka (*DYEvooshka*) means "young woman" in Russian and is also used to get the attention of a waitress or shop assistant. It is not considered rude to use this word to attract attention. The diminutive is *dyevochka*—"little girl." (In Ukrainian, *deevchynka* and *devchyna* mean "young woman" and "little girl," respectively, but they are not used for attracting attention.) To get a man's attention, you will say *mushchina*, meaning "man" in Russian. *Malchik* is "little boy."

Finally, *charka* is a shot, generally of vodka or *samohon*, which may lead to a *hopak*, a traditional Ukrainian dance.

Chapter Five

SETTLING DOWN

GET YOUR VISA BEFORE YOU ARRIVE

It sounds obvious, doesn't it? But tourist visas are available upon arrival at the airport—with one caveat. I've seen the airport visa office both open and closed. If it's open, you will need to pay a fee, surrender passport photos, and relinquish a letter of invitation. But if it's closed, you've surely made a long trip, and who knows how long you will have to stand in line? I've heard of people who were stranded at the airport for more than four hours because the visa office was closed. There have also been periods of several days or weeks when the practice of granting visas in-country was suspended. In short, unless you're headed to Kyiv on a brief, last-minute trip, I strongly recommend that you obtain your visa in advance of arrival.

Another warning: don't enter the country with a tourist visa if you really need a business visa. Chances are you will need the business visa if you're in Ukraine on a long-term basis. I entered with a tourist visa, expecting to be in Kyiv for one month only. Plans changed quickly, even before I had departed, yet I assumed (that dangerous word) that changing my tourist visa to a business one could be easily handled with some assistance from USAID, the United States Agency of International Development. (We were, after all, in Kyiv on the invitation of the Ukrainian Government and Ministry of Agriculture.) I was declined twice: both times I was told that it was categorically impossible to make such a change in class of visa. But the second official took pity on me and extended my tourist visa by three weeks. From a hotel employee, I learned that there was an office where I could pay $2 a day to extend my tourist visa indefinitely. But I wanted to be in the country legally and also to have multiple-entry privileges.

In the end I prevailed, and my six-month visa was granted. It cost me $200 in bribes (USAID project personnel are NEVER supposed to pay for visas in-country), five post-it pads, and a roll of scotch tape. Having had the business visa in the first place would have saved me undue aggravation; I was especially ticked off that I might have to leave the country at the last minute because of an avoidable error.

My subsequent business visa cost me nothing and was granted for two years, but it was merely an extension of my previous visa. (This would have cost money had I been outside of Ukraine.)

Tourist visas are easy to obtain with a faxed hotel confirmation, but many hotels won't provide these. I've heard of hotels that are now charging for this letter. But the letter will suffice in getting a visa, even if you later cancel the reservation. Naturally, it should include your full name, passport number, and the hotel reservation dates.

Many hotels won't accept you without an advance reservation, even if they have the space. It's a carry-over of the inefficiencies from

Soviet days. Even once we were in our hotel, we were required to type letters on our letterhead stating how long we would be extending our stay at the hotel. At the end of the period, literally to the day, the hotel staff would inform us that we had to check out. So we typed the letter again. We did this several times, because we didn't know how long we needed to stay. (All this was before our contract permitted us to rent an apartment, which was considerably cheaper.)

As for business visas, an invitation letter from a Ukrainian business entity or a governmental agency is necessary. For foreign firms, the letter should indicate the company's relationship to the Ukrainian firm. Is this company setting up offices in Ukraine or merely doing temporary business? If setting up offices, is this to be a legally registered company, meaning, among other things, that Ukrainian hiring practices are followed and taxes filed accordingly? Foreign governmental or aid organizations—American, Canadian, or European—in Ukraine will need an invitation from some sector of the Ukrainian government to implement a specific project.

There is a third class of visa called the private visa, where a Ukrainian invites an individual. Check with the Ukrainian Embassy or Consulate about this; I personally have never been aware of anyone who entered Ukraine on one of these, but I feel certain some of the diaspora are invited by family members in Ukraine.

One final note on visas: Ukrainian visas are stamped into your passport, whereas Russian visas are a separate document to be kept in a safe place with your passport (or on you).

CURRENCY EXCHANGE AND CUSTOMS DECLARATIONS

The old days of recording on your customs declaration every time you exchanged foreign currency for local currency are over. It is also unnecessary to keep receipts from these transactions.

While it is no longer possible to use dollars when you pay for goods or services, all the larger stores will have their own currency exchange facilities. I say dollars here, because in Ukraine the American dollar is still king. Obviously, for some purchases it pays to shop around for the best exchange rate. Also, it is possible to exchange German marks or Russian rubles at most currency exchange bureaux (called *obmyn valut*).

The airport will permit you to exchange dollars at bad rates; upon arrival you don't have much choice. Just exchange enough to get you to your hotel or where you are going. You can always exchange more money later on.

Chances are good that you can pay for your taxi in dollars. For years, I have heard that the cab drivers at Borispil International Airport (Kyiv) are completely overrun by the mafia whose rates to the city (20 miles from the airport to the city center) are upwards of $50. Anything close to $25 is extremely fair, and every first-time visitor should try to arrange to have a driver meet him upon arrival. Also, if the weather is bad, expect to pay more.

Customs may or may not be slow, and this is the way it is. Hold on to your declaration form during your stay; you will need it when you leave. You will also need to keep your small receipt from Immigration which looks like an advertisement on slick paper; it now tells you in fine print to hold on to it. When you enter the country for the first time, be sure to record all valuables, such as furs, expensive gold and other jewelry (I wouldn't recommend carrying these with you in the first place), computers, cameras, and videocameras, on your incoming declarations form. You'll actually make two copies— one for customs upon entry and one for customs upon departure. When you depart, you'll also fill in a new customs form that the officer will compare with your incoming declaration. Don't lose it!

A friend recommends xeroxing your incoming declaration after you arrive, because if you travel in and out of Ukraine, you won't be carrying all of your valuables with you on every trip. For example, your latest entry declaration might say nothing about your laptop computer if you didn't carry it with you on your recent trip to Vienna.

I had trouble with customs on only one occasion. I was trying to leave the country with more money than I had carried on me when I entered the previous time. This is one of the carry-overs of the archaic Soviet bureaucracy.

I was lucky this time in that logic, I think, prevailed. I was leading a Ukrainian delegation to the United States for three weeks. My interpreter recorded on his declaration that he was leaving the country with $200 in his wallet. At the time, he had closer to $800 as I recall (to partially cover his hotel expenses and because he had no credit card). I had close to $1000 on me, and on my previous (incoming) declaration I had entered the country with $800. I therefore broke the $1000 down on my outgoing customs declaration, indicating one-half of the cash as belonging to me (which was true), and one-half, company money intended to cover unexpected expenses in the United States. The interpreter was waved through, and I was detained. Standing for a long time in front of the curt customs officer, I feared that my honesty would cost me my airline seat that day. (One has to remember that Ukraine has archaic and sometimes surreal rules, and the customs officer really was trying to do her job. And I've found that getting mad or crying—even if the circumstance warrants—is rarely worthwhile. Be patient, polite, and stand your ground.) Finally, this customs officer exclaimed dramatically and with evident irritation: "This is not enough money to worry about!" and waved me through.

Obtaining currency in Ukraine is sometimes a nightmare. ATMs arrived, albeit reluctantly, in 1998; the machines at both airports, Borispil and Zhuliany, are currently the most reliable. The general situation should soon improve but there is still no American Express office (although a representative office is planned). You should prepare yourself in the event that getting cash proves difficult. (For example, unless you are employed by your embassy, you will not have access to check-cashing privileges.) Western Union is available in Ukraine. Far more common are wire transfers from Western banks. Many Ukrainian banks have working relationships with Western banks, and Crédit Lyonnais has been in Kyiv since 1995. A few others have followed, and the financial situation is gradually improving. In short, it is certainly possible to have more money upon leaving the country than upon arrival, but you don't want to report it.

One further concern is how much money you can carry with you when you arrive in the country. Know your own country's rule about declaring amounts over a certain limit. Into Ukraine, you can bring as much as you desire, but above a certain level, they will want to see and count it. I first arrived in Ukraine with entirely TOO much money, and the sad truth is that it belonged to my company and not to me. I wouldn't carry this amount again as it is too risky; yet at the time we needed immediate cash for hiring staff and drivers, renting office space, procuring office supplies, and so on before we could establish a bank account (an experience that turned out to be Kafkaesque).

When I arrived with all this money on me, the customs official asked me to go into a separate room where I could count out my money in front of an official. I was relieved to be able to do this in a private office and away from the public chaos of the airport. To my surprise, the private office included about ten bureaucrats sitting around wooden tables and smoking dispassionately. My entrance and my company's money aroused them from their reverie. I felt for certain I would be mugged as soon as I exited the airport. I wasn't, but I didn't forget the lesson either. To restate the obvious: foreigners with a large amount of cash are always a great target for robbery. (Foreigners without cash are also generally suspected of having lots of money.)

Another important point: bring only crisp, clean dollar bills to Ukraine. This means no bills that are well-worn, torn, or crumpled. I've had bills rejected because of very slight ink markings. Eventually you will be able to exchange your crumpled notes for better ones, but it's easier to start with crisp, new bills.

As for credit cards, we chose our hotel in part because it accepted plastic at a time when few hotels did. Fortunately, in Kyiv and the larger cities credit cards are often accepted so there are a number of options for foreigners now; elsewhere, acceptance of credit cards is not so widespread yet. (Problems still arise with Visa and MasterCard transactions. I've heard warnings to watch your statements for double billing. All Visa-type transactions until recently had to clear through Moscow, and hotels would therefore set limits on the amounts that you could charge. For example, a limit of $500 meant around three nights' stay at the standard expat rates in Kyiv, depending, of course, on your choice of hotel.)

One more point on leaving the airport: luggage carts are available for a fee, but there are no bellmen around to assist you with luggage.

LOST LUGGAGE

There were many times (most frequently when flying through Frankfurt) when our luggage to Kyiv was delayed by a day or two, and it once took Frankfurt a full week to send several bags to the United States. Once I received a nylon suitcase one day late that had been sewn shut in Frankfurt, but at least nothing was stolen! Fortunately, we always received our late luggage and without anything missing, but this meant returning to the airport and a lot of hassles to deal with. I say, avoid Frankfurt connections if you can, but that's one of my biases, supported by statistics from some Irish airline consultants. Only on a domestic flight was I aware of tampered luggage: a close friend had a pair of shoes and other personal items filched from his suitcase in transit.

WHEN WE WERE ALL MILLIONAIRES

The new currency, the *hryvnia* (say *HREEvnya*), was introduced in 1996. In the Middle Ages, the *hryvnia* existed in the form of silver ingots. Indeed, war erupted in Novgorod in 1462 when these were replaced by smaller, thinner coins.

The Russian ruble was the currency in all Soviet republics. After independence in 1992, Ukraine's interim currency called the *karbovanets*, or simply the *kupon*, was introduced and all coins were abolished. When the *hryvnia* was reintroduced in 1996, coins were also reintroduced. These are now Ukrainian kopeks, as opposed to Russian or Soviet kopeks, and one *hryvnia* is composed of 100 kopeks. (In the twelve-month period before the *hryvnia* was introduced, the *kupon* fluctuated from around 175,000 *kupon* to 195,000 *kupon* to the US dollar.)

How I loved the transitional currency! *Karbovanets* (Krb.) is difficult to pronounce (a friend jokingly called them "car payments") but easier than *hryvnia* (pronounced *gryvnia* in Russian), which followed it. In 1996, before the *hryvnia* was introduced, the largest bill in circulation was the million-*kupon* note, worth roughly $5.25. At that time, USAID recommended that contractors pay local staff in local currency. I thought of the stories of German wheelbarrows filled with worthless money during the 1920s, and declined the suggestion, which fortunately USAID did not follow either. They fell under the umbrella of the United States Embassy and followed the Embassy's guidelines. Since we were under the USAID umbrella, so did we, and the Ukrainian staff was all the happier for it. (Because there were no coins in the transition period, public phones were free! More on Lenin's dream of free telephones under Telephones below.)

The government had been unwilling to introduce the new *hryvnia* currency until it believed that inflation had more or less stabilized. The earliest *hryvnia* bills in fact show dates of 1992 and were locked in vaults until 1996. There were two variants of the one-*hryvnia* note, one produced in Canada and the other in Ukraine. The *hryvnia* was introduced at roughly 1.80 *hryvnia* (or 180,000 Krb) to the US dollar. I felt certain math scores in Ukraine would soar—once the "000" was lopped off!

The official symbol for the *hryvnia* is UAH. UA comes from the first and last letters of *Ukraina*, the Ukrainian name for Ukraine, and H from *Hryvnia*. The plural of *hryvnia* is *hryven*, not *hryvnias*.

One note about small change. Don't be surprised by the common practice in small groceries and Western-styled shops of giving gum or candy to customers when change is not available. With the reintroduction of coins, this should be a less common occurrence. I had a friend who once returned a stick of gum to a shopkeeper when she found herself a few kupons short. The shopkeeper was perplexed to find the tables turned!

OPENING A BANK ACCOUNT

If you want to open a personal account, it's quite easy to do. There are a number of banks, many of which I wouldn't trust, but there are good ones. The scenario is this: they'll take your money and charge you every time you want to withdraw any money. The rates used to be usurious, and now they are merely outrageous. It's part of the cost of doing business. Budget for this expense.

If you want to open a business account, it's much more difficult. My firm wanted me to open a personal account for company use; many other firms are successfully doing this. Just remember, Americans have to report all foreign accounts to the IRS. (What are the laws in your native country?) My stance is, I don't advise this, just as I'd now say don't carry a lot of company money when you enter the country. But I also know that imperfect decisions are made as temporary solutions to seemingly overwhelming obstacles. We can only hope that some of these systemic inefficiencies inherited from the FSU will die a natural death—and sooner rather than later.

For business accounts, you will need endless documents, including articles of incorporation and bylaws, translated into Ukrainian and notarized, another surrealistic all-day event. Stamps and seals are still regarded as very important in Ukraine and we nearly had our bank account frozen two months after we opened it, because someone realized we had no official company stamp. You can get around some requirements if you fall under one of the international aid umbrellas. This is to say that you are an approved development contractor (as opposed to a private enterprise) and therefore not subject to laws requiring legal registration of your firm. The Big Five accounting firms, for example, are in-country implementing international aid contracts; they maintain separate registered offices with standard business bank accounts for their consulting practices.

Once you've successfully opened your bank account, you'll have to deal with the exasperating process required whenever you enter the bank to do business. After passing armed guards, you will show your passport to a bank officer, who will enter your information into a computer. Guards will continue to monitor every step you take, and you won't be allowed into the room with the tellers until it's your turn. This means you'll stand with other patrons on the hallway steps as you wait. You should have a car and driver waiting, i.e., don't just have a cab drop you off, as shady types hang around outside the banks. If possible, bring a friend or driver/bodyguard into the bank with you.

My firm opted to put a vault in the office to minimize the time wasted at the bank. Compare the value of a vault against the risks of not having one in your particular case. For firms taking in cash receipts, there are endless rules and regulations about how much cash you can have on hand.

HOTELS BEFORE APARTMENTS

Before you settle into an apartment, you will probably spend some time in a Ukrainian hotel. Or you might travel to other Ukrainian cities on business. Ukrainian hotels are surely part of the expatriate experience. Interestingly, they are one of the few businesses that had contact with foreigners during the Soviet period but still seem stuck in their Intourist ways, which is to say, quite Soviet and far from service-oriented. But the situation is gradually improving. ("Intourist" is the name of the Soviet agency with which foreigners were obliged to make all hotel and travel plans during Soviet times.)

The vast majority of Ukrainian hotels are still Intourist-run and outrageously expensive. Kyiv, unlike Lviv, still lacks anything approximating a truly Western-style hotel. The Grand Hotel in Lviv stands out among Ukrainian hotels—it is considered one of the best in Central Europe—but there is an ugly story behind it. A Pennsylvanian heiress purportedly helped to restore the hotel to its former glory based on tales her grandmother had told her as a child. Once renovated, the American investor who needed a Ukrainian partner hired a Ukrainian relative to oversee her interest. The relative was murdered, and the investor quietly withdrew from the picture.

Doormen guard entry in the larger hotels and supposedly keep out the riffraff. There used to be a female attendant on each floor who would keep your key (*kliuch*) while you were away. The "floor mom" (*dezhernaya* in Russian; *chertoviy* in Ukrainian) is still present, but her role is less apparent. She cleans the rooms and provides hot water for tea, while she monitors the comings and goings of hotel guests on her floor. In those hotels and on those floors where prostitutes are active, the *dezhernaya* gets a cut for permitting the prostitutes access. The doormen do too.

As a female, I was usually placed on a floor where prostitutes didn't come knocking. On one occasion, the *dezhernaya* at the Hotel Rus stole my tampax. "Threw it out by accident," I was told when I threw, not by accident, an absolute fit. Tampax is now widely available, but I wanted to make my point. (The Tambrands plant near Borispil is Procter & Gamble's largest such factory in Europe.)

Another night the *dezhernaya* must have been paid off on my floor, as she was nowhere around, and several bodyguards were in the hall and noisy all night. They were there to protect an American all-girls pop band visiting Kyiv. In the early hours of morning, these guards were sprawled out in chairs in the hallway, heads thrown back, mouths open. Their blazers were open too, guns concealed the night before now clearly visible.

Most of the Intourist hotels look ragged around the edges, although sometimes you can tell how nice the hotel once was; this is especially true for the hotels reserved for Party deputies. Still, the Soviet architecture is generally gray and depressing; inside, dark murals adorn the halls, and large banquet halls serve stodgy, greasy

meals amidst a background of loud, scratchy speakers blaring sentimental music. Men at the tables down vodka in greedy gulps, and
couples glide across the dance floor.

As I mentioned above, if you work for your country's embassy (or
in some related capacity) and you are living abroad for a minimum of
twelve months, you may be eligible for what is commonly called the
green card. We called it the "get-out-of-jail-free card" because of the
reference on the back of the card to the Venice Convention of 1961
and diplomatic immunity. Holders of the card receive the diplomatic
hotel rate and reduced domestic airfares.

Intourist Travel Services

I've heard it said that Intourist retains its pro-Russian bias, meaning
not pro-Ukrainian; more likely, the problem is Intourist-speak (*tufta*)
in general. I don't know of expatriates relying on its travel services,
but the agency may be a source of information for hikers and campers
who enjoy traveling farther afield. I've met a few adventurous souls
who enjoy trekking in the Carpathians, and western Ukraine especially has well-preserved castles and several monasteries worth
visiting. If you want to visit or get suggestions for some of the better
places off the beaten track, perhaps Intourist can provide assistance.

There are also new private travel agencies that might have good
service, although they tend to specialize in overseas travel, to Turkey
and Cyprus, for example.

Dining at an Intourist Hotel

In the old days, you often wondered why the waiter didn't begin by
telling you what was unavailable and what you should therefore
order; it would have saved both you and the waiter a lot of time. Today
the food listed on the menu is generally available, or there won't be
a price next to the item. (Be aware that weights and measures for food
and alcohol listed on the menu may not be the same as the standard
serving amount that you'll get.)

If you are staying in Kyiv, more than likely you won't take so many meals at the hotel, given the dramatic increase in the number of restaurants. But eating out is expensive, whereas hotel dining rooms are not. I always recommend checking to see if there is borshch on the menu, very likely served with the tasty garlic rolls called *pampushky*. If borshch isn't on the menu, there may be other soups available, such as *solyanky* (see Chapter Four).

Soups are never eaten as a main course, although you can order as you like. The most common Intourist entree these days is greasy chicken or a pork cutlet with undercooked fried potatoes, also greasy and limp. Chicken Kiev is really a tourist item, but I enjoy it, especially when my cholesterol level is in remission.

Hotel Services and Phones

In my hotel room I had two telephone lines, but one was useless, and all I got was a staticky radio connection. We all had direct lines into our rooms, as these were easier to tap in the old days.

The good news now is that your international callers don't have to deal with Ukrainian hotel operators. Frequently, though, hotels make it impossible to place international calls using AT&T and other carriers by blocking the access numbers so that you are obliged to use the hotel services and hence pay the hotel for your calls. They leave a bill for you the next day; they even stopped me as I walked by to tell me about it. You must pay this bill in cash; it won't be added to your room charges.

If and when you can, it's a good idea to ask your family and colleagues to initiate international calls; rates from Ukraine are significantly more expensive.

On a silly note, when Price Waterhouse had a temporary office in the Hotel Rus, one consultant was given a whopping phone bill after three months but without a breakdown of any calls. She requested more details, whereupon she received the phone log of every call made in the hotel, not just calls from her office.

Hotel shops now stock very basic supplies such as shampoo, razor blades, cheap pens, city maps, alcohol, juices, as well as overpriced souvenirs, including amber and the ubiquitous nesting dolls called *matrioshky*. It's always better to buy the touristy items elsewhere. Buy some bottled water before you need it, or try the hotel's dining room if the shops are closed.

A hotel business office can assist you in sending faxes, and this service is sometimes absolutely necessary. The Hotel Rus Business Center earned genuine kudos for friendliness and helpfulness, in marked contrast to the hotel's other departments. Once, I was forced to pay for a hand-towel, which hotel staff insisted I had swiped.

The various telephone exchanges throughout any given city differ in quality. In Kyiv, they are generally best in the areas close to embassies. The 1998 renovation of Kreshchatyk promised, among other things, better communication lines. It is still sometimes impossible to get your urgent faxes through. Be kind to the business office staff; you might just be rewarded in spades.

FINDING AN APARTMENT

Urban Ukrainians live in apartments rather than detached houses. Houses tend to be out in the rural areas. The following sections apply to my experiences in Kyiv, but the basic considerations regarding accommodation would probably be the same for other cities.

The options for finding apartments largely depend on your needs and preferences. First, you'll have to decide if you want to pay for Western-styled conveniences in renovated apartments; good local standard but centrally located; or flats that are off the beaten track, where you may well save lots of money, but your Russian and patience had better be up to snuff.

Many Ukrainians today are eager to let their apartments to foreigners for a high rent. They move in with relatives or move out to the *dacha*, weather permitting, and make do. This is especially true for older Ukrainians who cannot survive on their meager pensions.

Beautiful archways adorn Kyiv's streets. (Photo courtesy of Meredith Dalton.)

I've heard that you should not rent an apartment on the top floor because deteriorating roofs cause problems. I never had this problem, but I know of one friend whose roof caught on fire, and his apartment on the top floor sustained significant damage. His personal art collection was spared, but the walls were badly damaged by water from the fire-hoses and subsequent molding.

On the other hand, I've heard of worse cases where the fire department could not properly respond to a fire because the city's charming, turn-of-the-century archways were designed for horse and carriage access, not for modern-day fire trucks. It is a good idea to bring with you or buy a portable smoke alarm. Your neighbors are

unlikely to have one, but you increase your own chances of survival in the event of fire, and you might even help save a neighbor's life in the process.

If you want to live in the city center, you can get advice and ideas from friends, and there are many real estate agents eager to help. Ask what their fee is: most common is 10% of the first year's rent or one-half of one month's rent. If you're staying under one year the 10% is based on the annual rent. Deposit requirements can be huge, but I've also found these negotiable. Kyiv is still no Moscow, thankfully.

Contracts—How Useless Are They?

Contracts are essentially non-enforceable, and clauses like "The landlord will give 72 hours notice before entering the premises" may well be disregarded. If you work for a foreign company, your employer may insist that you have a signed contract nonetheless.

In most cases, there will be two apartment contracts, one in Ukrainian, the other in English. The former will include a ridiculously low rental fee, and this is the one that taxes will be paid on, if paid at all. Our English contract stipulated that this version superseded all others (this was for my company's records). I also suggest an appendix to the contract that lists apartment furniture, just to be on the safe side. Because of the need for two contracts, the tenant may have some bargaining power on issues such as deposits, or a satellite dish. If you choose not to sign two contracts, finding apartments may prove more difficult.

As an aside, I have heard of scams where someone contacts you claiming to be a friend of the landlord; he needs to pick up a specific book. (Many apartments boast at least one central bookcase holding a large book collection.) Since you will have no idea where the (fictitious) book is, you may think to let the stranger in to look around. The person is not a friend of the landlord, but someone who wants to rob you. If you get a similar request, tell the person to come back in 72 hours, after you check with the landlord.

Logistics Companies

Logistics companies are a good solution for your needs upon arrival in Ukraine. Fees are high, but the logistics people can get you rolling. They will help you locate apartments for living and for office space, as well as find interpreters and drivers on a short-term basis. They'll even help you find long-term staff if you like. You might try to contact one and have their representative meet you at the airport the first time you arrive; probably you'll have an English-speaker to boot. You shouldn't have to pay any more than the airport mafia's taxi prices.

Remont

Remont is the Russian and Ukrainian term for reconstruction, renovation, or repair. As stated in Chapter Three, *remont* is one of those terms every expatriate knows and uses. I guess this is because it's more succinct than "renovation" or "reconstruction." Also, it seems to have a particular application: for example, if repairs end up taking longer than expected, it isn't all that surprising. It's *remont*, no?

To supply materials for growing construction needs, more hardware shops are appearing throughout the city.

Centralized Heating, Hot Water, and Other Utilities

Many Soviet-style homes display rugs on their walls providing decorative flourishes and some insulation. The latter can come in handy, since such homes are noted for their absence (or excess) of heat. You get it when it is turned on, often around the first of November. Be prepared to wait and see if your apartment windows can be opened, in the event too much heat gives you a headache. Regardless, expect to buy a space heater or two, and be wary of blowing fuses when you use the heater and run, for example, the television at the same time. Know where the fuse box is and what to do with it. All in all I was quite comfortable at home with my space heater, even during the coldest winter in more than fifty years.

A duvet helps. In Ukraine, bedcovers are often duvets made from two decorated sheets sewn together; a large diamond shape is cut out of the top sheet. Inside the duvet is typically a scratchy wool blanket. I purchased several duvets at TSUM (see page 214 for more) as gifts.

In the summer months, you may need to buy fans for your apartment. The absence of screens can be a problem. My little sister brought from home a couple of 99-cent fly-swatters and I didn't need to install screens. I once had a bat fly into my apartment in the middle of the night. My first thought was "intruder"; then I thought " bird;" finally, I thought about rabies.

Hot water, assuming you have it, comes from a central boiler house. Due to age and the shortage of parts, there will be frequent repairs, often for days at a time. In the summer, there is generally a period of about three weeks when designated parts of the city will have no hot water. It is then that the bulk of the annual repairs is made to the system. If you don't have a separate hot water heater, expect to take cold showers.

For your bathroom sink and tub, consider bringing extra plugs, just in case. Otherwise, you can improvise or find these at TSUM. (My sister also brought me a small oven thermometer so I could bake with greater accuracy.)

If you can, try to include the cost of utilities into your rent. It's not that they will be high (although your landlord may disagree), but payment is another hassle for you to deal with. If it is your responsibility to pay for your utilities, understand that you will receive a monthly bill, and you will have to pay this in person, standing in line at the post office. Your landlord may insist you pay him so he'll be sure that you paid. The bill is still in his family's name, after all.

Laundry Services and Dry Cleaners

Many apartments will have a small washing machine, and in many cases your landlady or housekeeper will do your laundry and ironing (and think you have entirely too much—no matter how much or little it actually is). My landlady didn't want me using her machine, so she paid a housekeeper (out of my rent money) to assist me not only with my washing but with ironing, cooking, and shopping if I desired.

If your apartment does not have a machine, it may well be worth the investment. I really don't know how Ukrainian women survive without washing machines, what with all the cooking, shopping, cleaning, and other work that they do. I vaguely recall a public laundromat, but it was not convenient to downtown Kyiv. A far better idea would be to find someone who wants to earn a little cash on the side. Ask at your office for suggestions.

The number of Western-styled dry cleaners is steadily increasing with good locations throughout the city. As economic principles would have it, their formerly outrageous prices have started to come down. The American Dry Cleaners has several branches, including one on Kreshchatyk, but there are other decent firms as well.

Housekeepers and Domestic Help

Many apartments come with maid service; that is to say, the housekeeper is often included as part of the rent. Frequently, people rent out their apartments fully furnished to foreigners and therefore want someone to watch over their possessions. How better to do this than to build into the rental price the services of a maid? In many cases, the housekeeper will be the landlady. In my case, I had my apartment cleaned, my clothes washed and ironed, and borshch prepared when I requested it. My housekeeper also made the best dill pickles I ever tasted! Obviously, contract terms, like landlords and housekeepers, will vary.

It is often hard to communicate the concept of privacy (or lease) to landlords. I insisted that the landlord inform me, the tenant, in advance of periodic visits. While this should be written into your lease agreement, remember that contracts aren't enforceable. I've heard of bad landlord situations, but most are manageable with some diplomacy and a cup of hot tea (or maybe the occasional glass of vodka).

ON TELEPHONES

Cell Phone Junkies

The Soviet joke in Chapter Three about having a refrigerator delivered in ten years (on precisely the same day that the plumber was coming) didn't make reference to Soviet phones, I think, because it would be more painful than funny. The stories about waiting for phones—and then no phone books or city maps to assist in locating people—are legion. Even today, waiting for a phone is still a huge problem and exorbitantly expensive.

The attractiveness of apartments often relates to the number of phone lines, especially if the apartment is to be used as office space (these are generally rented without furniture). Also, as stated earlier, some parts of the city have better exchanges, meaning much clearer phone lines.

For long-distance calls, there is now UTEL, a Ukrainian-Dutch joint venture, and Western companies like Sprint and AT&T are in Ukraine. Still, the network in place is not always able to cope with current demands. As a result, many Ukrainian and foreign business-men in Kyiv and other cities are forced to purchase cellular phones.

Seedy mafioso types are not the only ones carrying cell phones, especially now that prices have become more affordable. You can lease cell phones in Kyiv. Check the Kyiv Business Pages (available for free or for sale in Kyiv, but also on the Internet); prices in late 1998 were $7/day plus calls. (Nokia is the most aggressive advertiser on Jay Leno's The Tonight Show, piped in via satellite.)

Although I highly recommend cell phones in this day and age, and sometimes they seem absolutely necessary to conduct business here, you should note that business is never conducted solely by phone. The phone is used to set up (and confirm) appointments and to let someone know if, for example, you are stuck in traffic. Business etiquette still requires that the parties meet face to face.

Telephone Etiquette

The old practice of hanging up the phone if the call wasn't for you is not entirely a thing of the past. Even today you can see this in business meetings, and sometimes it's hard to stifle a chuckle. There you'll be in a meeting with a bureaucrat whose desk is covered with old-fashioned rotary phones. (Five or more in a row is not uncommon.) One phone rings, and a silent hand reaches discreetly for it, raises it a centimeter or so, and quietly drops it back on the hook. Almost imperceptibly. Except first you heard a phone ring, and then the hand scurried across the desk. The face in front of you never acknowledges a thing.

When you place a call, you normally hear one of three responses:

Allo, much like the French use of the same. It is never used as a greeting in the street, per se. It is reserved for telephone usage.

Da, which simply means "yes," is common.

Ya slukhayu, which translates as "I'm listening."

Often you will hear someone say "*Allo, allo*" repeatedly if there is a pause in conversation. Irritating in any language, this is a carry-over from the days when cutoffs (as well as wire taps) were frequent, and you might as well hang up if you are disconnected.

As in many parts of the world, Ukrainians divide telephone numbers into thirds, thus 229-3841 becomes 229-38-41. You may well have to repeat and/or record telephone numbers a lot, so it's good to practice your numbers in Ukrainian or Russian early on.

A Digression

My favorite story about Ukrainian telephones stems from Lenin's dream of a day when all phones would be free in the new world he envisioned. During 1992–96, the years of the interim currency, *karbovanets*, there were no coins in Ukraine. (By contrast, Russia retained kopek coins during this period; in Moscow in 1992 the two-kopek coin was the most sought after because it was used in public phones. A few enterprising types would stand by public phones and sell them at a premium—often pretending to have no other change.) By the mid-1990s, half of Ukraine's pay phones weren't working; the others were free of charge due to the absence of coins. All this began changing in late 1996; phone cards appeared around the same time that kopek coins made a comeback. But for that one short period in Ukrainian history, Lenin's dream of free phones had become a reality in coin-free Ukraine.

Local and International Telephone Calls

Local calls from pay phones now require phone cards that are sold at the post office.

Note the emergency access numbers from all Ukrainian phones:

01—fire

02—police

03—ambulance

When placing long distance calls, dial 8 and wait for another dial tone. When calling within Ukraine, dial the following city codes followed by the local number. Always include the initial zero with the city codes: for example Kharkiv is 0472, Kyiv is 044, Lviv is 0322, Odesa is 0482, Sevastapol is 0692, and Yalta is 060 or 0654.

International callers have several options. They may dial direct or use AT&T, Sprint, or one of several other services now available in Ukraine. It is no longer necessary to book in advance international calls to Asia; however, expatriates from the United States and Europe should investigate call-back services for international calls where you place a call directly to the United States, enter a personal code, and hang up. Immediately you will receive a call back, whereupon you will enter the telephone number of the person whom you are calling. When signing up for this service you will pay for calls in advance, but the savings will be substantial.

To place an international call directly from an apartment, dial 8, then pause for the second dial tone. For the United States, dial 101, followed by the area code and number. For Europe, dial 8, pause, then dial 100, followed by the specific country code and number.

To access your AT&T operator, dial 8, wait for a new tone, then dial 10011. You can then speak with an operator in English. The English code for a Sprint operator is 10015.

Be forewarned: landlords are very wary of expatriates' phone bills and will even discourage phone use by saying your calls will be tapped. I promised my landlady to use a credit card; she was skeptical but allowed me the use of her phone because she liked me (and also my large monthly rent payments).

How To Pay Your Telephone Bill

All bills must be paid in full within 10 days. You must go in person to the post office and queue. You may enjoy this sort of "Soviet" experience once, but after that you will probably think of better ways to spend your days in Ukraine. It is good if you can send a housekeeper or office employee to stand in line for you and pay your bills.

INTERNATIONAL SCHOOLS

Education for Ukrainians begins at age six, and primary school lasts four years. Secondary school lasts seven more. A diploma is awarded upon completion of ninth grade or ninth form. Those remaining in secondary school for the final two years are preparing to enter a university or technical college. There are also technical courses available upon leaving ninth form.

Instruction is now in Ukrainian with foreign language classes offered in Russian, English, and other languages. A sixth-form student today has more classes in English than Russian or Ukrainian, as well as introductory German. Soviet textbooks were in Russian and are now being translated into Ukrainian. One high school student described his difficulty in learning Latin, precisely because the instruction is in Ukrainian, formerly a foreign language to him!

There are over fifteen universities in Ukraine. (One-third of these were established recently, and some are not yet accredited.) College admissions are competitive. Stories of bribes are not uncommon, but many students earned their places. The level of education in Ukraine is very high and may be one of the best incentives for considering doing business here. Ukraine also boasts high computer literacy. Kyiv was considered a center for computer programmers in the Soviet era.

For international families living in Kyiv, the city now boasts several international schools. They are very expensive, but the majority of expatriate children attends one of them. Compensation packages for Western employees of some companies include private tuition for their children.

HERE'S TO HEALTH

Pre-Departure Health concerns

The Center for Disease Control (CDC), at (404) 332-4565, provides Americans with up-to-date information regarding recommended immunizations before leaving the country. You can also check their website at www.CDC.org.

It is a good idea to consider purchasing SOS or Medevac insurance before you leave. It's cheap and provides peace of mind. If you are the holder of an international student identity card, the annual fee includes SOS insurance. This is medical evacuation insurance. In the event of a medical emergency, you will be flown to the nearest acceptable medical center. This does not mean the United States, Canada, or Britain. It will more likely be Vienna, where I was flown for a dental emergency in 1995. (SOS had wanted to send me to Moscow, but I objected strenuously, as this had not been done before. I was worried about dental care at that time as well as last-minute visa requirements.) The SOS service was highly professional, and I recommend this insurance. SOS does not pay any hotel, hospital, or other medical expenses. It is purely for evacuations. I have heard of special clauses providing for mafia-related evacuations—probably not exactly what you wanted to hear.

Testing for AIDS is still not required for long-term visitors to Ukraine, although it is for Russia. If possible, have your test results translated into Russian (in most places easier to do than Ukrainian and just as acceptable) and signed and stamped, if possible, by a medical professional. Remember: the more official the better, but still be prepared for bureaucratic hassles.

Hospitals

I've heard lots of stories about the necessity of bribing Ukrainian doctors; most foreigners will use the Western clinics if given half a chance. There is now a Swiss-Ukrainian joint venture for dental care, and other facilities are cropping up. These are the latest recommendations, but check with your embassy and other expats for more recent suggestions.

The American Medical Center now offers dental care in addition to its standard medical services. Again, in the event of dire emergencies or should local treatment be unavailable, your SOS insurance will provide necessary medical evacuations. There is a large chain of dental offices throughout Kyiv with the same name. Not all these offices were created equal, so check with your friends or call the staff nurse at your embassy.

If you are sick, be prepared for unsolicited references to herbal and homeopathic remedies. My suggestion is to hear the ideas out. Some of the remedies may be worth trying.

Pharmacists (chemists to some of you) are called *apTYEka*; think of the word "apothecary" where you can buy most medicines without a prescription, assuming that they are available. There are several quasi-Western-style pharmacies, including one Swiss joint venture on Passazh off Kreshchatyk.

An Aside: The Good News About Hospitalization

In 1996, some of the government officials with whom we were working were accused of corrupt practices. In one day, four arrests were made in the Ministry of Agriculture. The head honcho disappeared, and we heard no news of him for several days. It turned out that he was fine, and just recuperating in the hospital. In Ukraine, you cannot be arrested if you're hospitalized!

SHOPPING GUIDE

Grocery Shopping: Western-style and Local-style

It is in grocery shopping that the dollar/*hryvnia* economic zones become most apparent. Most ordinary Ukrainians will not patronize Western stores or expatriate restaurants. They frequent the state stores

Bessarabskiy Rynok off Khreshchatyk. (Photo courtesy of Meredith Dalton.)

with their simple but now plentiful food. There is even a disdain, in a distinctly Soviet, almost anti-material way, for these Western grocery stores and restaurants and those who frequent them.

This is not to say that Ukrainians aren't to be found in the more expensive restaurants, but a lunch at many of these may well cost half a day's salary for those who are working for an expat firm. It is simply impossible on most local salaries. So the people you encounter here will most likely be young entrepreneurs, the bilingual staff of Western firms who were introduced to these establishments by their colleagues, and mafia types doing whatever it is that they do.

As an expatriate living an expatriate life you'll also shop in the local stores. A *hastronom* is the state equivalent of a grocery store. It typically carries pasta and local products. You may have to queue here three times to buy your products: in the first queue you will select the product and request a receipt indicating its price; you will then pay at another counter where the receipt is marked as paid; in the final queue you will hand over the receipt in exchange for your purchased goods. This is also the practice in pharmacies and lots of other stores. Sometimes you will not receive a receipt at the first step; you'll ask the price, then tell the cashier how much your item costs. She'll give you a receipt for that amount, which you'll then trade for the item.

You'll likely spend more time at the *rynok* than *hastronom*. *Rynok* means "farmer's market" and is a popular word among expatriates (like *remont*). Here you won't be dealing with all these silly receipts; you will pay the seller directly. I love to hear the sound of clanking abacus beads in some of the *rynok* stalls.

For those living or working near downtown Kyiv, the Bessarabskiy Rynok is where you and your fellow Ukrainians can buy cheese, eggs, and a wide range of sausages as well as most vegetables and fruit. Don't worry if you forget to bring plastic bags; you can always buy one from the many old women who sell them. The bag designs are generally wholesome; flowers, smiling couples, children or their beloved pets predominate, but the occasional half-clothed beauty sneaks her way into the available choices. While standard backpacks are much sturdier, some folks recommend that you carry plastic bags like a local and blend in more.

The Western stores also carry fruit and vegetables at premium prices. More importantly, this is probably your best source for imported cheeses, frozen entrees, smoked salmon, soup mixes, pasta sauces, olive oil, Irish beers, and expensive gin—essentially many of the food products you'll want, although not always when you want them. Even peanut butter has arrived, although the brands are a little strange for American tastes.

For everyday shopping, often your housekeeper can help. She can negotiate good prices on vegetables, for example; but I've also been refused certain items that were not a good buy, according to my housekeeper, even though I requested and needed them.

TSUM on Kreshchatyk is the Kyiv equivalent of Moscow's famous GUM. TSUM stands for Central Department Store. (Photo courtesy of Meredith Dalton.)

The *univermag* (say *ooneeverMAHG*—from *universalny magazin*, or universal store) is a department store selling select groceries, hardware, household appliances, clothing, children's toys, and other goods. Modeled after Moscow's celebrated GUM, for *Gosudarstveny* (or State) *Univermag*, TSUM, for *TSentralny* (Central) *Univermag*, was its equivalent in Ukraine (and in all Soviet cities). All the cities in Ukraine still have one. In addition to selling egg crates and duvet covers, you can find sweet chocolates, sweet Soviet champagne (as it is still called) or the deep red, Crimean champagne, alongside corkscrews, batteries, light bulbs, videotapes, coffee grinders, and much more. Greasy cream pastries served on slips of coarse paper are sold on little carts near the entrances.

Kiosk Culture and the Free-Standing Vendors

Kiosks have sprouted like mushrooms in the cities around metro stations, train stations, and on major thoroughfares, as well as in the underground passageways. These kiosks were one of the earliest forms of post-communist private enterprise. In many places, the government has cracked down on the number of street vendors.

Originally, "kiosk," taken from the French, referred to Soviet billboards that displayed newspapers and Party propaganda, as well as opera and theater schedules. Today's kiosks resemble glass and metal sheds. Magazines and sundries are sold, but food and drink items are the most common—imported cookies, juice, European beers alongside Kyiv's Obolon, and a wide array of vodkas and imported spirits. There are even plastic cups of vodka covered with aluminum foil lids and Stolichnaya vodka (from Russia) in cans. Kiosks selling non-food items such as inexpensive watches, jewelry, and Chinese knock-off Swiss Army knives are often found in the underground passageways.

Alongside kiosks both at and below street level, vendors set up stands using portable tables, stacked fruit crates, or boxes. Their array of food and cosmetic products is often the same as that carried by the kiosk vendors. Mars and Snickers bars (sometimes past their expiration date), imported bubble gum, shampoos, inexpensive caviar, olive oil, and razors are common items. Kiosks stick to non-perishables, while freestanding vendors sell perishables such as bananas, pineapples, kiwis, and plastic bags of milk. Underground, you'll find artisans selling a range of products including handcarved wooden combs, lovely wooden boxes from western Ukraine, origami mobiles for children, and handmade potholders. Artists will display their works for sale; some will sketch you in charcoal. There are several artists to choose from, and their portrait prices are very reasonable. You will also see cigarette sellers, usually older women, who carry trays suspended from their necks like vendors at a baseball game. There are also the flower vendors, of course.

Separate stands are devoted to books, bootleg videotapes (mostly in PAL VHS format), or bootleg compact discs with typos on the xeroxed notes. It is easy to find CD-ROMs that include huge libraries of bootleg computer programs. (The joke that China has only one registered copy of any Microsoft product seems equally valid here.)

There are also small tables set up with various types and sizes of batteries for calculator and watch repairs. You can find shoe repair shops, locksmiths, and shops that specialize in developing film.

Shopping for Clothes and Cosmetics

Benetton came early to Ukraine and today has stores in Kyiv, Odesa, Lviv, and elsewhere. There are guards posted outside Kyiv's Kreshchatyk store to control what are sometimes artificial queues (à la Hard Rock Café), intended to create a sense of excitement. Most foreigners still prefer to bring in from the West the clothes that they will need. Shopping in Kyiv simply cannot compete with Warsaw, Moscow, and St. Petersburg. The good news is that most foreigners will save money, certainly in terms of impulse buying.

Italian shoes are available for a small fortune at Fendi, and new places are cropping up; I advise bringing boots from home, as well as

215

sensible shoes for pounding the pavement. (Know that whatever shoes you bring will be ruined by trampling the streets.) An extra supply of pantyhose is also a good idea. Some inexpensive shoe polish and a small sewing kit I took along also proved handy; these are available but convenient to have on hand. Shoe repair is generally easy to find throughout the city.

Cosmetics are becoming big business in Ukraine, with Lancôme, Avon, and others now available. Prices are high, but the women of former Soviet republics are a good market opportunity after years of greedily devouring the slick pages of cosmetics advertisements found in then-contraband *Cosmopolitan* and *Vogue*. There are now Russian-language versions of these publications, along with Russian *Playboy* and other popular Russian and Ukrainian magazines.

Hair Salons

So you want to get your hair cut? There are state salons, worth at least one visit. How good are your language skills? And don't be scared off by the older women with henna or even bluish Soviet hair dyes if all you need is a simple cut. I knew a USAID worker who would only get her hair cut when she left the country, which seems extreme.

Don't expect to find a Western salon atmosphere in Kyiv yet; and salons in the other cities will probably have even less to offer. You might feel more comfortable checking with the hotel hairdressers, where fees are higher, but they are used to Western clients and their demands. Like so much other advice, talk to friends, expat and local.

I went once to a hair-cutting school, right off Kreshchatyk near Passazh, recommended by my office assistant. We had to wait a long time because the woman we wanted was booked up. I ended up with a young male hairdresser, who boasted he could cut my hair faster than any cut I had had in the United States. I told him that being the fastest was not the most important point when it comes to haircuts, but speed seemed at the time to be more of a challenge than a client's request. The cut was fine. I also had a woman come to my apartment once, but I wasn't too pleased with her blunt scissors or the haircut. But I'm not a great judge on this topic. I think I let down "the fastest haircutter in the East" by my lack of salon knowledge; he certainly knew a lot more about American shampoos and styles than his first American client!

Gifts for Friends and Family

Ukraine is noted for its handicrafts, and there are several good options for buying these.

The *Berioshka* ("birch" in Russian) stores, from the Soviet days were the hard currency stores where only tourists shopped, since it was illegal for Soviets to own foreign currencies. This also limited contact between foreigners and local citizens. *Kashtan* (meaning "chestnut") is what these state stores were called in Ukraine; this seems appropriate given the number of chestnut trees lining Kreshchatyk Avenue on which the Kyiv store is located. The stores carried in addition to very limited food items like sweet Soviet champagne and chocolates, tourist items like *matrioshky* (nesting dolls) or Russian lacquer boxes, both well known in the West. The days of the *Berioshka* are over, although you may see *Kashtan* stores in Ukraine. They are usually uninteresting post-communist stores.

For souvenirs I would recommend that you first visit Kyiv's winding, picturesque Andriyivskiy Uzviz (or *Spusk* in Russian, meaning "descent") where you'll find artists and vendors selling their paintings, ceramics, handicrafts, and jewelry. Small statues of Lenin, and other Soviet memorabilia such as badges, military medallions, and stamps are also available. There are lacquer boxes from Palekh, Fedoskino, Mystera, and Kholui (the four celebrated centers for these, all Russian) as well as Ukrainian variants with their own schools. Be wary of stenciled designs or transfers—if you choose to buy these, you should clearly not be paying the price for the hand-painted boxes. The brightly painted wooden spoons and candlesticks make good small gifts.

The ubiquitous *matrioshka* doll, popularized as typically "Russian," has distinctive Ukrainian variants, and is most easily identified by its Ukrainian folk dress or musical instruments. There are also *matrioshky* clearly developed for the Western market—Bill Clinton, Michael Jordan and Chicago Bulls dolls are especially popular.

You can also buy hockey jerseys with the Cyrillic CCCP (literally, SSSR in Russian letters which stood for USSR) and with the names of popular players; Kyiv Dynamo, one of the foremost teams in the Soviet era and now, is the most popular. There are T-shirts designed for the Western market, and slowly the quality is improving as the designs become more varied.

Like samovars, be wary of buying old icons, as it is illegal for any objects made earlier than 1945 to leave the country; customs officials take this seriously. If you buy post-1945 art and plan to take it out of the country with you, you'll need to have receipts for the objects, and, of course, there are separate forms that you will have to fill out and additional taxes to be paid. (This applies to art, not souvenirs.) Ask for details at the time of purchase.

If you can carry them home safely, I would recommend buying *pysanky*, the Ukrainian eggs that are first blown empty and then dyed with rich colors and in painstaking detail. The figurative and more common abstract designs (including modern and traditional patterns) are truly fantastic. Eighteen of twenty-four survived one of my harder trips, and the rewards were well worth the hassle.

Amber jewelry (actually from the Baltic states) is another popular gift item. Also pay attention to the fine Ukrainian embroidery: table runners, placemats and napkin sets, and small wall hangings. Wonderful wooden boxes with inlay of diamond-shaped straw are uniquely Ukrainian, as are the beautiful wooden plates, carved or painted with abstract and representational designs. I gave my mother a lovely miniature *bandura* (*bandurka*), similar to the painted balalaikas one finds in Russia. The *bandura*, a Ukrainian folk instrument from the lute-zither family, is a work of art in itself, even if never played.

Look for Sasha on Kyiv's winding Andriyivskiy Uzviz (Andrew's Descent); he'll cut you a good deal if you mention yours truly. (Photo courtesy of Meredith Dalton.)

On the Uzviz, you can find inexpensive, military hats if you want one. I bought myself an expensive fur hat in TSUM.

Among Ukrainian souvenir shops (*Suveniry Ukrainy*) is a good one in Kyiv near the Pushkin metro stop on Chervonoarmyiska vulytsia (Red Army Street). It offers a wide selection of traditional Ukrainian shirts with embroidered collars. If you want a decorative plate, souvenir shops have larger selections than you might find on a random stroll down the Uzviz. Shop around. But the standard rule of souvenir shopping prevails: if you find something you really want, buy it now. It may not be there when you go back for it.

On the grounds outside St. Sophia's Cathedral, there are two souvenir stores; one specializes more in Russian souvenirs, the other in Ukrainian. In these, you can buy many of the same objects you'll find on Andriyivskiy Uzviz or in the Ukrainian souvenir shops.

Art for Sale

In many of the former Soviet museums, the ubiquitous elderly woman who stands guard will turn on and off the lights as you enter and exit each gallery. The museums of Ukraine cannot compare with the spectacular wealth of St. Petersburg and Moscow, but there are many worth visiting, including some off the beaten path. There are significant fine arts, folk art, and ethnographic collections; don't forget the collections housed in the monasteries.

The fact that Ukraine's trove of fine arts is diminishing is especially disturbing. Given the absence of money for salaries and operating expenses, the survival of both the performing and fine arts is at risk. (Every major city has an opera house, but how well can ballet and opera be supported without improved economic conditions?)

Museums suffer even greater losses with limited funding. Unscrupulous museum directors claim that a lack of money for salaries and maintenance in the post-Soviet era justifies selling selections from their permanent collections. Taken to extremes, money for salaries and everything else won't be needed when there is no longer art to venerate and conserve.

In the West the process of de-accessioning art from permanent collections is well-established and at times necessary. However, the museums follow rigid guidelines: de-accessioning funds, for example, are used for new acquisitions. We can rule out this possibility in Ukraine today, but will staff members really benefit, or are a few individuals lining their pockets? These works of art are not sold via art auctions or public sales, but clandestinely to private collectors.

In 1998 one of Copernicus's invaluable volumes was stolen from the National Library in Kyiv. Only four such volumes were ever produced, and the theft of this priceless treasure is vexing. According to museum officials, a uniformed man came into the non-lending library and requested the Copernicus volume and five other works. The staff didn't question him out of fear of his uniform, which connotes clout to many in the FSU. The man examined the books and left them on the table. He returned a second time; however, when he left this time there were only five books remaining. He had escaped past two guard stations with the irreplaceable volume. One wonders whether library officials really had, as they claimed, no part in the theft.

For Those Who Travel a Lot

You may want to carry either a portable dry iron or steamer with you. Inexpensive small hair-dryers designed for travel have dual-voltage settings (those from Conair are very convenient). You may also want to bring one of the small, dual-voltage hot water heaters for preparing tea or instant soups; again, remember to use bottled water or boil tap water for a long time. (Norelco makes inexpensive folding travel products that can be used with 110 or 220 voltage; you don't need a converter, but you will need to bring adapters so that the plug will fit the local outlets.)

Ukraine uses plugs with the two straight but round pins (type B). I suggest attaching adapters to your appliances in advance, so you will have them when you need them. Most American travel stores charge about $4 apiece for these, but you can also easily buy these at TSUM (on Kreshchatyk in Kyiv) for about $1 each. Bring at least a couple with you. You'll find all the abovementioned products in stores catering to the traveler.

When shopping for converters, buy the better ones that have two settings, so that, for example, CD players and most small appliances can be used with the lower setting, and printers, the higher frequency/voltage (1500). Most laptops and videocameras require no converter, only the two-pin adapter.

PUBLIC TRANSPORTATION

Flights

International flights to Kyiv are increasingly available from major European cities. British Airways, KLM, and Lufthansa are probably the best established carriers, but Malev, Lot, Austrian Air, and Swiss Air have also arrived. Ukraine International alternates every day with Lufthansa from Frankfurt and is perfectly fine. Also, occasionally it is cheaper to buy international airline tickets in Ukraine than abroad due to associated taxes.

Ukraine Air offers flights within Ukraine and the FSU and strikes me now as dodgy. They use former Aeroflot airplanes, often grungy inside and more than a bit frayed. One friend forgot to unbuckle his seatbelt to reach into the overhead compartment. *Nemaye problem* (or in Russian, *nyet problema*), the seatbelt merely moved with him as he stood up! With that said, the airline has not had any major catastrophes in recent years. With domestic prices so high now, Ukrainians don't tend to fly much; for those who need to, Ukraine Air has no competition. Aerosveet is another domestic airline, but it is actually part of Ukraine Air and virtually no different for passengers.

Trains

Ukrainian trains run close to schedule time, and they should as they are incredibly slow. Almost every train is an overnight one, even to travel short distances. You never know if you will be comfortable, freeze to death, or be overheated to severe headache proportions. But such is life in Ukraine. At least if you get this far (i.e., you are on the train), that means you have successfully garnered a ticket. The ticket mafia used to have this area well sealed up, but today there are more options throughout the city for buying tickets in advance.

Fortunately, the old days of two train rates—expat and local—are diminishing. If need be, have a Ukrainian friend buy your ticket for you. Sometimes they will overcharge foreigners if they think they can get away with it. If you show up at the station to buy your ticket just before departure, you will find yourself at the mercy of the train station mafia. They set the rates, and a green card is useless. Your Ukrainian friends won't be much help in this case.

You can only buy tickets that include your starting point. You can't buy a ticket from Lviv to Odesa if you're in Kyiv, and this also means you can't buy three-way tickets: Kyiv to Lviv, Lviv to Odesa, and Odesa back to Kyiv. You can buy one-way or round-trip.

The *providnytsia* (or male *providnyk*) on trains is like the *dezhernaya* (floor mom) in hotels. One hears frequently that she is corruptible. What does this exactly mean? Is this how folks get robbed on overnight trains? Do remember: if you reserve a berth and not the entire car, you can't control who shares the berth with you. There are sleeper cars for two or four people. I've been in both, and they are not all that different. If you are worried about your belongings, they'll be sealed shut beneath the lower berths. Also, bring the right sleeping clothes and slippers.

The *providnytsia* will come by and rent you your overnight sheets, which are not included in the price of the berth. She can bring you coffee or tea in one of the metal tea holders, both in the evening and in the early morning. Learn to travel like a Ukrainian: this means always be prepared for delays. Bring extra food with you as well as extra drinking water and booze should you want it. Toilet paper, handiwipes, and a Swiss army knife are always handy.

My earlier fears about sharing a compartment with strangers have lessened with time and experience. I prefer sharing with three people to one. I have never had problems, and I have often met charming traveling companions.

The Lviv Grand Hotel now owns a special car on overnight trains to Kyiv and Odesa from Lviv. This is a very non-Soviet experience. Many foreigners and wealthy Ukrainians are quite willing to pay the extra dollars for the decor, friendly service, and a clean bathroom! Not only will your bed be made before you depart (with a chocolate left

223

on your pillow), you won't have to wake up to music blaring in your compartment. The Grand Hotel staff has apparently learned how to reduce the radio volume for its passengers.

Cabs in Ukraine

A key part of the Ukrainian experience is sticking out your arm (palm down) and hailing a cabbie—who is really a driver headed in your direction, or he will, for the right fee. I say "he" because almost all drivers in Ukraine are males, with the exception of some tram drivers. Usually, you'll open the passenger door and state your destination. If he's interested, you negotiate the fare. Do this before climbing in. It's polite to climb in the front seat but always smarter to climb in the back. You may offend the driver by using the seat belt, but do it anyway.

The new, official yellow cabs cost slightly more than gypsy cabs, but are very comfortable and worth the price. Some people still prefer to negotiate the fare in advance. If you choose to take a cab from one of the taxi queues at the hotels, the fares will be significantly higher.

Sometimes you have no choice but to walk a few steps more to hail a gypsy cab. The longer you are in Ukraine, the less you will think about the dangers inherent in hailing a gypsy cab, when you have no other options. For the most part, gypsy cabdrivers are good-natured, even when lost. It's when they insist on an unfamiliar "shortcut" that I get nervous, shift closer to the door, and speak up. The truth is I have never had nor heard of problems with gypsy cabdrivers.

My mother (of all people!) most enjoyed my gypsy ride tale although this took place in Moscow, not in Ukraine, and is included here for some lessons I learned from the experience. It was very late, and my friend and I were having trouble hailing a cab when a van pulled up. My friend spoke to the driver and told me to climb in; I thought she would follow, but she was headed in another direction.

That night, I ignored the cardinal rule of never getting into a cab with more than one person. On this occasion, I was so relieved to find a willing driver that I foolishly let down my guard. Inside the van were two women and a man, all friends of the driver, it turned out. I consoled myself that these women were there; naturally, they were the first ones dropped off. I moved closer to the door handle. The men were very courteous, and one offered me a cigarette, which I declined. "Menthol or regular?" he asked. "Juice or beer?" he continued, but he too was soon dropped off. I was able to relax a little. With me as the only passenger, the driver pulled off the road and turned off the engine. He took the bottle opener from his keychain and popped open a warm beer for me. He restarted the car, and I realized now that I was safe but silently cursed my foolishness. Though it was hardly important now, we had also failed to negotiate my fare in advance.

When the van pulled up to my door, I offered the driver a generous fare. He refused my money. He said that he was not a cabbie; he was going my way and wanted to help me out, especially since it was so late. It turned out that he and his companions ran a kiosk on the outskirts of town, which was where he got the drinks. Never since has a gypsy driver refused my money and, despite this driver's kindness, I have never since gotten into a cab with more than one man. Observe the rule of numbers, and be safe. (Also, be wary of sharing elevators; trust any suspicious instincts that you have and act on them. I know an American who was assaulted and robbed on an elevator.)

One night in Kyiv an American friend and I were simply unable to hail a cab. We found ourselves in a deserted area, so we opted to walk briskly to a better lit and more traveled road to find a cab. We were lucky. Public transportation ends sometime after 1:00 a.m., and a city bus, moonlighting as a gypsy cab, stopped for us. We were delivered home safely and in style!

The Metro, Trams, Trolleys, and Buses

Both Kharkiv and Kyiv have metro systems, each with three connecting lines. Some of the stations are lovely Soviet structures (not always oxymoronic!), and while they may have lost some of the luster of Soviet times, vestiges of their glory days remain intact.

The Kyiv metro is one of the deepest in the world. It is said that all stations are on the same level; hence, sometimes it takes two excruciatingly long escalators to reach the metro itself. It is also designed to function as a bomb shelter should the need arise. Presumably construction of the metro lines continued uninterrupted even during the German occupation.

The metro is an inexpensive form of transport. You buy a token (called a *zheton*), and drop it into the turnstile to enter the metro. At the base of each long escalator is a woman seated in a booth; her duty is to see that there are no problems on the escalators. The rails and steps operate at different speeds, which means if you stand rigid from the beginning while holding the rails, you will be stretching to maintain your position at the end.

Public street transportation includes the trams (or *tramvai*), which are streetcars traveling on rails with electric wires overhead. A *trolleibus* (say *troLAYboos*) has wheels like a bus and is attached to

Metro stop, Dynamo Station, Kyiv. (Photo courtesy of Meredith Dalton.)

two overhead wires. An *avtobus* is a bus. For street transportation, you will need a ticket called a *talon,* sold in booklets or individually. There is an honor system aboard; you will stamp your ticket yourself in a small machine or pass it to someone closer to help you out, as frequently it is quite crowded. There are periodic ticket checks to make sure everyone adheres to the honor system.

While the tickets cost the same, there are separate tickets for buses and another for trams and trolleys. I was reprimanded once for using the wrong one, but a gallant Ukrainian spoke up for me, sternly admonishing the attendant that I was a foreigner, and that this was an innocent mistake. I wasn't fined.

You may also buy monthly passes which are available for several days at the beginning of each month. These passes are available for all forms of public transportation: for only the metro, or for only ground transportation.

DRIVING

My first advice to everyone is "hire a driver." I'd opt for that in the United States if it was truly feasible or in any other country for that matter. But Ukrainians are erratic drivers, and the number of cars has expanded vastly since the early years of independence. The streets clearly weren't made to handle the current amount of traffic, and as elsewhere in the world the situation only gets worse with time.

It is possible to rent a car in Ukraine, but would you really want to? Avis arrived recently to compete with the smaller firms already here. Rates are very high, but if you insist on renting a car, call around for quotes.

Whether you drive or are driven, you'll see drivers barreling down sidewalks. You'll also see U-turns in the most unexpected places and more than once I've been in a car when traffic was headed in both directions in a single lane! With such erratic driving, pedestrians should always assume that the driver has the right of way. I know of people being hit in several cases, and I have heard of and witnessed bad car wrecks. Ambulances can be slow in arriving. Honking your horn isn't permitted. (The car alarms going off throughout the city will more than make up for no horns.)

Even in the cities, parking is not the problem one would expect given the rising number of cars. A painted yellow curb, yellow sign, or sign with a red X means "No Parking." A diagonal red stripe means "Temporary Parking only." Most hotels have parking lots, and there are paid parking lots around town. Shady types will try to charge drivers for what appears to be ordinary city parking; sometimes they're successful. But the most enigmatic to me is all the parking— and driving—on sidewalks! (Naturally the drivers who remain near or in their parked cars can simply move off elsewhere if necessary.)

If you have a driver, this is a good opportunity for practicing Russian or Ukrainian (or teaching English, as the case may be). My driver knew where to get fire extinguishers, space heaters, and a 200-pound vault; he also took my shoes to a friend for re-soling, and it didn't cost me a dime, though I tried to pay. My driver assisted in buying and carrying groceries, and I am certain he would have procured more groceries and other favors had I asked. He carried my heavy suitcases and bags whenever necessary and occasionally offered me nicknacks. But more than this, he was a friend and a sort of personal bodyguard, and he would escort me on foot at times when traffic or practicality precluded the possibility of driving. (He also knew who paid his salary, and the concept of *blat* sometimes involves giving small gifts to your boss.)

There are embassy staff who have their cars shipped over, and they don't seem to object to driving as stringently as I do. They also have diplomatic plates, which may help if they are ever pulled over by the dreaded traffic police, known to be among the most corrupt officials; they wave their batons and stop cars at random. If your papers are in order, there isn't much of a problem. But I recall several occasions when my driver returned to the car infuriated that the officer expected a bribe when no violation had been committed.

Driving on Empty

It is a common sight to see drivers refilling their vehicles with gas reserves that are carried in the trunk of their cars. It always made me think that rear-end collisions must be deadly. Our salaried drivers always drove close to empty, and while it bothered me, we only ran out of gas on two occasions that I recall. Since extra gas was in the trunk, it was only moments before we were on our way again. Turning off the engine and freewheeling downhill isn't all that unusual either.

Prices for gasoline (*benzin,* say *benZEEN*) are high by local standards, and there is no unleaded fuel. You won't see the queues from the old days. Still, gasoline is hard to come by, and Kyiv regulates the number of filling stations within city limits. Many gas stations are found on the outskirts of Kyiv, for example on the road to the airport. But drivers know where to find gas within the city.

Incidentally, the road to Borispil Airport, 20 miles outside of Kyiv, is in fact one of the best in the country. It was re-paved in the early 1970s before Nixon's visit. It always reminded me of a Potemkin village, in this case, a smooth Soviet road fabricated to mislead one of the world's leaders. (Nixon should have appreciated that.)

Car Theft

Car plates in Ukraine identify where a car is registered. KV on the plate tells you that it's from Kyiv; LV for Lviv; KR for Crimea; OD or OA for Odesa; and so on.

Sometimes one cynically wonders how many of the cars on the road are stolen vehicles. There are lots of Mercedes and Jeep Cherokees among the many Ladas and Zhygulis. The Jeeps are supposedly a favorite among nouveaux riches and gangsters and hence a possible theft target. I heard of a Danish woman whose Jeep was car-jacked. She was pregnant and thrown out onto the ground with her small child.

Ukrainians are concerned enough about theft that they remove the wiper blades at night. Many don't bother to have radios, just as many Americans choose to buy removable radios for their cars. One night I had a driver from Moldova stay in my apartment, as there was some mix-up with his hotel reservation. The poor man couldn't sleep for fear of damage to his car, which he would be driving back to Chisinau the next morning. His reaction may have been a legitimate reflection of car theft and crime in general, which are reported to be high in Moldova, or just the ordinary concerns of being in a different country.

Car alarms and removable wheel-locking devices are used as common deterrents against car theft.

General Safety Precautions

More than car theft, the greater concern, clearly, is safety. One of my colleagues described a horrible snow storm south of Kyiv as "the most harrowing road experience of my life." He was visibly shaken and adamant that the trip could have been avoided or postponed. So many cars (close to 400 by newspaper accounts) ran out of fuel or were stranded that the army was called in to assist on that occasion. There was a genuine fear that people would freeze to death in their cars. Our colleague and his crew were able to drive through a tunnel carved out of the snow, but in fact this was not even on the road itself but off to the side. The lesson in hindsight is, don't drive, or let your driver proceed, if the situation is hairy. And ALWAYS INSIST on wearing your seatbelt, regardless of the weather, and even though you may even insult your driver.

Most accidents befall Ukrainians and foreigners alike due to adverse driving conditions such as unsafe roads or alcohol-related accidents. If you drive out of town, you will see fenced-in "car graveyards" on the sides of the highway. These propagandistic displays of hideously wrecked cars are meant to discourage unsafe driving practices.

CLUBS AND ORGANIZATIONS

For expatriates in need of moral support or business advice from other expatriates, there are several important organizations. An international women's club caters more to the housewives of working expatriates than to working women, but both groups are represented. The American Chamber of Commerce and the British Ukrainian Chamber of Commerce are here, as are Alliance Française, Amnesty International, and Alcoholics Anonymous. Various religious organizations are also represented.

Some embassies host happy hours on a regular basis, and most celebrate their country's national holidays. Embassies of NATO countries may invite citizens of other NATO countries to their assorted social functions, provided that guests show their passports.

Being a non-club sort of person, I've always preferred occasional functions to club membership. But one club I've joined is the Hash House Harriers which has chapters around the world and been dubbed "the running club with a drinking problem." In Kyiv, the Hash organizes bi-weekly runs—or walks for those choosing not to run. The Hash is a sort of scavenger hunt; participants have to locate the course through symbols made of ribbons or flour thrown in handfuls on the ground. When those around you locate clues, they shout them out so you need not worry about losing the group or the trail if you are falling behind. There are many arcane rules about behavior during the

Ukrainians and other nationals enjoying American Independence Day, 1998.
(Photo courtesy of Meredith Dalton.)

Hash. The drinking comes later, to the accompaniment of silly and often bawdy songs. A lot of beer is drunk from plastic bowls, or Cokes for those who don't imbibe, and what remains at the end of the song ends up on your head. But it's all done in good spirit.

The Kyiv Hash provides a great way to see different parts of a lovely city replete with green spaces and to meet friends from the international community. There are also Ukrainian members, often introduced to the Hash by their foreign co-workers or friends. Most appear to be bilingual (or even trilingual), though sometimes Hash humor eludes them.

The Hash for the first-timers is free; it's $5 thereafter. Give it a spin, even if neither running nor beer is your thing. Currently the Hash assembles in Kyiv on alternating Sunday afternoons at O'Brien's Bar; the exact time (1 or 2 p.m.) varies according to the season.

ENTERTAINMENT IN KYIV

Restaurants and Nightclubs

New restaurants are constantly cropping up in Kyiv. You may not consider dining out as entertainment per se, but a lot of expatriate social life takes place at restaurants. However, it's difficult to give specific restaurant recommendations here, since venues are constantly changing. The variety of ethnic food available gets better all the time, and there are also more fast food options. It used to be quite difficult to find good coffee in Kyiv, but the situation has improved greatly. Good pastries are available in a few select locations.

In the springtime, Kyiv takes on a vibrant atmosphere; cafés, with white plastic chairs and colorful umbrellas, offering vodka, beer, and limited menu items, sprout alongside city sidewalks. Most restaurants set up tables outdoors if possible. The parks and Independence Square (*Maidan Nezalezhnosty*) fill with people of all ages.

Although Ukrainians don't dine out with the same regularity as the expatriate community, in any given restaurant there will be a mix of locals and foreigners. In the Western restaurants, you will be seeing the more well-to-do Ukrainians, since for average Ukrainians, dining out is exclusively reserved for special occasions, and usually meals are taken in Ukrainian rather than Western restaurants.

The expatriate bar scene is alive and well in Ukraine, and a great place to meet other foreigners. This network is easy to tap into and provides a familiar support mechanism that you may need and welcome periodically.

The nightclub scene does not appeal to everyone's tastes, but many foreigners find themselves (possibly dragged) in an all-night discotheque at some point. Chances are you paid a steep entrance fee and were frisked in the process. If the pulsating rhythms and heavy clouds of smoke don't immediately drive you away, sit back and watch the people. Here is a good opportunity to glimpse the younger Ukrainian set, especially those with some money to burn.

You may be invited to join a Dnipro boat cruise for dinner and drinking. The cruise is generally good fun and a pleasant way to see the city from a different perspective. On most night cruises, the top deck will function as a dance floor with disco lighting along with a disc jockey for at least part of the evening's entertainment.

Live music is frequently heard in the subways, where accordion music seems especially popular. For the best folk music, presumably you should head to Lviv, although Odesa too has a long tradition of lively folk music. An Andean band that moved throughout Kyiv was especially popular for a period.

There are also casinos all over town, and some of the nightclubs include a casino in addition to the dance floor and bar areas. I don't know how frequented these are by the expatriate crowd; I personally have fed tokens once to slot machines adjacent to one of River Palace's bar areas. In big-money gambling in Ukraine, I've been told that there is only one thing worse than losing—and that is winning. If you do win big or show a lot of money trying, expect some thugs to start watching your movements.

Sports Facilities

Pool tables are available in several of Kyiv's more popular bars, and bowling has recently arrived, pleasing some expatriates who tire of the restaurant and bar scene. Bowling alleys have full bar facilities.

A Western health club opened in Kyiv in 1998. The facility has standard weight machines and trainers to assist you; aerobics classes are offered on a regular basis, and a pool is under way. Membership is very expensive. (Lviv's exclusive Grand Hotel has an even fancier facility: its pool has a wave machine, and patrons swimming laps are surrounded by palm trees and singing canaries! The new complex also has a casino, a virtual reality club, and even a ski machine.)

You can go cross-country skiing and horseback riding within Kyiv's city limits near the Hippodrome. Ask around about other venues.

The water park at Hidropark. (Photo courtesy of Meredith Dalton.)

Hidropark

You'll encounter the Ukrainians in more sedate environments like the numerous parks and green spaces throughout Kyiv. One of my favorite places is Hidropark (also spelled Hydropark) where people go to relax. In the summer evenings and on weekends, the place is alive with activity. You will see all ages enjoying themselves; there's even an area where older folks congregate to gossip and dance to accordion music. There are several restaurants on the park's grounds. You may prefer to eat outdoors at one of the many *shashlik* stands, the smell of *shashlik* sizzling over hot coals wafting through the air. Elsewhere, couples move over to dance-floors as the night progresses and the speaker volume is turned up.

In Hidropark you can stroll along the Dnipro's banks, swim, or sunbathe. Lounge chairs and small paddle-boats can be rented. A water-slide is popular in the warmer months. There is an outdoor gym

235

facility with lots of weight machines attracting body-builders in tank tops. For children, there are old-fashioned outdoor amusement rides. Vendors throughout the park sell ice cream, soft drinks, and standard alcoholic fare; you can also buy the popular dried fish (also available at the *rynok*) that tastes as fishy as it smells.

Hidropark is a great place to wander and people-watch; and when you're ready to leave, you hop back on the metro since Hidropark is directly on the metro line.

Movies and Theaters

One of the newer additions to the world of entertainment in Kyiv is the large, upscale movie house a few footsteps off Kreshchatyk. The new facility features assigned seats with Western-style refreshments and prices. The films are typically the latest American releases dubbed in Russian. Films are shown, also at Western price levels, in English at one of a couple of popular movie theaters in central Kyiv; these theaters don't hold a candle to the newest cinema. They also tend to show releases from recent years but not current ones.

Older Ukrainian theater halls are large and often drafty; unlike opera houses and most restaurants, they could not care less if you wear your overcoat inside—and you'll probably need it. These show mostly Russian releases (or foreign films dubbed in Russian) at reasonable prices. Check the *Kyiv Post* for all the current listings.

The Kyiv Circus and Opera or Ballet are must-sees when they are in season. They are generally closed in summer months. Ticket prices are very reasonable.

There is a celebrated Puppet Theater on Shota Rustaveli. This theater shares the building with a synagogue, which has led to minor conflicts in recent years.

Bootleg Galore

You may buy bootleg videotapes on the street, formatted for PAL VHS. The quality of dubbing is awful in some cases; one voice will translate all voices into Russian with snippets of English still audible in the background. Worse are some videos that were copied by means of a hand-held videocamera in the movie theater. You can guess the results. As for bootleg CDs, there may be no liner notes, and sometimes the album is entirely different from the packaging. However, you can generally listen to the CD before you purchase it, whereas videos are sealed.

You can buy multi-system video-players that will read any video format; this is useful if you bring videos from abroad and also intend to watch locally produced films.

Cable television has finally arrived which is good since until now a satellite dish was practically necessary for the foreigner's survival. If nothing else, news in English is always a relief, and the channels and films coming out of Europe are much appreciated.

European Access

Finally, take advantage of Ukraine's location if you can afford it. In most cases, you should be saving some money, at least on clothes, while in Ukraine. (Then again, if you are dining out a lot, or depending on your apartment rent situation, any savings may be a wash.)

Many expatriates claim that they have a psychological need to travel outside of Ukraine from time to time. For some of us, it's necessary to revitalize by getting away every three to six months, if only for a long weekend. Western Europe is an easy flight away, and both Turkey and Cyprus are popular tourist destinations. Make sure your visa allows for multiple entry into Ukraine.

SAFETY

Before you go, you might want to arrange for someone to have limited power of attorney in your absence. Get all your insurance papers in order. Consider getting an international driver's license in the event that you will want it for Ukraine or elsewhere. Leave most of your credit cards at home. Bring some extra passport photos just to be on the safe side (although they are easily obtained here). Put a card in your wallet that identifies your blood type and any allergies to medicines. Maybe you want to bring some hypodermic needles that you definitely know are sharp, safe, and unused?

Avoid night arrivals, and check out hotel escape routes in the event of fire. Register with your embassy upon arrival. They will need a local phone number for contacting you in the event of emergencies at home or should political evacuations become necessary, and the name of the person to contact on your behalf, if need be.

Always lock your doors, and never answer the door without first asking "Who is there?" (*Khto tam?*) Teach your kids the same. Make sure that they and any babysitter never say on the phone that you are out. Only say that you are unavailable, and take a number so that you may call back.

Safety Precautions While Street-Roaming

In Ukraine, pay attention to your style of dress. Don't insist on standing out or talking too loudly. Make a habit of surveying your surroundings; watch your jewelry and beware of pickpockets. Learn to identify the most familiar car makes.

Carry your ID, green card, and/or copy of your passport with you as you roam the streets. I never had any problems, but I know men, especially younger ones with darker skin, who had problems with the transit police. Like the traffic police waving their batons at unsuspecting drivers, the police can demand to see your papers without giving a reason. Their selection of when, why, and who they stop is random (but less random if your skin is dark).

Always assume that the driver has the right of way—or will seize it. It appears that there is growing courtesy toward pedestrians, but with the sharp increase in cars, impatient drivers are out in full force.

Be careful on all those granite steps, especially after rain or when they are icy. Watch the pavement for missing manhole covers, and watch overhead for rotting balconies and unruly icicles. People have been killed by falling icicles, and the weight of snow and ice led to the collapse of the portal by the main post office in 1989, just off Independence (then October Revolution) Square. Eleven people died.

It's not all gloom and doom here, just an ounce of prevention. By staying alert, you'll also notice a lot more around you.

Safety Alert

One spring evening just after dark, a close friend and her male companion, who had been enjoying an evening stroll outdoors, had a horrible experience after buying vodka from a kiosk vendor. The only thing my friend could figure out later was that the vendor must have slipped a drug, probably rohipnol, into their glass of vodka. Their mistake was in not buying the bottle and taking it elsewhere. Rather, they let the kiosk vendor serve them in plastic cups and even join them in a drink. (Remember the tradition of drinking in threes, cited above.)

The woman recalled being dizzy; she and her friend remembered nothing else until later back in her apartment. The vendor had come home with them. Neither could recall either walking the short distance to the apartment or inviting the vendor into the apartment. She later recalled going in and out of consciousness, which supports the

239

rohipnol theory. In the morning she awoke to find out that she and her companion had been robbed. She had also been sexually assaulted. She never contacted the police or her embassy. When asked why she didn't contact the *Kyiv Post*, she would only say she regrets not doing so. She wanted me to include her story here so that this kind of incident might be avoided in the future.

The American Embassy has reported similar offenses involving drugs; there are also stories of people being drugged and robbed on trains. As stated above, I never personally knew anyone who had had trouble on trains or with gypsy cabdrivers. Nevertheless, it is wise to be wary of accepting drinks from strangers.

— *Chapter Six* —

DOING BUSINESS IN AND SURVIVING UKRAINE

Several points in earlier chapters bear repeating here. Ukrainians don't like to be called Russians, any more than Southerners in the United States like to be called Yankees or Scots, English. Indeed the name Ukraine may originate from a Slavic word meaning "border-land," but that doesn't mean it is one any more. Nor is it Southern Russia or Small Russia. Ukrainians today prefer the name "Ukraine" to "the Ukraine" as the latter suggests to them a geographical region, presumably under the yoke of another country. Ukraine's history is a troubled one, and Ukrainians are both proud and at times divided.

Left-Bank Ukraine and Right-Bank Ukraine continue to exhibit marked differences in language, history, and customs. Time will tell if these differences are too divisive and how nationalism will prevail.

In 1991 the nationalists achieved their primary goal. Independence proved intoxicating, but its implementation remains tentative. However slow the many reforms seem to outside observers, they are under way and will not be revoked willingly. Meanwhile, satellite television and Internet access have changed lives and redefined Ukraine's borders in today's "global village."

Much of what can be said about modern Ukrainians is equally applicable to modern Russians, at least those from Russia's western regions around Moscow and St. Petersburg. Russia and Ukraine in the early 21st century may exhibit more divergent paths. Ukraine's challenge now is to work within its own borders, while striving to be a good neighbor. But these are my opinions.

Ukrainians say they tire of expatriates who occasionally treat them as if they are a vanquished people. Ukrainians are certainly not that. However, my fascination with Ukraine is often matched by my frustrations. Those who accept the challenge to work in Ukraine must consciously strive to work within its perplexing, undulating parameters. Accept that your advice and opinions will not always be welcome and that friendships reign supreme. You as the foreigner are perceived as being rich; money issues should be trifling, and your attitude toward graft is rather naive. Corruption is cultural and as ingrained as excessive drinking. The Ukrainian government and the Ukrainian people are not, however, one and the same. All this has been said before, but it cannot be ignored. Some slide too deeply into harsh criticism and accusations; then it is surely time to leave Ukraine.

MY FAVORITE SAYINGS

Throughout this text, I've mentioned several popular sayings. Here are some that I think are very relevant to life in Ukraine:

1. *At home do as you wish, but in public do as you are told.*
I said earlier that this was an improvement on "When in Rome do as the Romans do," since it underscores the existence of two different, yet overlapping, worlds. You need to know something about both the private and public worlds, especially if you intend to do business here. Establishing solid relationships, especially business contacts, requires that you navigate a steady path between these two worlds.

2. *We pretend to work, and they pretend to pay.*
This was a cynical—or realistic—perspective of working within the Soviet system. You will encounter Ukrainians who still maintain this perspective, but you cannot assume that this is always true. You will no doubt find many different profiles of working Ukrainians.

3. *May he live on his salary!*
This Soviet curse is linked to the last saying. It underscores the gross inadequacy of most salaries both in the Soviet and post-Soviet eras. Scrimping is a way of life for most Ukrainians, filching a common problem in the workplace. Often companies keep extra office supplies under lock and key, even though no one wants to have to do this.

For some Ukrainians, moonlighting has been an option for supplementing paltry incomes; however, underemployment is more likely an issue. That bureaucrats abuse their positions of power and demand bribes to perform their tasks as public servants is partly a result of pitiful salary levels, but not a justification.

4. *More men are drowned in a glass than in the ocean.*
Any questions?

5. *An American (or Westerner) is not just a future spouse but a means of transportation.*

I'm not sure if this last one is for the cynics or the healthy skeptics among us:
6. *There is no disputing a proverb, a fool, or the truth.*

ATTITUDES TOWARD MAKING MONEY

Those coming to Ukraine to do business should be aware of the various attitudes toward making money. Making money used to be considered inherently evil, and this surfaces in some of the anti-Semitic sentiment. Historians have cited, for example, cases where Jewish landlords seized the key to the church as mortgage, allowed peasants to run up huge debts, and then demanded immediate repayment; similar tales recounted swindling or stealing property from drunken peasants. Jews (and other foreigners in the cities) were also accused of using inaccurate weight measures in their businesses. Armenian Christians were accused of like offenses but were never so vilified as the Jews. Georgians were also commonly the butt of Soviet jokes involving money, and a *spekuliant*, meaning a speculator or simply a person who makes money, still retains derogatory nuances.

During the Soviet era the concept of *uravnilovka* established equal pay for the same work regardless of effort, resulting in what some foreigners have bemoaned as a culture of "good-enoughness" rather than one that pursues excellence. A friend offered the example of mixing cement in freezing temperatures as recounted in Solzhenitzyn's *One Day in the Life of Ivan Denisovich*. Ukrainians themselves have expressed dismay and even embarrassment with the shoddiness of certain Soviet products, and improving quality standards is one of the stronger incentives today to adopt (or adapt) Western practices.

Younger generations have a decided economic advantage in independent Russia and Ukraine, especially if they are able to make the leap to free market thinking. Many have traveled abroad (primarily to Europe) and are learning foreign languages, especially English. They are attracted to the West and want to see Western business practices adopted. They recognize that this will require reducing the widespread corruption that exists today.

Consider this: ten years ago, none of Russia's ten or twelve so-called oligarchs had a net value of $10,000. Just before Russia's stock market plummeted in August 1998, the wealthiest of these had a net value of $1.6 billion. (He was 37 at the time.) Further, only one of the top twelve was born prior to World War II, and another, in 1946. The others were born in the 1950s and 1960s.

TIPS FOR BUSINESS SUCCESS: AN OVERVIEW

Dress

Westerners should wear business attire to all business meetings. This means conservative suits for men. Avoid lighter colors, which to some are an indication of a lazy or unreliable person. Do not remove your suit jacket without first asking. Generally follow the lead of your Ukrainian counterparts or hosts. (Of course you will remove hat and overcoat; ladies will have their overcoats removed for them in most cases.) Women should dress conservatively and even femininely.

If possible, dress in layers in an effort to combat the sometimes oppressive centralized heating or the sometimes freezing offices you might encounter. This is true not only for winter but spring and fall; and don't forget your umbrella.

Business associates and pickpockets will pay attention to the shoes that you wear. So should you polish them or not? Expect in any case that the soles will quickly be ruined by the grime and the pounding of city streets. For business purposes, I generally stick to simple black flats, and I pack a ziplocked bottle of shoe polish in my suitcase.

Food and Drink

Chances are very good that whenever you visit someone's office for a meeting, you will be served a demitasse of highly sweetened Nescafé or a cup of black tea with sugar on the side; chocolates or a few cookies should also be available. If there is mineral water on the table, you should finish any open bottles that are near you before you open a new one. (If you are hosting the meeting in your office, you should likewise provide coffee or tea and cookies.)

Depending on the nature of your meeting, you may be served alcohol, always accompanied by at least a small bite. Open-face sandwiches are also likely in this case; however, in most office settings, you shouldn't expect more than a few toasts. In a banquet setting, it's another beast entirely.

Business breakfasts are still unusual and won't be initiated; however, if you propose the idea, it will not be declined. Business dinners rarely include spouses.

Smoking Happens

The joke is that there are two sections in every Ukrainian restaurant: smoking and chain smoking. So you must add endemic smoking to the list together with corruption and drinking. It doesn't mean that you will succumb, but you must be aware of its prevalence.

People will also smoke during your business meetings. You may be offered a cigarette, but you shouldn't ever expect to be asked whether you mind someone else smoking. And you should not respond *yes* if asked. It's merely a feigned courtesy because you are a foreigner, and this is where *vranyo* (the white lie) is necessary—irrespective of your position on smoking.

Business Card Formalities and Tips for Meetings

Arrive on time for all business meetings and dinners. As stated earlier, never shake hands across a threshold, and always remove your gloves first. Men will initiate handshakes with women. Kissing on alternate cheeks three times is not an uncommon greeting.

To all meetings, you will need to bring an abundance of business cards, printed in English on one side and in Ukrainian (or Russian if you insist) on the reverse. Do not underestimate the importance of the exchange of business cards; be respectful of this ceremony that officially kicks off most meetings. Even if you speak Russian in your meetings, Ukrainian is the politically correct language. Thus, if you are also doing business in Russia, why not carry two sets of business cards? Your company's name, address, contact numbers, and e-mail address should be standard on business cards. For Ukraine (and Russia), you should also include your degrees after your name, with your company title or position printed below in the standard manner.

Next, the person who called the meeting will proceed with summarizing the reasons for the meeting. There will probably be some small talk at the beginning, but unless you are meeting with established friends, don't expect more than perfunctory niceties. Don't ask personal questions or give any details about yourself or your family that seem to indicate any sort of problems. Moreover, you should be aware that, as you form closer alliances with your business contacts, some will feel responsible for your problems in-country, just as most of us hope that foreign visitors to our own country will have a good experience and depart with a favorable impression. Be careful not to overburden Ukrainian business acquaintances and friends with your problems.

Bring an ample supply of letterhead stationery, although some variant is easy enough to generate with all the fonts and formatting features available on today's word processors. (When writing letters in Ukrainian, the phrase "Respected" is used as opposed to "Dear." Envelopes are addressed in inverted form, beginning with the city,

247

country, and zip code on the top line, followed by the address below, and finally, the recipient's name on the bottom line.)

In most cases you will be working through an interpreter, and this requires extra time and organization of your thoughts. You should probably begin the meeting by apologizing for not speaking Russian or Ukrainian, if appropriate. Then you should summarize your points before you go into specifics. To wrap up your meeting, you should reiterate your main points and suggest topics for future consideration. This will include, of course, any subjects that were inadequately resolved in the current meeting.

All this naturally takes longer than conducting meetings in a single language; in fact, it will take more than twice the time, given the need for both interpretation, repetition, and clarification. That your Ukrainian counterparts are often loathe to make decisions is another issue altogether.

Also, you may notice during your meeting that, like the people you encounter in the streets, your Ukrainian counterparts or hosts don't tend to smile much. Don't interpret this as a sign of anything. Joviality in meetings may be viewed as inappropriate and even insincere, although after a meeting people will lighten up.

It is never acceptable to call someone *tovarish*, meaning "Comrade," and diminutives are discouraged in business situations where ideally patronymics are used. Rather, diminutives should be reserved for close friends. In all cases, it is inappropriate to adopt a diminutive for business associates without permission; this is simply too informal. Standard protocol is that you show respect to age and rank.

Avoid a hard-selling technique as it will not be well received. You should stress your desire to make a contribution to Ukraine, rather than your desire to quickly repatriate profits. At the same time, don't be deceived: your Ukrainian counterparts want to work with you because of your foreign currency (as well as technical expertise).

Foreigners should expect excruciating delays: never expect to waltz into town, sign a contract in short order, then fly out. Negotiations are always lengthy. You will also encounter red tape that boggles the imagination—you'll wonder at the need for all the official stamps, bells, and whistles. Some foreign firms refuse to work in Ukraine for these reasons, but if you intend to stay here, you should accept the system, as it may not change any time soon.

Most Ukrainians are unaccustomed to playing the role of decision-maker. Still, some of those you encounter will be dictatorial and authoritarian, and find admitting mistakes quite difficult. Ukrainians typically prefer to think as opposed to respond or act; better yet, they may try to pass you on to someone else. For this reason, you should always strive to work with the most senior person available to you. In theory, this should save your firm some time. Your company should also utilize its senior people whenever possible, as older businessmen (and I mean men) are considered more experienced and preferable. Sometimes the young whippersnappers put forward by consulting firms can be an affront to their Ukrainian counterparts. Relationships take time and Ukrainians want to work with a steady counterpart, rather than be shuffled among various consultants flying in and out of town; whoever is selected should not be changed mid-course if possible. It's a matter of respecting one another.

Ukrainian women are expected to be unassertive. They are still undervalued in Ukrainian society and in business relations. Foreign women are treated with considerable respect, but this might prove equally frustrating in light of the standard sexist treatment toward Ukrainian women. Equal pay doesn't exist in this male-dominated society, but there are increasing numbers of women in important roles. Today the vast majority of Ukrainian women work, although the wives of the New Rich do not.

In business situations Western men should not flirt with Ukrainian women, although Western women should be prepared for men who may flirt with them. Don't take this seriously if it happens. Also, because Ukrainian men are afraid to not be gentlemen, some foreign women might use their femininity to their advantage. In all cases, expect that your cigarettes will be lighted, your coat removed, and doors opened for you.

Business Telephones

Get a cell phone, but don't expect to conduct any business by phone. All business must be done in person, but you'll need a phone because existing phone lines are insufficient and the quality of lines poor. Even if you can get through, oftentimes you'll reach a busy signal on the other end. With a mobile phone (*mobilniy telefon*), you can alert people when you are stranded in traffic, although you should always plan for delays. People give out their cell phone numbers and leave their phones on. It's not uncommon to be given home numbers, in which case it's okay to contact people there. This is partly done since it's sometimes hard to get through on the office phone lines.

Hiring Local Staff

Upon arrival in Ukraine, hire a driver and a translator. Recognize that the most valuable staff members have added value in general information—how to get around red tape, where you can get keys copied, purchase a fire extinguisher, or notarize a document. While the *Yellow Pages* and *Golden Pages* (see below) available in bilingual versions are useful, people rely most heavily on staff, friends, and other people. (See the section below on Procuring Equipment for a caveat to this.)

You will also need to know the local labor laws.

Protocol for Interpreters

Always place your interpreter next to you, but look at your counterpart, not at your interpreter. Refrain from making statements such as "Please tell him ..." Organize your comments in advance, and pause frequently to give your interpreter a chance to translate. Avoid slang and jargon, including sports analogies, which may be misinterpreted or simply translate poorly.

Never say anything in English that you don't want understood by everyone present; you might also assume that telephone lines are tapped. No paranoia here, but take necessary precautions.

When hiring interpreters, look for those who love languages and especially this career field. Many interpreters want to use their language skills as a springboard to other positions, especially in a Western company where salaries tend to be significantly higher. Over time some interpreters slip into their desire to speak for themselves, rather than serve as the mouthpiece for another person. I have encountered interpreters who, after repeated conversations, were eager to demonstrate their familiarity with the subject and sometimes pre-guessed what was about to be said. This is not the purpose of an interpreter and can only lead to inaccuracies; words will literally be put in your mouth, and if you don't speak the language well, you may never know it. As authoritarian as it may sound, one needs an interpreter who speaks only when spoken to and then translates as accurately as possible.

Some interpreters tend to sanitize more awkward conversations, and this is not desirable either. You may want to work with several interpreters to identify one with whom you have a better rapport.

There are some related cultural issues. I have encountered a few expatriate men who were uncomfortable traveling out of town with female interpreters. We have also had interpreters who were cowed by some of the frankly intimidating higher officials in the Ukrainian government. Your firm or team will not want to project an image of being easily intimidated.

My company initially decided against setting strict guidelines regarding interpreters imbibing alcohol at business functions. But excessive alcohol intake on several occasions resulted in a revised policy strongly discouraging interpreters from imbibing on the job.

Finally, it is always a good idea to have someone in your party take notes of the meeting. Ideally, this will be someone who understands both languages and can monitor the accuracy of the translation.

251

BUSINESS HOURS

Occasionally, the operating hours of a business will be changed without notice. This can be frustrating to say the least. Generally, shops and some restaurants post their operating hours near the entrances, but for unknown reasons, doors will close for extended, unannounced periods throughout the day (for an office birthday party, for example); or a store will close for lunch in the middle of the day precisely when many of its customers want to do their shopping. For the most part, the hours posted will be accurate and shouldn't hamper planning your day's schedule.

BANKING, ACCOUNTING, LEGAL MATTERS

As stated in Chapter Five, opening a bank account may be hazardous to your mental health. Once you have succeeded in opening your account, you will have to show and register your passport or identification every time you enter the bank's premises. You will then pay a fee for the privilege of withdrawing your own money, which does not accrue interest for you. (You may decide to install a vault on your premises to cut down on bank visits.)

At the bank, those waiting in line for the tellers stand in the hall and stairwell; this gives you a fair idea of the non-service mentality of banks; perhaps it also reflects concern for both your safety and the bank's. (When exchanging dollars for *hryven*, you won't see the person in the booth without stooping to peer through the window. I personally like to see whom I'm dealing with, so I find this setup disconcerting.)

Prior to arriving in the country, you should be in contact with knowledgeable accountants and lawyers who can advise you and your firm on specific needs. Many smaller firms that in the West would not do so will elect to hire in-house lawyers and accountants on a full-time basis; these professionals can assist in complying with local labor and tax laws, following standard hiring practices, registering the company, and so on.

RENTING OFFICE SPACE

You can buy office space but most firms still view this as an investment (or risk) they would prefer to avoid. You may nonetheless negotiate a lease that allows for substantial renovations to the space.

Office space available for rent ranges from fully modernized, Western type offices at very steep prices to residential flats, unfurnished or sometimes partially furnished, depending on the arrangements made with the landlord. Most domestic apartments (except for the most expensive ones) are rented fully furnished, which simplifies the furniture issue. It is a good idea to append to your lease contract a list of major furniture items in the event of any disputes. Some employers will require it.

Remember that some parts of the city have better phone lines. There are many real estate agents now who can provide the most current information and price lists.

PROCURING EQUIPMENT AND SUPPLIES

In Ukraine you can find reasonably priced computers and generally overpriced office supplies and furniture at various places throughout town. Your best options are to ask other expatriates, check the listings in the *Kyiv* (or equivalent) *Business Directory* (now available online; see below), or ask your local staff. The third option has a caveat: be wary of kickbacks to staff who direct sales to their friends at particular stores, although this may not be important to you so long as the price and/or quality is right.

You might note that WordPerfect is not the word processing program of choice; Microsoft Word is what people in Ukraine know and use. You'll need the Russian or Ukrainian edition of any program you use.

INTERNET AND E-MAIL ACCESS

The Internet is alive and well in Ukraine. The greatest challenges are access to sufficient phone lines and the quality of these lines when available. Efforts are under way to solve these problems. In some areas you can now purchase telephone lines from UTEL; they are expensive, but you won't spend years on a waiting list.

E-mail services are widely available now; even America Online (AOL) has local access numbers in Kyiv and Odesa and will soon expand to other areas. You do have to pay a surcharge above your standard monthly fee. Likewise, Ukrainian Internet providers charge according to the minutes spent online, with varying options depending on expected usage. (In our case, we wrote all e-mails offline to reduce online fees to transmission time; we still had a problem with phone lines that frequently didn't disconnect properly.) You will need to select from the various local companies depending on whether you need e-mail services or full Internet access. Choose a plan that makes the most sense for your anticipated online usage.

COURIER SERVICES AND THE POST OFFICE
DHL, Federal Express, and UPS are now available in Ukraine. They are expensive but do a good job. I was very pleased with DHL, whose staff was well trained and courteous. Check to see which companies provide services and fees matching your needs both within and outside Ukraine.

In addition to basic services, the Ukrainian post office sells phone-cards and accepts payments for utilities and telephone bills. You may also send telegrams and faxes and place international calls from here.

JOINT VENTURES AND LOCAL PARTNERSHIPS
There is no simple answer to this problem. I say problem, because I know of cases where a JV was more or less required for entry into a Ukrainian market, but the foreign investor in the end got the short end of the stick, and sometimes ended up with no stick at all. Identifying the right partner is half of your challenge, and one of the foremost reasons for investing time in your relationships is to locate this ideal

person or organization who will help you with the second half of the challenge—which is to (further) unravel the byzantine Ukrainian business world. Naturally, should you meet someone early on who seems too eager, trust your instincts.

MAFIA

Concerns about the mafia were voiced in previous chapters. To me, it's a bit like excessive drinking. If you think you have a problem, you probably do. Think safe sex and safe business all the way. At the same time, don't let the foreign press or your friends who are unfamiliar with the territory dissuade you. (Think of how non-natives often view New York City.) If you've done your homework, and this means extensive research including due diligence, proceed with caution.

HOLIDAYS

Ukrainian Independence Day is celebrated on August 24. The year 2001 will mark the tenth anniversary of independence. August is generally good weather for outdoor celebrations. The Soviet tradition to appease workers on selected holidays continues today, and probably entirely too much state money is spent on Independence and Labor Day (May 1) celebrations.

The other big celebration during Soviet times was October Revolution Day, celebrated on November 7, according to the Julian (or old) calendar. It is hard to say whether this will be celebrated in a given year. Technically, it is not observed now, but it still is by many, and the state doesn't know how to treat it. I have been in independent Ukraine when it was celebrated and when it was not.

Officially recognized holidays include New Year's Day. (From the communists' anti-religious standpoint, January 1 was the most important holiday, and this is when gifts were exchanged.) "Old New Year's" is unofficially observed by some on January 14, or more likely the celebration of Old New Year's Eve. In general, expect no work in Ukraine from our Christmas (I've heard it derogatorily

255

called "Catholic Christmas") until after Ukrainian or Orthodox Christmas, celebrated on January 7.

Early May is also filled with holidays. May Day is Labor Day (International Workers Day), followed by another holiday on May 2. (It is quite common for Ukrainian holidays to last two days instead of one.) This second day was explained to me as a day to recuperate from the previous day's drinking, but in reality it often became a day to continue to binge, carouse, and play. May 9 is Victory Day, very important in the FSU where so many lives were lost in the Great Patriotic War.

It is also not uncommon for the government to start a holiday weekend early, for example, Friday and Saturday may be declared the official weekend to follow a Thursday holiday; then it's business as usual on Sunday!

March 8 is International Women's Day, which is treated as a sort of egalitarian Mother's Day; the difference is that the custom is to congratulate all women, not just mothers. This day is a public holiday, and there will be parties with flowers, champagne, fruit, and chocolates. Traditionally, men give flowers to women.

Flowers are also given, on a much smaller scale, on March 1, which is considered the (unofficial) first day of spring. Other seasons start at the beginning of their respective months.

April 1 is April Fools' Day in Ukraine. With its milder, seaside climate, Odesa has a longstanding reputation as the Ukrainian center of humor and fun, and is known for its April 1st festivities. April 1 is not one of the officially recognized holidays, but there is a joke that May Day in Ukraine is International Workers April Fools' Day.

SO CAN YOU MAKE IT?

Expect to make a faux pas now and then. Ukrainians recognize culturally sensitive foreigners and tend to forgive them readily.

The most obvious steps for making the most of your visit have been stated above. A few important themes are worth repeating.

Learn the Language

Buy cheap phrasebooks and a Russian pocket dictionary. A Ukrainian-English dictionary may be easier to find in Ukraine, but start with phrasebooks before you go. Plenty of these are available for learning Russian phrases and a few for Ukrainian; you should purchase both if chances are good that you will be working with the government in some form. If you are headed for western Ukraine, concentrate on Ukrainian over Russian. Ultimately, since all students are now taught in Ukrainian, this will in turn influence eastern Ukraine.

Do Your research

Read up on the history of Ukraine; buy a guidebook or two. Fodor's has one called *Moscow, St. Petersburg, and Kiev*. This provides a history of Kyiv and recommends tourist sites and walking tours. You may find other guidebooks on Russia that include a back section on Kyiv—invariably spelled Kiev.

Lonely Planet has a book called *Russia, Ukraine and Belarus*. This gives a better history of the region and offers details on cities and towns besides Kyiv. I'd recommend both of these books if you have the space to pack them.

Research Current Events via the Internet

Start with *The Kyiv Post*, the English-language newspaper: www.thepost.kiev.ua has two online editions per week, one on Tuesday and one on Friday. The free paper version of the *Post* is available in Kyiv twice a week at popular expatriate hangouts. There is also an *Odessa Post* that covers local events in Odesa for the expat community besides reporting national news.

For general information on Russia and CIS countries in general, look at the online journal, www.russiatoday.com; this is updated daily. The focus is clearly on Russia, but Ukraine receives coverage. (This same group produces daily journals called *Eastern Europe* and *Inside China*; in both cases, type the name as one word.)

There is a new publication called *Transitions*. Its website posts articles two months after publication.

For general information, check out www.uahoo.com; it's like yahoo but with UA for Ukraine in the name.

The Kyiv Business Directory is online. The online version operates essentially as a phonebook. The telephone number of a firm is provided by category (e.g. car rental, then Avis), but no additional details are given. The paper version is better, with good maps of the city, a brief history, and lots more information. Try to find this when you arrive in Kyiv; sometimes it is made available for free in Western grocery stores, or hotels typically charge $5. It is updated quarterly. I called the company directly to find out how to get the latest copy.

Also available in Kyiv now are at least two yellow page directories. One is called *Yellow Pages*; another is called *Golden Pages*. These are also available in select bookstores and at hotels.

For regional current events, try *The New York Times*, *The Financial Times*, *The Economist*, and sometimes *The Wall Street Journal*. Check their websites for more information regarding subscription rates and online access. *The Eastern Economist* has detailed information; their website tells you how to order it. *Interfax News Agency* is a news source faxed to subscribers on a daily basis. These last two are more expensive than most of the above suggestions and also more specialized; they may well be worth the cost depending on your needs.

HIGHLY SUBJECTIVE TOP TOURIST SUGGESTIONS

This is not a guidebook, but here is my top ten list, which you'll notice really stretches the concept of ten numbers. Some of the ideas are lumped together unfairly. It all depends on how much time you have. Even if you are not posted in Kyiv, you will probably have the opportunity to visit Kyiv where most of the following are located.

- The Monastery of the Caves (*Pecherska Lavra*) and St. Sophia's Cathedral *(Sofiyivskiy Sobor)*, both in Kyiv; *Pochayiv Lavra* in the

Ternopil region in western Ukraine.

- An opera or ballet performance at one of several grand opera houses throughout Ukraine; a performance by the Kyiv Circus; and a football match showcasing Kyiv Dynamo.
- The Ukraine Museum of Folk Architecture, outside of Kyiv in Pyrohovo (about 8 miles from the city center).
- Hidropark and Andriyivskiy Uzviz, both in Kyiv.
- Babi Yar and the Chornobyl Museum, also in Kyiv.
- Try out the transport: a train ride to Lviv (perhaps contrasted with a return in the Grand Hotel's car?); a race up the Potemkin steps in Odesa; a ride on a tram, trolley, or bus; a ride on Kyiv's or Kharkiv's metro; any gypsy cab ride; and a stroll down Kreshchatyk.
- An (expensive) night on the town starting with a typically Ukrainian dinner, followed by a visit to an expatriate hangout, and ending up in an all-night discotheque.
- A Sunday with the Hash House Harriers and a Dnipro boat cruise with friends.
- A visit to a Ukrainian home or *dacha*. Consider yourself honored to be invited.
- For those seeking adventure off the beaten track, there's skiing in the Carpathians, medieval ruins and castles in western Ukraine to explore, underground caves in Crimea, and Yalta's celebrated Swallow's Nest, the picturesque castle perched high on a cliff overlooking the Black Sea.

UKRAINE IS NOT YET DEAD

Two points always come to mind when I speak about Ukraine. First, Ukraine is not for everyone. Many Ukrainians are dissatisfied and eager to emigrate. Many foreigners are eager to see a part of the world they've been missing—then flee. Second, Ukraine is not Russia, despite strong links between the two countries.

Russia's financial and consequent social crisis in the summer of 1998 had significant and dire ramifications for Ukraine, and the long-term effects are far from known. To date, one of the reasons that Ukraine has fared somewhat better than Russia in the aftermath of August's financial crisis is that the international investment community was extremely slow to invest in Ukraine. Rather, Russia to Ukraine's east, and Poland, Hungary, and the Czech Republic to the west, have received considerable investment and attention. Ukraine, by contrast, has received principally international aid since independence. Frankly, much of this had to do with Ukraine's arsenal of nuclear weapons (now relinquished) and nuclear power plants, including the most infamous in the world—Chornobyl.

My advice for doing business in Ukraine includes many caveats. To succeed in and enjoy Ukraine demands a knowledge of its many cultural traditions, its peculiarities, and its strengths and weaknesses. The focus in the present text is on customs and etiquette. Your decision to further explore business in Ukraine at this juncture must be predicated on solid business research and personal circumstances.

Specifically, you must decide if Ukraine makes sense for you and your family, and your company must decide if Ukraine makes sense for the long run. If it doesn't, more than likely it won't for the short term either. Companies must further consider the specific business, legal, and political issues relevant to the work that they aim to do.

The 1998 publication of *Doing Business in Ukraine* is helpful and necessarily vague, as so much information becomes quickly outdated. With its considerable advertising, the book aims to attract business to Ukraine; it therefore paints a rosier picture than the present text. My purpose is not to sell you on Ukraine but, rather, to share observations of expatriates working in a variety of situations.

More than a few reliable and savvy resources have stated matter-of-factly that no foreigner should attempt to enter the oil and gas industries in Ukraine, where personal safety may be an issue. Limited fuel resources in Ukraine have made Ukrainians dependent on alliances with the Russians, who also produce the nuclear fuel necessary to run Ukraine's Russian-made nuclear plants. Because so much of Ukraine's agriculture is bartered for Russian fossil fuel, and since bartering circumvents tax collection, neither country receives income for these products or tax revenues from these transactions. Moreover, when countries cannot regularly pay salaries to their armed forces, world safety may be (further) compromised.

While much of Ukraine's wealth derives from her celebrated soil, Ukrainian agricultural production is less than half of that produced in Soviet years. The concept of a market economy is still so far from being fully implemented; obstacles in banking and finance reinforce this. Transportation infrastructure is likewise in a state of disarray verging on crisis proportions.

It is overwhelming to grasp the magnitude of areas of Ukrainian life demanding improvement as well as the incipient changes that have been implemented since independence. These include, but are not limited to: coal mine safety; nuclear reactor safety; air traffic control; airport, road, and rail construction; conversion of coal-powered plants to gas; military reform; security and defense conversion; telecommunications; development of independent media; civil society; rule of law; criminal justice system reform; the development of political parties, fair elections, participatory political systems, grassroots organizations; tax reform; bankruptcy code; pension reform; local government and finance; labor-management relations; labor statistics; tax accounting; customs reform and border controls; international trade and investment; entrepreneurship and small business development; banking; promotion of agricultural development, including exchanges and training, non-governmental grain storage facilities; private land ownership and real estate markets; public health and hospital management and finance. The list goes on and on. In 1999, Ukraine was ranked among the ten worst countries for journalists to access information. Re-education and training must therefore become insistent priorities.

So am I gung-ho on Ukraine? Ukraine is (more than Arkansas!) a land of opportunity, and its neighbors to the west, in particular Poland,

Hungary, and the Czech Republic, have in recent years exhibited tremendous progress. However, none of these countries was a Soviet Republic, although none avoided the Soviet sphere of influence, either. Despite the promising successes of these former Eastern Bloc countries, it is more apt to compare Ukraine to Russia, whose future looks just as uncertain as Ukraine's. For both countries, wiping out several generations of communist mentality may take several more.

Ukraine's singular strength is her 50 million people rather than her under-producing soil. The population is declining, and social ills that have escalated since independence have converged on Ukraine practically in lockstep with democratic reforms. Particularly in light of mafia and corruption charges, reform must begin at government level, despite past disastrous experiences stemming from an all-powerful central government. (It is easy to blame all current problems on the Soviet system and its legacy, but this is too simplistic.)

Ultimately, my greatest hope for Ukraine's entry into the 21st century rests with the young, entrepreneurial set, regardless of their motivation. Today's New Rich must be distinguished from Ukraine's growing entrepreneurs, who tend to be young, well-educated, and ambitious; they are members of the emerging middle class and the new risk-takers in their society.

The example of the Internet perhaps offers an analogy for the near future in independent Ukraine. Worldwide, the Internet seems to be teaching, not just Gen-Xers but multiple generations, that change is accelerating, and those who are willing or able to adapt quickly will not be left behind. In Ukraine, the beneficiaries of this thinking are largely limited to the younger and more flexible citizens.

Expatriates wishing to remain in Ukraine for an extended period should have respect for Ukraine's history and strive not to judge so harshly the obstacles facing Ukraine in this transitional period. It is important to examine Ukraine today in light of some 2000 years of history. I don't want Ukraine to be another America, although sadly a lot of my Ukrainian contemporaries seem to want just that.

I will close as I began this text. Ukraine is not for the meek. Ukrainians are not meek; they are a proud people with a troubled history. They are survivors and deserve far better than they have fared. For true entrepreneurs and mavericks, there are exciting opportunities in this country whose great people sing aloud:

Ukraine is not yet dead, nor its glory and freedom,
Luck will still smile on us brother-Ukrainians.
Our enemies will die, as the dew does in the sunshine,
and we, too, brothers, we'll live happily in our land.
We'll not spare either our souls or bodies to get freedom
and we'll prove that we brothers are of Cossack kin.
We'll rise up, brothers, all of us, from the Sain to the Don,
We won't let anyone govern in our motherland.
The Black Sea will smile yet, Grandfather Dnipro will rejoice,
Yet in our Ukraine luck will be high.
Our persistence, our sincere toil will prove its rightness,
still our freedom's loud song will spread throughout Ukraine.
It'll reflect upon the Carpathians, will sound through the steppes,
and Ukraine's glory will arise among the people.

CULTURAL QUIZ

QUIZ A

When visiting a Ukrainian home, it is inappropriate to:
1 bring non-alcoholic drinks.
2 bring cakes and cookies.
3 give two flowers to the wife of the host.
4 give three flowers to the wife of the host.
5 give flowers to the wife of another.

QUIZ B

In business meetings,
1 it is appropriate to serve alcohol without a small bite so long as alcohol is not served before noon.
2 it is appropriate to serve alcohol without a small bite so long as everyone is seated.
3 it is appropriate to serve alcohol without a small bite so long as everyone clinks their glasses together in toast.
4 you must always serve alcohol with a bite.

QUIZ C

A woman should not sit at the corner of the table, as superstition has it that ...
1 she will not marry for seven years.
2 bad luck will be brought upon all the guests at the table.
3 all her money will fly out the next open window.
4 a woman should be seated at the head of the table.

QUIZ D

At all but one of the following, you will check your coat in the coatroom upon entering:

1   upscale restaurants.
2   movie theaters.
3   opera houses.
4   ballet performances.

QUIZ E

The second largest city in Ukraine is:

1   Kharkov.
2   Kharkiv.
3   Odesa.
4   Dnipropetrovsk.
5   Lviv.
6   Donetsk.

QUIZ F

To export 19th century art (e.g. an icon) from Ukraine, you will need

1   to pay a bribe.
2   your own personal jet.
3   to register the art, pay a fee, and receive the official stamp to show the customs officials upon exiting the country.
4   to trade in your conscience.

ANSWERS TO QUIZ A–F

A Alcoholic and non-alcoholic drinks, cakes, cookies, and flowers (yes, to the wife of another) are all appropriate gifts. Just make sure that you bring an odd number of flowers since even numbers are reserved for funerals: (3) is unacceptable here.

B (4). If possible, you should serve tea and coffee with a bite of something, but it is imperative to serve a small bite with alcohol.

C (1): She will not marry for seven years.

D (2). Movie theaters were traditionally large and drafty, and the moviegoers kept their coats on. This may change with the arrival of large, Western-style movie theaters. In that case, expect to receive a dirty look if your coat lacks a loop for hanging!

E The answer is both (1) and (2): Kharkov is the Russian name for the city and the one most often heard, while Kharkiv is the Ukrainian name, and technically this is the proper name. In the book, I use the Ukrainian spelling though Russian is overwhelmingly the language of the streets here. For the capital city, I use Kyiv, not Kiev.

F This is a trick question. Only (3) is definitively wrong. Since it is illegal to export items made before 1945, you cannot go through legal channels, pay a fee, and receive an official stamp.

SELECT BIBLIOGRAPHY

Here's a list of selected texts from my library and other sources.

Suggested Introductory Reading

The following three books make for good reading as an introduction to Ukraine and Russia.

Traveling Companions by Friedrich Gorenstein, trans. Bernard Meares (New York: Harcourt Brace Jovanovich, trans. 1991). This is an interesting fictional account of two men who meet on an overnight train in Ukraine. The playwright protagonist tells his tragic life story by interweaving tales of the occasional simple pleasures amidst the larger, bitter experiences in his Ukrainian village. He recounts the horrific German occupation that initially he believed might prove superior to life under the Soviets. After the war, life continued in its bleak fashion under Stalin and included a seven-year sentence in a labor camp. Gorenstein's tale is hard-hitting all the way but told in compelling storyteller fashion.

Imperium by Ryszard Kapuściński, trans. from Polish by Klara Glowczewska (New York: Vintage Books, Random House, trans. 1994). Kapuscinski is the Polish journalist who has written extensively on Latin America, Africa, the Middle East, and the FSU. This is a very readable, if meandering, text wherein Kapuscinski recounts colorful vignettes from the disparate Soviet republics. This composite profile reminds us that the various cultures with their separate histories and cultures were never fully subsumed by the attempted wholesale Sovietization.

267

In Search of Melancholy Baby: A Russian in America by Vassily Aksyonov, trans. by Michael Henry Heim and Antonina W. Bouis (New York: Vintage Books, Random House, 1989). This is a fast-paced and enjoyable autobiography by a dissident writer who emigrated to the United States in 1985. The author's observations, along with his comparisons and contrasts between America and the Soviet Union (but really Russia), are compelling.

Russian History and the Soviet Peoples

A History of Russia by Nicholas Riasonovsky (Oxford University Press, 5th edition, 1993). This is one of the classic college texts and a good standard reference source.

Russia and the Soviet Union by Warren B. Walsh (Ann Arbor: University of Michigan Press, 1958). From my grandmother's collection, still one of the better overviews of Russian history just after Khrushchev's denunciation of Stalin, i.e. pre-Brezhnev.

The Russians by the Pulitzer Prize-winning correspondent Hedrick Smith (New York: Ballantine Books, revised 1984). I always recommend this as one of the best examinations of Soviet life during the late Brezhnev era. Smith was traveling to Russia and speaking to the Russian people long before most Westerners had access. The people he met were often too scared to give him their home phone numbers, if they were so lucky as to have a phone. Read this great book, then follow up with Smith's sequel, *The New Russians* (New York: Avon Books, revised 1991). This brings us up to date through Gorbachev's reign and the final days of the Soviet Union. The Avon version was updated to include the failed coup of August 1991.

David Remnick's Pulitzer Prize-winning *Lenin's Tomb: The Last Days of the Soviet Empire* (New York: Vintage, updated 1994) describes life during the break-up of the Soviet Union. Recommended in all circles, it is an excellent book to throw in your suitcase. Many contend that Remnick is the best American writer on Russia today.

Remnick's most recent book, *Resurrection: The Struggle for a New Russia* (New York: Vintage, revised 1998), is also highly praised. Life under Gorbachev and Yeltsin in the early through middle 1990s is his focus here. Unfortunately, no book exists to explain the leadership in post-Soviet Ukraine, but the above four books by Smith and Remnick are invaluable for understanding Ukrainians and recent Soviet history.

The Dream that Failed: Reflections on the Soviet Union by Walter Laqueur (Oxford University Press, 1995). This is another account of what went wrong in the later years of the Soviet Union. The text is more academic than the above books (and hence not as easily readable) and does not focus on personal testimony per se, but it is useful for those readers in search of insightful political analysis.

"The Russian Question" at the End of the Twentieth Century: Toward the End of the Twentieth Century by Aleksandr Solzhenitzyn (New York: Farrar, Straus and Giroux, 1995). This was written by the famous dissident writer and intellectual, best known for the weighty *Gulag Archipelago* and *One Day in the Life of Ivan Denisovich* (always highly recommended).

Russians in the Former Soviet Republics by Paul Kolstoe (Bloomington, Indiana: Indiana University Press, 1995) is useful for statistical purposes. Conflicts in Crimea and Transdnistr are touched upon, and these are important topics in Ukraine today.

Ukrainian History
Ukraine: A History by Orest Subtelny (University of Toronto Press, revised 1994) is an excellent history of Ukraine. Others also recommend *A History of Ukraine* by Robert Paul Magocsi (University of Washington Press, 1996). Magocsi also wrote *Ukraine: A Historical Atlas* (University of Toronto, 1986); this is a valuable source of history as reflected through Ukraine's many borders (and hence these maps) changing over time.

Kiev: A Portrait, 1800–1917 by Michael F. Hamm (Princeton: Princeton University Press, 1993) is useful for history and information about the capital city and its inhabitants, and the book's photo reproductions are a welcome addition to the text. The history of Jews in the capital city is also well documented.

The Black Sea

Black Sea by Neal Ascherson (New York: Hill and Wang, 1995). This great book traces the region's long and complex history from the time of Jason and the Golden Fleece until the fall of communism. This unique study of the Black Sea highlights its bridges between European and Asian culture and provides insight into both past and current tensions.

Stalin and the Terror-Famine

There are many books now available on Stalin. *Stalin: Breaker of Nations* by Robert Conquest (Penguin, 1991) is a very readable account from the author who has written many other related books. One of these is on the famine, *The Harvest of Sorrow: Soviet Collectivization and the Terror-Famine* (Oxford University Press, 1987), and several are on the Great Terror, including *The Great Terror: A Reassessment* (Oxford University Press, 1987).

For another account of the famine, see Myron Dolot's *Execution by Hunger* (New York: W.W. Norton and Co., 1987). Both this and Conquest's books give very detailed histories of the 1932–33 famine, deliberately engineered by Stalin as a means of bringing about Soviet collectivization of Ukraine.

Jews and Babi Yar

The Jewish Traveler: Hadassah Magazine's Guide to the World's Jewish Communities and Sights, ed. Alan M. Tigay (New York: Jason Aronson, revised 1994). The book provides great information on Kyiv and other cities throughout the world.

Babi Yar: A Document in the Form of a Novel by A. Anatoli (Kuznetsov), trans. by David Floyd (New York: Farrar, Straus and Giroux, 1970 uncensored version of 1966 censored version). This is a fascinating book on several levels. Currently out of print, the later version shows text that was censored by the Soviet government. The author was a young witness to the events and determined then that he would record his horrific memories as a testament to those who were killed here. Contrary to some accounts, the author was not Jewish.

Soviet Women

Soviet Women: Walking the Tightrope by Francine du Plessix Gray (New York, Doubleday, 1990). This is a very informative book that helps to explain both the plight of Soviet women and the sexist culture in which they still find themselves.

How We Survived Communism and Even Laughed by Slavenka Drakulic (New York: Harper Perrenial, 1992). Written by a Croatian, this is one of the great books about Eastern European life, especially for women. Contrary to its title, this book is not a humorous account, but I highly recommend it.

Also, contrast *Moscow Days: Life and Hard Times in the New Russia* by Galina Dutkina (New York: Kodansha America, 1996) with Jennifer Gould's *Vodka, Tears and Lenin's Angel* (New York: St. Martin's Press, 1996). Dutkina is a Russian woman (born 1952) who describes post-Soviet life as lived by so many contemporaries. Gould is a young Canadian Jew whose expatriate lifestyle (and privileges) rings true for another section of the population.

Chornobyl

Here are three books that I suggest for information on the world's deadliest nuclear accident (to date):

Chernobyl: The Forbidden Truth by Alla Yaroshinskaya; trans. Michelle Kahn and Julia Sallabank. (Lincoln: University of Nebraska,

1995). This was written by a Ukrainian journalist who fought for several years to publish material on Chornobyl. Not only was such discussion not allowed in the aftermath of the disaster, it was deemed a criminally punishable offense.

Journey to Chernobyl: Encounters in a Radioactive Zone by Glenn Alan Cheney (Chicago: Academy Chicago Publishers, 1995). The American author was in Ukraine when the Soviet Union dissolved. He traveled illegally into the radioactive zone to talk to pensioners who had returned there against the orders of the government. He also spoke with Kyiv residents about their personal experiences immediately following the world's deadliest nuclear disaster.

Also by Cheney is *Chernobyl: The Ongoing Story of the World's Deadliest Nuclear Disaster* (New Diocene Books, Macmillan Publishing Co., 1993), a more statistical account that lacks the strong narrative component of *Journey to Chernobyl*.

Vodka

A History of Vodka by William Pokhlebkin, trans. Renfrey Clarke (London, New York: Verso, 1992 translation of 1991 text). From a Marxist historian's perspective, this book documents the history of vodka in the Russian Empire and presents compelling arguments for government action to curtail the rampant alcohol abuse that has long plagued Russia and the FSU, especially since World War II.

Travel Guides

In general, you are far more likely to find information on Russia than Ukraine. Sometimes Kyiv is still thrown into travel books on Russia, since it was the third largest Soviet city and historically the "mother of Russian cities."

Lonely Planet Russia, Ukraine and Belarus (Lonely Planet Publications, 1996). The best generic guide available. I highly recommend bringing a copy with you.

Fodor's Moscow, St. Petersburg, Kiev (Fodors, 3rd edition, 1997). This book covers only these three cities, but it is also worth bringing along for the Kiev (sic) section.

For information specific to Ukraine (which is extremely rare!), look for *Hippocrene Language and Travel Guide to Ukraine* by Linda Hodges and George Chumak (New York: Hippocrene Books, 1994). This is more of a language than travel guide.

(Russian) Etiquette and Customs

The following books are all quite helpful:

From Nyet to Da: Understanding the Russians by Yale Richmond (Yarmouth, Maine: Intercultural Press, revised 1996).

The Russian Way: Aspects of Behavior, Attitudes, and Customs of the Russians by Zita Dabars with Lilia Vokhmina (Lincolnwood, Chicago: Passport Books, 1995).

Put Your Best Foot Forward Russia: A Fearless Guide to International Communication and Behavior by Mary Murray Bosrock (International Educational Systems, 1995).

Ukrainian Cooking (and Customs)

There are various books on Russian cooking, many expanded to include the best of Ukrainian and Armenian recipes, since these were sometimes adopted as Soviet cuisine. I highly recommend my favorite book on Ukrainian cooking, *Festive Ukrainian Cooking* by Marta Pisetska Farley (University of Pittsburgh Press, 1990). In addition to recipes, old folk traditions are recorded here; many of these have disappeared, while others have been better preserved in Ukrainian emigré communities than in rural Ukraine.

Dissident Humor

Jewish Humor: What the Best Jewish Jokes Say about the Jews by Rabbi Joseph Telushkin (New York: William Morrow and Co.,

1992). This is a great book in many respects, although clearly the dissident jokes are most relevant. One of the strengths of this book is that the author always presents his jokes in a didactic context.

Language and (Ukrainian) Phrasebooks

Bilingual dictionaries are readily available in the country. If you want to buy one before you go, Russian language dictionaries are always easy to find, and Ukrainian ones are becoming more available.

The Atlas of Languages: The Origin and Development of Languages throughout the World edited by Bernard Comrie, Stephen Matthews, Smaria Poinsky (Facts on File, Inc., Quarto, Inc., 1996). This is a great book for people who are interested in the interrelations between various world languages and their roots.

Lonely Planet Ukrainian Phrasebook by Jim Dingley and Olena Bekh (Lonely Planet Publications, 1996). This and the Ukrainian language book produced by Rough Guide are small enough to fit in your coat pocket. I would recommend that you bring one with you.

For phrasebooks in Russian, you will have many more choices. Barrons publishes one that is also pocket size, and which I especially like, called *Russian at a Glance: Phrase Book and Dictionary for Travelers* (Barrons Educational Series, 1991).

Business Information

Whereas books on doing business in Ukraine are very difficult to find, there are books on doing business in Russia with titles increasing regularly. Many of these may be relevant, and you should visit a bookstore with a good international travel or business section. There is a recent book on Ukraine, which includes a lot of upbeat business propaganda. It presents a rosier picture than actually exists, but it is still useful. This book, *Doing Business in Ukraine*, edited by Adam Jolly and Nadine Kettaneh (London: Kogan Page Ltd, 1998) was published before the 1998 crisis.

The Mafia

Comrade Criminal: Russia's New Mafiya by Stephen Handelman (New Haven: Yale University Press, updated preface 1995). The best source of information available on the subject.

Folk Traditions

Evenings on a Farm near Dikanka by the famous Ukrainian writer Nikolai Gogol was originally published in the mid-19th century. Gogol's appreciation of his country's folk traditions is reflected in this book.

Ukrainian Music

World Music: The Rough Guide, edited by Mark Simon Broughton (Rough Guide Publications, 1995), is a great book for all sorts of world music, as the title suggests. A 1999 revised edition is available.

THE AUTHOR

Anne Meredith Dalton first visited the Soviet Union in 1982 while attending the University of Edinburgh in Scotland as an exchange student. She received both a B.A. and an M.A. in art history from the University of Texas in Austin. The focus of her master's thesis was Russian and Ukrainian art of the early 20th century. After serving as curator and director of the Oklahoma City Art Museum, Meredith entered the Wharton School of the University of Pennsylvania as an MBA candidate. During the summer of 1992, she interned in Moscow with the Russian Privatization Institute funded by financier George Soros. After receiving her MBA, she joined a DC-based consulting firm specializing in USAID contracts. This work, combined with previous experience trading commodities and financial futures, landed her in Kyiv, Ukraine, beginning in 1995. The project in Ukraine was designed to assist grain exchanges in the development toward a viable market economy. The establishment of forward and futures contracts for wheat and other agricultural commodities remains a top priority in Ukraine, formerly hailed as the breadbasket of the Soviet Union.

Meredith was born in Richmond, Virginia, and lived in various places before her family settled in Oklahoma City in 1971. She continues to travel frequently. Her latest trip to Ukraine was in 1998.

You may contact her with questions or comments via: Meredith.Dalton.WG93@wharton.upenn.edu.

INDEX